STAND!

A Complete Guide to Showing Your Dog from Companion to Champion

TRISH HAILL

THE CROWOOD PRESS

First published in 2015 by
The Crowood Press Ltd
Ramsbury, Marlborough
Wiltshire SN8 2HR

www.crowood.com

British Library Cataloguing-in-Publication Data
A catalogue record for this book is available from the British Library.

ISBN 978 1 84797 993 3

Dedication
This book is dedicated to my husband, Steve Haill, for his support and putting up with being
dragged along to most of the dog shows I've attended, and to my son, Michael Haill, for his
encouragement and help.

And of course I can't forget Bess (Snuggler Honey Pie over Smokeywater), without whom I
wouldn't have started showing at all.

Acknowledgements
First and foremost I have to thank Gill Tully (Highclare), whose encyclopaedic knowledge
of the dog showing world has been fundamental in ensuring this book is as accurate and
informative as possible. I thank her for her time, help, ideas and encouragement, both with
the book, and in the show ring. Without her practical, no-nonsense approach and support,
this book might not have been written!
I have been overwhelmed by the amount of advice and encouragement given freely by so
many people . . . I thank them all, but in particular I'd like to mention David Alcorn, Kim
Black, Sue Brown, Katherine Bull, Olivia Carty, Julie Frost, Georgina Harrison, Jane Heggie,
Vicki High, Paul Meakin, Helen Moore, Amelia Murray, Virge Neary, David Paton, Graham
Peers, Jamie Read, Val Rottger, Gillian Serpa and Carla Young; and Sharron Dyer (Sharnphilly), who suggested ringcraft classes, and the Central Essex Dog Training Society, which
set me off on the right path!

There was a huge response to my call for photographs, for which I'm extremely grateful. It
was a very hard job sorting through them all, and I apologize that I was unable to use all the
photos submitted. I did enjoy seeing them all!

In addition, I have to thank the various Breed Clubs which so kindly responded to my
requests for Breed Showing information, and the Kennel Club for so patiently answering my
queries about the less obvious interpretations of the regulations.

Finally I'd like to thank Pat Brown who initially suggested that I enter the show world.

Disclaimer
The authors and publisher do not accept any responsibility in any manner whatsoever for any
error or omission, or any loss, damage, injury, adverse outcome or liability of any kind incurred
as a result of the use of any of the information contained in this book, or reliance upon it.

Typeset by Jean Cussons Typesetting, Diss, Norfolk
Printed and bound in Malaysia by Times Offset (M) Sdn Bhd

CONTENTS

FOREWORD

After reading *Stand!* by Trish Haill, my first thoughts were 'What a well written and suitably illustrated book'. It would have made life easier for me when I first entered that exciting world of dogs many years ago. I had so many questions to ask but nobody to answer them. Sometimes people gave you incorrect information but you could not check it and so just believed it (as people still do).

In my early days the people who did know the answers were so far up the ladder in the chosen breed that you felt you could not even speak to them. As the years went by, some of these people became good friends and were always happy to share their knowledge.

But with this excellent book you can find out all you need to know from the beginning. One sentence especially rings true: 'You hope that one magic day you'll reach the point when you "know everything"! But I suspect there are very few people, if any, who could legitimately make this claim.' This book will help you in your quest and will always be to hand.

Valerie Foss

Valerie Foss has had sixteen UK Champions and Champions in Europe with her two breeds, English Setters and Golden Retrievers (Elswood). Being extremely busy in the canine world, she has personally not bred or shown for ten years.

A renowned judge, she awards Challenge Certificates in the Gundog, Hound, Working and Pastoral Groups, regularly judges Groups at Championship Shows, including the Gundog Group at Crufts in 1995, and the Pastoral Group in 2014, culminating in being the Best in Show Judge at Crufts in 2010. She judges all over the world as well as in the UK. She has had eleven books published, and is President of the following organizations: the Young Kennel Club, the Manchester Dog Show Society, the English Setter Association and Scottish Breeds.

Valerie Foss, Best in Show Judge at Crufts 2010, and her winner, Hungarian Vizsla 'Sh CH/AUST CH Hungargunn Bear It'n Mind'. With Moray Armstrong, Jock Bettie and John Thirlwell. (© The Kennel Club)

PREFACE

Many years ago I bought a pedigree dog, and the breeder asked me if I would show him. Piece of cake, I thought, so I trotted along to a Companion Show. I hadn't heard of ringcraft, had made no preparation, and hadn't a clue what to do. My dog was miserable, with his tail between his legs. I wanted the floor to open up and swallow me and I was disillusioned when the judge didn't place us. Despite owning more pedigree dogs, I didn't go back to the show ring for about twenty-five years!

Fast forward a couple of decades and I acquired an Irish Setter and decided it was time to try again. This time I decided to learn something about dog showing first, but I found that however hard I looked, I really couldn't find all the information I was looking for in one place, either in books or on the internet. Even though I'd gone to ringcraft training, there seemed to be a lot of practical gaps in my knowledge – this was only too apparent when I arrived at my first show and didn't even know what a ring number was, let alone how to obtain one!

Knowing that it would have been helpful to have understood the details before I set foot in the show ring, I decided to write the book that I felt was missing to help newcomers to the sport enter the show ring with more confidence. My background in research and in interpreting legislation came in useful when trying to understand the show regulations, and with the expert advice from knowledgeable friends and contacts *Stand!* gradually emerged.

As I was writing and talking to people, it became clear that many exhibitors have learnt from the famous 'sitting with Nelly' method, and there were lots of conflicting views and interpretations about what the showing regulations actually mean, even among experienced show-goers. So I've taken the time to try to cover most (I wouldn't dare to say all) topics in the dog showing world, and hope that *Stand!* will act not only as a basis for newcomers, but also as a reference book for those already actively engaged in the sport.

There is no doubt that dog showing will change over the next few years, and some possible changes are discussed in the final chapter. It's an interesting time, with newcomers actively encouraged to join in the sport, giving everyone owning or thinking of taking on a pedigree dog an opportunity to show off their beloved pets, to make new like-minded friends and to engage in the canine world in a way which has a positive benefit to dog health and welfare.

For newcomers, I hope that *Stand!* gives you the knowledge you need to enter that first show ring with confidence; for more experienced exhibitors, I hope it will be a book that can be dipped into to refresh your memory.

As things never stand still, there may be some changes after this book is published. Keep an eye on my website, www.trishhaill.co.uk, through which I will endeavour to keep you up to date with anything new in the show world.

Trish Haill

'Snuggler Honey Pie over Smokeywater' (aka 'Bess') and the author.

INTRODUCTION

This book is for anyone who's involved in, new to, or just thinking about showing their dog. As well as the mechanics and rules of exhibiting, we'll be looking at the reasons why we show dogs at all, and what showing means to the dog world in general. If you're just starting out, the book will give you the information you need to enter your first show with confidence, and for more experienced exhibitors it will act as a reference guide making the showing regulations more accessible.

Showing off our canine companions may not quite be as old as time, but certainly man's (and woman's) desire to prove that they have the best hunting, racing or fighting dogs goes back far longer than records have been kept. Mention of actual dog shows appears in records from the second half of the eighteenth century but the change really came in 1835 when dog fighting – up to then the most popular dog sport – was made illegal. Law-abiding folk started to concentrate more on showing off their dog's conformation, breeding and looks, rather than their fighting skills, resulting in the kind of shows that we take part in nowadays. When the Kennel Club was formed half-way through the reign of Queen Victoria, dog shows were given a more formal structure and the regulations that were brought in at that time are still largely in place today.

Seasoned exhibitors, who have been showing all their lives, have learned and absorbed most of the various rules and practices which surround the hobby and which have evolved over the last century and a half. But for the newcomer, something which should appear simple (you turn up, enter your dog in the ring, and hopefully win a prize) becomes more complicated the longer you're around the show ring. You hope that one magic day you'll reach the point when you 'know everything'! But I suspect there are very few people, if any, who could legitimately make this claim.

Over the 140 years since the first showing regu-lations were introduced, custom and practice have lent them an interpretation that can be difficult for a newcomer to understand. So this book sets out to try to demystify the world of dog showing and to help make sense of the sport. It is important to remember that an understanding of the regulations is vital for anyone who shows: every time you sign an entry form you confirm that you will comply with the official rules for dog show-ing – which may prove difficult if you don't know what they are, or have simply relied on word of mouth as to what they actually say!

The Kennel Club is currently undergoing a review of the dog showing regulations to bring the sport into the twenty-first century and make it more attractive and participative. Certain changes are being trialled from January 2015 for a period of two years, after which they may or may not be confirmed by a rewrite of the rules, or perhaps some other changes will be brought in instead. This book reflects the changes that were to be trialled in early 2015, and where these appear there will be an indication of where to check for the latest information. Updates can also be found by visiting www.trishhaill.co.uk.

When I first started exhibiting, I found there were a number of questions that even a thorough knowledge of the regulations wouldn't answer. For example, what is a ring number, and how do you get one? Which classes, and how many of them, should you enter? What is the dress code for various shows? And then, even when I knew the basics, there were a myriad of other questions I wanted to know the answers to. For example, what is a beaten dog? What is, and how do you achieve, a Junior Warrant or Stud Book number? Or to put it simply, what is the whole point to dog showing other than turning up at a show and hopefully going home with a rosette?

During my forays into the hobby, I found I wasn't the only person ignorant of the bigger picture, or even of some of the minor details. People come into showing in a number of ways. A breeder might suggest showing a promising puppy. Some people actively set out to buy a puppy from a top showing kennel with exhibiting in mind. People may have shown an unregistered dog at Fun or Companion Shows and, having enjoyed the experience, decide to take up showing more seriously. A friend might say an older dog is looking really good and should be shown. Someone in the family might show. Sometimes it's as simple as just being a dog owner and wanting to learn more about, and to improve, the breed they love. All of the above share the same dismay when they find that everyone else seems to know what they are doing, and they feel they are the only one who doesn't. Well, that certainly isn't true, but this book will, I hope, give you more confidence and help you know what you are doing, and why!

Taking your first step into the dog show scene could mean stepping onto the initial rung of the ladder leading to becoming a Champion or even Best in Show at Crufts. Of course, you may not do it with your first dog, or your second, or your third – or at all! But to get the most out of showing, you will benefit from an understanding of what it's all about, and what you should, or shouldn't, do according to the rules that govern the sport, and from learning how to avoid the many mistakes that can be made.

Dogs in the UK

In the UK we're not known as a nation of dog lovers for nothing! A quarter of households in the UK own at least one dog, and it's estimated that the total dog population is approaching eight and a half million. Nearly a quarter of a million pedigree puppies are registered with the Kennel Club each year, which suggests that there are in excess of two million pedigree dogs at any one time that are eligible to enter conformation shows. Annually a staggering 22,000-plus dogs are exhibited at Crufts in the breed judging, all of which have to first compete at other shows in order to qualify and be eligible to enter the most prestigious dog show in the world.

CHAPTER 1

DOG SHOWING AND SHOW DOGS

So where's the best place to start with a book about dog showing? We could start with how and where to buy a puppy specifically to show, but it's possible you already have a potential Champion sitting beside you as you're reading! And even if you're setting out to buy a show dog, having knowledge of the show world will give you important pointers as to what you need to be looking for. So while how to acquire a show puppy definitely should be covered, and will be in Chapter 8, here we'll begin with which dogs can be shown and some general points about dog showing. Whether you're thinking about exhibiting with your current dog or puppy, or buying one to show, or are already involved in the sport, we'll provide some context as to why we exhibit dogs in conformation shows, and give an introduction to how dogs are judged and the sport's influence on canine health and wellbeing in general.

HOW IT ALL STARTED – A BRIEF HISTORY

Put simply, a dog show is an event where people who share an interest in dogs meet to show off and compare their dogs with others. The origin of such meetings and get-togethers goes back to the time when dogs first became domesticated. It began out of necessity, when the best dogs were required for guarding, hunting and herding as part of daily life in order to survive. Then, as people began to move from the countryside to urban areas in the eighteenth century, they wanted to keep something of their rural life and many took to keeping dogs – no longer to herd or hunt, but as companions.

There are no records of formal dog shows until 1775, when John Warde's passion for fox hunting led him

Fig. 1.1 The first recorded Hound Show in 1775 was primarily for Foxhounds, and Hound Shows continue to this day. Foxhound 'Haughmill Prefect'.

Fig. 1.2   Beagles can qualify for Crufts in conformation shows, and also by coming first in a Hound Show held by the Masters of Harriers and Beagles Association. (Photo: Graham Peers)

Who shows dogs?

One of the reasons for the sport's popularity, then and now, is that it has always cut across class boundaries. Poachers had lurchers to help them hunt; the aristocracy had toy breeds as a mark of prosperity or gundogs to work; and in the north whippet racing was the province of the working class. The one thing uniting all these spheres of life was pride in their stock, and the desire to show that their dogs were the best example of the breed! And this is still true today, with shows attracting exhibitors from all walks of life. Compared to some other sports, dog showing is also relatively inexpensive.

to hold hound shows with acquaintances who shared his interest. During the latter years of the eighteenth century Agricultural Society Shows began to emerge, with Durham being the first to be held in 1783, primarily to show off livestock but including classes for dogs. This practice continued for many years, with some shows evolving to hold Championship Dog Shows alongside the competitions for pigs, cattle and sheep. It's only in recent years that the Agricultural Shows have ceased to include a dog show as part of their event, due to the size of area needed to accommodate the large entry of dogs. But the tradition continues in that many Championship Shows are still held on land belonging to the Agricultural Societies.

Fig. 1.3   The Duchess of Windsor and her Champion Borzoi 1903 – demonstrating that even the aristocracy were involved in the sport of dog showing.

Fig. 1.4 Whippets coursing. Whippets were originally miners' dogs used for rabbiting and racing, and the breed is extremely popular in the dog show world today. (Photo: Robert Moore)

From the early 1800s dog shows started to change and evolve as the Victorians embraced the sport with a passion. Local and small shows for working hounds and pet dogs continued, but larger shows for all breeds began to sprout up all over the country, facilitated by the advent of the railway. By the mid-1800s almost all major towns could be reached by rail, making travelling over longer distances possible. Some shows even arranged special train carriages to carry dogs and exhibitors.

The first recorded mixed breed dog show, which benefited from the new mode of train travel and thus appealed to people from a wider area, was held over two days in June 1859 at the Town Hall in Newcastle upon Tyne. The entries at this first show were twenty-three pointers and thirty-six setters. It was hailed as a complete success (although in fact it was a financial failure), and this sparked larger exhibitions in the following years, which began to cater for ever-increasing numbers of breeds and exhibitors.

Fig. 1.5 Victorian people, including a vicar, at a dog show. From Punch, vol. LXVIII (68), published in London in 1875. Dogs were benched for public viewing.

Fig. 1.6 The concept of benching hasn't changed over the last 140 years, although nowadays it's only at Crufts where the public come in numbers to walk around to see the dogs.

The origins of many of today's Championship Shows date back to this period – for example, the Birmingham National Dog Show was established in 1860, the Manchester Dog Show Society in 1863, Bath Canine Society in 1877, and Southern Counties in 1870; in 1894 the Ladies Kennel Association was established to run shows for ladies, by ladies, to address the male domination of the sport that had existed up until then.

The Kennel Club itself was founded in 1873, and promptly introduced the showing regulations that are still the basis for those used today in all Kennel Club Licensed shows in the UK. In 1891 the first ever Crufts show took place – there is more about this renowned show in Chapter 10, but it will suffice to say here that by this juncture dog showing had become so popular that this first major show even attracted royal patronage. Queen Victoria herself entered some of her dogs, and won with her Toy Pomeranian called Gena and with her Collie, Darnley II. Royal support continued and in 1897 the Prince and Princess of Wales entered six dogs, which all won prizes (although whether the

judge was looking at the owners or the dogs is open to conjecture!). Participation at the very highest levels of society wasn't restricted just to British royalty – eighteen Borzois belonging to the Tsar of Russia attended the 1897 show, demonstrating that by the end of the nineteenth century UK dog shows were attracting international attention. Crufts has been run regularly ever since, except during the world wars, with increasing numbers of entries each year. Until 1942 it continued to be run by the Crufts family but when it recommenced in 1948 after the Second World War, it had been sold to the Kennel Club, which has been responsible for putting on the show ever since.

Dog showing continued to grow in popularity, with local canine societies springing up to run Open and Championship Shows, and we now have twenty-six General Championship Shows throughout the year, together with a wide range of Group and Breed Championship Shows. Open Shows, let alone Companion and Fun Shows, are too numerous to count and would run into thousands. Dog showing remains a popular and participative sport.

Fig. 1.7 It may have changed from the first show in 1891, but Crufts remains the world's greatest dog show. (© Kennel Club Picture Library)

What is a pedigree/purebred dog?

A pedigree or purebred dog is one whose parents – both sire (father) and dam (mother) – are of the same breed. This might seem an obvious point to make, but nowadays some cross-breeds are being given rather fancy names, and in many cases are becoming known, inaccurately, as 'breeds' – Labradoodles and Cockapoos, for example. And, buyers beware! Do not be fooled by adverts which state these dogs are 'pedigrees and come with papers'. As lovely as it might be, a Puggle (a Beagle crossed with a Pug) will never be able to exhibit in the conformation rings at Crufts. Although it is possible to establish a new breed, it takes many years and many generations of dogs, not to mention the dedication of extremely knowledgeable breeders who are experts in genetics before a cross can breed true. And there is already a vast range of pedigree dogs to choose from.

WHICH DOGS CAN BE SHOWN?

So, how can you take part in this centuries-old sport? First, you need a dog. There are opportunities for any dog to be shown at a variety of different shows. But if your ultimate aim is to show your dog in the breed classes at Crufts, and have a shot at winning the top accolade of Best in Show, you will need a pedigree dog that has been registered with the Kennel Club.

Cross-breed or non-pedigree dogs, or pedigree dogs that have not been (or cannot be) registered, can enter Fun and Companion Shows. Large numbers of these shows are held up and down the country every week and it's far from unusual for someone to get their first taste of showing in a local informal setting, find they enjoy it, and make the decision they want to show more seriously.

Dogs can start showing either as puppies, or as adolescents or as mature adult dogs. There is no upper age limit. There's nothing wrong with beginning to show an older dog who has matured very nicely, or even starting off with a veteran over seven years old!

We'll have a brief look at Fun and Companion Shows as these are good starting points for novice handlers, but in the main we'll be concentrating on the shows and regulations for pedigree dogs.

Fig. 1.8   An example of a pedigree dog: English Setter 'Arabin Street Party'.

Fig. 1.9   A pedigree dog is one whose parents were the same breed. This is Papillon 'Sunshoo Jeremy Fisher'.

Fig. 1.10   'Teddy' is a lovely Cockapoo, but as one parent was a Cocker Spaniel and the other a Poodle, he is not a pedigree dog.

THE KENNEL CLUB

The Kennel Club (KC) is the body that regulates the registration of purebred dogs in the UK. It also operates an activity and companion register for cross-breed dogs. Although the Kennel Club has a much wider role, being dedicated to the health and welfare of all dogs, whatever their breeding, its spheres of influence in which we are primarily interested here are its functions with regard to the show exhibitor. These include its responsibility for maintaining the breed standards, recording health test results on breeding stock, running the Assured Breeders Scheme and last, but by no means least, producing the show regulations that govern the majority of dog shows in the UK (exceptions being some shows in Northern Ireland which are run under the Irish Kennel Club Showing Regulations, and Fun Dog Shows).

Although originally drawn up by breeders as early as the nineteenth century, today it's the Kennel Club which owns the breed standards of all the 210 breeds currently recognized in this country. A breed standard can be defined as a word picture of the perfect example of the breed. The standard describes looks and physical features, size and character, and every dog of that breed is measured against it. The basis of judging in dog shows is the comparison of each dog to the standard. A dog is said to have good conformation when it is a good match, but poor conformation if it deviates significantly from the standard. All the breed standards can be found on the Kennel Club website.

Other countries have similar bodies to the Kennel Club, all looking after dog health, welfare, registration and showing. Eighty-nine countries (including most of Europe and Northern Ireland) are members of the Federation Cynologique Internationale (FCI) – the Worldwide Canine Organization – which governs registration, breed standards, show regulations and judges in all of its member countries. In America the American Kennel Club (AKC) has this responsibility.

Kennel Club registration

Registration of show dogs, and of cross-breed dogs competing in various disciplines, is important as it is a unique identifier of that dog. When registration is coupled with a microchip, we can be absolutely sure of a dog's identity, which is important when conferring awards or recording the results of health tests. Microchipping of all dogs will be mandatory by 6 April 2016 in England and Scotland, and is already a requirement in Wales and Northern Ireland.

Who can register a puppy?

Puppies are normally registered by their breeder soon after birth, and the buyer receives a transfer of ownership form when they go to collect their puppy. The Kennel Club will then send the registration certificate to the new owner. Some people wanting a puppy just as a pet don't bother about transferring ownership into their name, but it is mandatory if you are going to show, as the owner's name goes onto entry forms. You can pay for a five-generation pedigree at the same time as transferring ownership and it's a useful document to have. You'll be surprised how often you'll be asked about your dog's breeding by other exhibitors at shows.

Registration of puppies is only possible if both their sire and dam are registered, and only the breeder can complete the registration; it's not something the new owner can do. Registration can be done after you've collected the puppy (if he's entitled to be registered), but a late registration fee (currently £60) is payable after twelve months and needs a letter of explanation as to why it wasn't done earlier. So having a piece of paper in your hand (or at least checking online) at the time of purchase is far better than an airy promise that it will be done at a later date.

There are a few circumstances where pedigree puppies cannot be registered with the Kennel Club, so make sure you check before you commit to a purchase. If you're offered a puppy which has not been registered, it's often a sign that you should avoid that breeder.

Puppies which cannot be registered with the Kennel Club

Usually the only circumstance where purebred dogs with long pedigrees cannot be registered is when they are an imported breed, and owners and breeders have not yet applied for the breed to be recognized by the Kennel Club. This applies to a tiny minority of dogs in the UK. Worldwide there are many breeds that are popular in their country of origin, but are rarely, if ever,

Fig. 1.11 'Mr Wizzy' is a pedigree Powder Puff Chinese Crested but he wasn't registered by his breeder. He is shown in companion shows, but cannot be shown in breed shows.

Fig. 1.12 English Shepherd dogs are recognized in other countries, but owners/breeders in the UK have not applied for the breed to be recognized here. 'Edenvillage Harris'.

Registration when parents are not registered

There are exceptional circumstances where a puppy whose parents were not registered can nevertheless itself be registered. However, this happens very rarely and needs a lot of supporting information. It is only likely in breeds that are very small in number, and where such registration is likely to benefit the breed. This is not something that would be attempted by newcomers or even by most established exhibitors, and it only tends to be applied for by breeders/exhibitors with an in-depth knowledge of their breed, and the lines within it.

seen in the UK. The breeds currently recognized by the Kennel Club are listed in the Breed Showing Information Guide at the back of this book.

It is a sad fact that all too often puppies cannot be registered due to disreputable breeding practices. The Kennel Club, in its role to improve the welfare of dogs, has certain criteria for registration. They will not register more than four litters from one bitch in her lifetime. They will not register litters born before the bitch is one year of age, or after she turns eight, or where the relationship between sire and dam is too close (for example, father/daughter, brother/sister) except in exceptional circumstances. They will also not register puppies if breeding restrictions have been placed on the sire or dam – sometimes breeders have endorsed the puppy and don't want it bred from, for example, if a fault or possibly hereditary disorder has been identified in the line or individual dog. Reputable breeders will follow these guidelines, but unscrupulous breeders, such as puppy farmers who use bitches as breeding machines, or anyone who sees breeding as a way of making money, may breed more than the recommended number of litters, or ignore the faults in their breeding stock. They may well be producing 'pedigree' puppies, but these can't be registered and therefore will not be able to be shown. Sometimes the excuse is given that registration is expensive, but in reality it currently costs the breeder just £16 per puppy (£14 for Assured Breeders), which is very little compared to what they'll be charging for each of the litter!

Whether or not you are thinking seriously about showing when you buy a pedigree puppy, make sure you get the Kennel Club registration papers when you collect him, or at least have confirmed that registration is in progress. You can check online – the easiest way is to check for the progeny of the dam.

It goes without saying that no person with a love of dogs would want to support unethical breeders who are exploiting their bitches or selling puppies which may end up leading unhealthy lives. So if you are buying a pedigree puppy, please be sure that it can be registered.

And lastly, a warning! Be extremely careful: to get round the lack of registration papers, some puppies are offered with 'Pedigree Papers'. An example of the official Kennel Club registration document which the breeder should provide you with is shown in Fig. 1.15.

Fig. 1.14   This is what 'Io' was expected to turn out like. Pedigree Rottweiler bitch, 'Alldenria All That Jazz'. (Photo: Dave Gaffney)

Fig. 1.13   'Io' was bought as a purebred Rottweiler, but without papers. As she grew, it became obvious that, although a lovely family pet who excels at agility, she is a cross-breed.

It may not look as pretty as some of the fake papers, but this is the one you should be given.

Kennel Club registration certificate

Formerly, the official Kennel Club registration certificate was A4 size, but it recently changed to A5 size. The document shows the current registered owner; the dog's registered name and any previously registered name (an affix might have been added); any titles he may have achieved; his breed, date of birth, colour and sex; and the breeder's details. It also shows the dog's registration number, stud book number, DNA profile and any microchip or tattoo number, and the results of any health screening. (For a puppy, a lot of these fields will be blank.) It will also show if there are any

Fig. 1.15   Example of an official Kennel Club Registration Certificate.

endorsements, and the details of the sire and dam are recorded, along with any results of the parents' health testing. You will need the sire and dam's registration details when you complete any entry form for a Kennel Club licensed show.

The reverse of the certificate has a change of ownership form which the breeder must sign if you are transferring ownership into your name.

Explanation of the dog's registered name (kennel name)

Your puppy's unique kennel name will initially be his breeder's affix (the registered kennel name of the breeder) and the name they have chosen for your dog.

As he goes through his showing career, his name might change in various ways:

- You might decide you want your own kennel name, which can be added at the end of his name using a preposition such as 'of', 'over', 'for', etc.
- He might win awards such as a Junior Warrant (JW) or a Show Certificate of Merit (ShCM), which can be added at the end of his name.
- He might win a title such as Champion or Show Champion, a working title or even titles abroad, which can be added at the beginning of his name.

If a dog is imported to the UK, then 'IMP' will appear at the end of his name.

| Champion Title (s) | → | Breeder's Affix | → | Dog's Name | → | Preposition | → | Owner's Affix | → | Awards | → | IMP |

Fig. 1.16   *How a kennel name is made up.*

Endorsements

There are two endorsements that can be placed by the breeder. One is to prevent any progeny being eligible for Kennel Club registration, and therefore to discourage the puppy being bred from, although often a breeder will lift this endorsement if they are assured that the puppy has developed into a good example of the breed, and all relevant health tests have been done. The other endorsement is that the puppy is not eligible for the issue of an export pedigree; unless this is lifted, the dog cannot be registered by an overseas Kennel Club, and subsequently cannot be shown abroad. The endorsements are encouraged by the Kennel Club to ensure dogs are responsibly bred, and that they are not sent overseas to countries whose concern for dog welfare does not match the UK's. Endorsements can obviously not prevent dogs being bred, or being sent abroad, but they do act as a deterrent.

Fig. 1.17   *A sign of a very good breeder. Four-week-old Greater Swiss Mountain Dog puppies have an outside playpen to provide them with plenty of stimulation. (Photo: Swisshaven)*

WHAT IS THE PURPOSE OF SHOWING DOGS?

Showing your dog in conformation shows may well cater to your inner competitive streak, but it also has a more important function than an individual dog simply getting placed and being in the line-up to receive a rosette. For a beginner, this may suffice as a first goal, but here's a glimpse of the bigger picture. Breeders continually try to produce dogs that match their breed standard as closely as possible. If a dog does not match the standard exactly – possibly he has a wavy rather than a straight coat – this is called a fault, or a deviation from the breed standard. Breeders strive to eradicate

Assured Breeders Scheme

The Kennel Club's Assured Breeder Scheme is certificated by UKAS (the United Kingdom Accreditation Scheme). Breeders can join this scheme if they abide by the criteria set out for their breed; these include the recommended ages between which a bitch can be bred and the relevant health tests that should be carried out before breeding. There are also general conditions about how the puppies should be brought up, their early socialization and training. Assured Breeders have inspections to warrant their compliance with the breeding standards. There are some fantastic breeders who are not part of the scheme for a number of good reasons, but unethical breeders are unlikely to be able to show they conform to these requirements.

Fig. 1.18 Winning Reserve Best in Show, this Wire Fox Terrier 'Ch Travella Starcraft' is a very good match to the breed standard. (Photo: Graham Peers)

that fault in their lines by a careful selection of dogs to breed from, although it may take many generations to remove the fault entirely. No dog, however, is ever a complete match to the standard, and all deviate from it to a greater or lesser degree.

'Proving' a dog in the show ring means judging him not against all other dogs present, but against the breed standard. The dog who best matches the standard (in that judge's opinion) will win 'Best of Breed' and may go on to win Best in Show, where he will have been measured against the top dogs in all other breeds.

Originally the main purpose of conformation dog shows was for breeders to show off their breeding stock, and to identify the best quality dogs to continue their lines. But there is nothing wrong in an exhibitor just wanting to show their dog for the fun of it, and not having any breeding plans whatsoever. There's always the chance that the dog winning Best of Breed, or even Best in Show, may not come from a top breeder's show kennel at all.

SURGICAL ALTERATIONS

When you sign the entry form for a show you are confirming that any operation which alters the natu-ral conformation of the dog has been reported to the Kennel Club and that you have a letter granting Permission to Show.

Neutering

If you're not even contemplating wanting to breed at some point in the future you may be considering neutering your dog. Don't be put off by the myth that neutered dogs cannot be shown. The Kennel Club recognizes that nowadays neutering is seen to be a responsible act on the part of the owner. While most pedigree show dogs are kept entire, it is acknowledged that wins by dogs which can no longer be bred from still reflect the quality of the line. It has become common practice for most vets to recommend that all dogs are neutered, and some routinely neuter at around six months. Neutering is encouraged in the pet community to prevent unwanted puppies being brought into the world, and ending up in our already over-populated rescue shelters.

There are, however, other considerations in the show world that need to be taken into account. Neutering is a serious operation that should not be undertaken lightly. Anyone contemplating neutering their dog should research both the pros and cons of spaying (for a bitch) or castration (for a dog), and also consider the best age for the surgery. Neutering before the dog's growth plates have closed can result in a tall, lanky specimen that no longer matches the breed standard. There can be behavioural changes (some for the better, some worse), and it may alter the conformation of the dog, as well as, in some breeds, turning a smooth coat curly. In the case of show dogs it is advisable to speak to someone knowledgeable in the breed to find out the likely effects of neutering on your show prospects. It is also important to discuss it with your breeder – particularly in less numerous breeds – as taking a potential Champion out of the breeding pool might have implications for that line.

We will be discussing what it's like to live with an entire dog or intact bitch in Chapter 8, but if you do decide to go ahead with neutering you will need to obtain a letter from the Kennel Club granting Permission to Show. The form to request this is available from the Kennel Club website. You do not need to take the form to shows, and when applying for permission you do not need to state the reason why neutering was performed.

Neutered dogs and bitches are judged in the same way as entire dogs, but the fact that a castrated dog does not have two normally descended testicles, or any other effect in which neutering causes a deviation from the breed standard, may be taken into account during judging in just the same way as any other fault may be considered.

If a neutered dog gains its Stud Book number the letters NEUT will appear after its name in the Stud Book.

Docked dogs and cropping

Cropping of ears is still practised in some countries, but in the UK no dog with cropped ears can be shown in a Kennel Club licensed event.

Docking is a thorny subject. It is a practice that can trigger a range of reactions – dismay in those who like to see their dogs as nature intended, complete with full tails; and anger in those of the sporting fraternity who know the injuries that can be caused to the tails of gundogs which spend much time running through thick undergrowth. So let's just stick to the facts in relation to dog showing. In England and Wales there is a ban on docking apart from working breeds, that is, Spaniels, Terriers, Hunt Point Retrieve (HPR) dogs or any cross of these breeds, but there are restrictions as to where they can be shown. A dog which had his tail docked after 28 March 2007 cannot take part in shows where the public are charged an entry fee, even if he was docked legally as a working dog, or if he had his tail removed for medical reasons, for example, after injury. The schedule for the show will specify if dogs docked after the legal date may not be entered for that show. If you have a dog whose tail has been legally docked, there will still be a number of shows which you can enter. This includes some Championship shows where your dog could be made up to be a Champion, but nowadays a docked dog can never be shown at Crufts.

In Scotland there is a total ban on docking, but a docked dog can be shown if he has had his tail amputated for medical reasons. In Northern Ireland the position is similar to England and Wales in that there are exceptions for working breeds, but the effective date is different (1 January 2013). It is permissible to show docked dogs who were docked prior to this date, and in working ability tests. But otherwise docked dogs cannot be shown where the public have to pay for admittance to the show.

Fig. 1.19   Brittanys are an example of a breed which can be born with bobbed tails or tailless. 'Sh CH Highclare Flaming Nora'.

Tailless and bob-tailed dogs

It can be confusing in some breeds where dogs look as if they have been docked when they haven't. The Bulldog and Boston Terrier, for example, have very short tails. The Old English Sheepdog and Brittany are examples of dogs often born without a tail, or with bob-tails. Where bob-tails turn up in breeds which normally have a longer tail, this is not necessarily seen as a fault. However, bob-tailed dogs should only be bred from by experienced breeders. In some lines it is not a problem, but in others it could cause spinal or other issues in resulting progeny.

Operations which alter the natural conformation of the dog

In order to be registered, or to continue to be registered, any operation that alters a dog's natural conformation must be reported to the Kennel Club by the veterinary surgeon who performed the procedure. This includes where bitches require a caesarean section when giving birth. This helps to identify breeding lines where hereditary defects might be occurring or where dogs are having difficulty whelping naturally, and means that judges are not rewarding dogs in the show ring whose faults have been covered up by corrective surgery. We'll be looking more into improving the health of dogs – particularly those with identified issues – in Chapter 7.

HOW DO YOU KNOW IF YOUR DOG IS GOOD ENOUGH TO SHOW?

The first time that you may have thought about showing perhaps came when the breeder suggested that the puppy you are buying might be a good prospect for the show ring, and asked if you would show him. The breeder's thoughts on an eight-week-old puppy, unfortunately, don't guarantee you success as the puppy may not go on to fulfil his potential. But such encouragement from the breeder is obviously a good start to your showing career.

Dogs which have success in the show ring don't always come from a breeder with experience of exhibiting. Pet bitches are often mated with Show Champion dogs and, while there is no knowing how well the bitch matches up to the breed standard, sometimes very good show dogs appear from pet homes. In these circumstances you don't have a knowledgeable breeder to guide you, so it's a matter of trying to interpret the breed standard and being as objective as possible when evaluating your puppy or dog against the criteria. Going to shows, looking at the dogs in the ring and mentally comparing your dog to others will also give you some pointers as to whether he could have any success. If you have knowledgeable friends, then you could ask them to look at him for you.

Fig. 1.20   *Bought originally as a pet dog, 'Snuggler Honey Pie Over Smokeywater' showing at Crufts. (Photo: Kasia Czapla)*

Fig. 1.21   'Garshakers Treasure' ('Skipper') is a handsome purebred Parson Russell Terrier. His coat is too heavily marked for the show ring, as the breed standard calls for it to be predominantly white.

Fig. 1.22   A show quality Parson Russell Terrier. (Photo: Michael Trafford traffordphotos.com)

Unless your dog is quite obviously not a good match to the breed standard, there is no substitute for actually getting into that show ring yourself. Even if you don't have success, you will have put your training into practice and have gained valuable experience that you can use at a later date if you decide you want to buy another dog specifically to show. And in the meantime you can enjoy yourself competing at Fun

Champions on your pedigree document

Don't be taken in by the number of names written in red on your pedigree document. Red ink indicates that a dog is either a Sh Ch (Show Champion), a Ch (Champion) or maybe a FTCh (Field Trial Champion). Champion dogs are very popular as stud dogs, and most pedigrees will have a smattering of red names throughout. This does not necessarily mean that the puppy you are buying has inherited the desired traits from these dogs, particularly if the dam was not proven in the show ring herself. But on the other hand, there is nothing to say that your puppy may not be a throwback to his famous great-great-grandsire, even if his parents have not achieved anything themselves.

Fig. 1.23 'Sh CH Highclare Flaming Nora' in the mud, hardly looking like the Champion she is! Compare this picture with Fig. 1.19 to see how she looks on a show day.

Fig. 1.24 Border Collie 'Cadiz Miss Independent' after a good walk.

Fig. 1.25   Rough Collies playing. (Photo: Julie Growcott)

Fig. 1.26   Cairn Terriers having fun. (Photo: Mike Huolman)

Fig. 1.27 Crufts 2009 (CC, BOB and Gundog Group 2) 'Sh CH Ansona Gamekeeper at Aarranz JW ShCM' ('Logan'), owned and handled by Lynne Danneau. (Photo: Carol Ann Johnson)

Fig. 1.28 The relationship between dog and handler shines through. (Photo: Carol Ann Johnson)

and Companion Shows with the knowledge that you are always taking the best dog home.

ARE SHOW DOGS PET DOGS?

It's easy to get so involved with the idea of showing that you forget that show dogs will be spending up to fifteen years of their life with you and your family. Even if you show every weekend, it's still only a minor part of the time you'll spend with your dog. Your show dog will be first and foremost your family pet. It's key to remember this if you are setting out to buy a puppy to exhibit, as the breed you think you could have success with needs also to fit in with your lifestyle and home. There's no point getting carried away and bringing home a giant breed if you only have a tiny garden, or a long-haired breed if you hate grooming!

Some people seem to think that show dogs are wrapped in cotton wool and are not allowed to get dirty and muddy, swim in rivers or the sea, or play like other pets. These pictures are of show dogs – but not how they look on the day of a show!

As we'll see later on, in the show ring a judge needs to feel all over the dog, and one thing they are looking for is muscle. A dog that is not exercised will not have firm, defined musculature, and therefore may lose out to another which has. A regular and consistent exercise regime is at least as important to a show dog as to any other canine!

Some show dogs do live in kennels, particularly if they belong to a large breeding kennel. But the vast majority of show dogs live in the house as pets. Diet, exercise, attention, training and love are as important to preparing a dog for the show ring as any grooming and pampering before a show. A dog which does not enjoy life will show it in his demeanour in the ring. A winning dog is a happy dog, who enjoys being shown and being with his handler. A good happy partnership between handler and dog will stand out and will not go unnoticed by the judge! This is evidenced in Figs 1.27 and 1.28, of which pairing the Group judge at Crufts stated, 'We often have good dogs and good handlers, but when they are bonding together and combining as a team they produce that extra special magic.'

Fig. 1.29   Grace Batt, aged six, achieved third place in the Junior Handling (6–11 years) class at Guildford and District Open Show with Papillon 'Bows Barleybright'. (Photo: Fran McWade)

Fig. 1.30   Dog showing can involve the whole family, as seen here with Grace's nan, Marie, handling Papillon 'Barleybright Moustache'. (Photo: Fran McWade)

AT WHAT AGE CAN AN EXHIBITOR START SHOWING?

We've spoken a bit about the dogs, but before we move to showing it would be useful to think about exhibitors. Exhibitors come from all backgrounds and from every age group. There are special classes for young handlers, and children can join the Young Kennel Club from the age of six. Many now-seasoned exhibitors started showing by handling the family dog in junior handling classes.

And at the other end of the spectrum, you are never too old to start showing!

Getting involved in showing without a show dog

It is possible to get involved with the sport even if you haven't got a dog with show potential. Buying a pedigree dog is expensive, and you might want to gain experience while you're saving up, or waiting for that special puppy to be born. You can volunteer to help out at shows, perhaps to be a steward, or you could make yourself available as a handler if you've got the knack – many exhibitors are nervous, and find their dogs behave better with another handler. Some exhibitors cannot run as fast as their dog, and appreciate someone else moving with them. You can join your local ringcraft club and watch the dogs being handled. You may be lucky enough to find someone who will let you handle their dog in the class.

So now that we've covered some of the background to dog showing, let's get on to the sport itself, starting with how to prepare your dog for the show ring.

CHAPTER 2

PREPARING TO SHOW YOUR DOG

Whether you've just collected an eight-week-old puppy or have an adolescent or older dog, there's a lot of preparation to do before you even think of stepping inside a show ring. It's not just knowing what to do, it's being able to do it. The effort and training you put in from the time when you first collect your puppy will pay dividends in your showing career.

WHAT AGE DOES MY DOG NEED TO BE TO START TO SHOW?

Most shows are licensed by the Kennel Club and run under their rules and regulations. Until your puppy is six months old you will not be able to exhibit him at most Kennel Club licensed events, but there is no upper age

Fig. 2.1   A litter of Labrador puppies (Tarimoor). (Photo: Joanne Elrod)

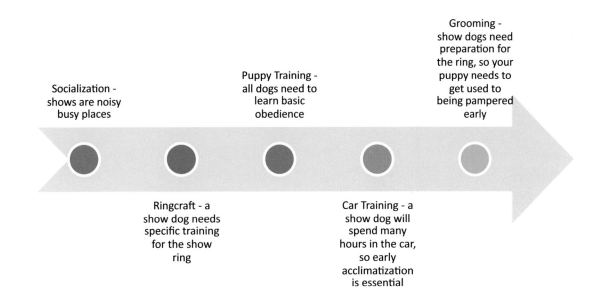

Socialization - shows are noisy busy places

Puppy Training - all dogs need to learn basic obedience

Grooming - show dogs need preparation for the ring, so your puppy needs to get used to being pampered early

Ringcraft - a show dog needs specific training for the show ring

Car Training - a show dog will spend many hours in the car, so early acclimatization is essential

Fig. 2.2   Steps to prepare your dog for his first show.

limit – dogs can start showing at any time in their lives. If you have a young puppy, that first show can seem a long way away, but there's a whole list of things you can do in the intervening time to prepare him, and you, for your first formal show. If you're considering showing an older dog, you'll both benefit from training before entering the show ring.

SOCIALIZATION

Whether or not you end up showing your puppy, it is essential that you start to socialize him as soon as you bring him home. This means getting him used to as many sights and sounds as possible. The experiences he has during his first sixteen weeks of life will have a great influence on his character and behaviour as an adult. A show dog, in particular, needs to be able to act appropriately around other dogs and strangers, including both adults and children. Shows are noisy and busy places. There will be the general hubbub caused by a large number of people chatting, tannoys announcing classes and people clapping the winners. There will be people, dogs, crates and trolleys being pushed past where you are standing. You'll find pushchairs, wheel-

chairs, mobility scooters and people with walking sticks at shows, and your dog needs to be able to stay calm and untroubled while they are going by.

Even before your puppy has completed his vaccinations, he can be carried out and about to expose him to new situations. Let different people stroke and fuss him. He will need to get used to judges going over him so he mustn't flinch away from strangers. Try to make sure he meets children of all ages, and people of all skin colours. Some people recommend taking him to somewhere like a car boot sale, where there will be a host of different activities going on, and where a cute puppy will attract attention from young and old alike. Some breeds are easier to socialize than others, and a naturally aloof breed might take a lot more effort to prepare them for the show ring. But the more you expose him to at a young age, the less scared and fearful he'll be of new things as an adult.

You may consider taking your young puppy to a show just for the experience. Local fun shows, which are not run under Kennel Club rules, are generally less strict when it comes to puppies, and are good places to take him to familiarize him with the hustle and bustle of the show environment. He may even be able to enter

Fig. 2.3   Borzoi puppy 'Cwmcoed Yefrem' enjoys an outing to an agricultural show where he's faced with people and animals as part of his socialization.

Fig. 2.4   All sizes, shapes and manner of dogs attend ringcraft. It's a good place to help your dog learn to behave around other dogs as he should in the show ring.

a puppy class before he's six months old. Be careful that you don't overwhelm him though – his first experience should be positive and fun, as you don't want to put him off showing for life! Once your puppy is four months old you might, at the discretion of the society running the show, be able to take him to any Kennel Club licensed show as a 'Not for Competition' dog. This means that you will probably have to pay an entry fee to take your puppy in, but you will not be able to compete. If it's a benched show, he will usually be allocated a bench. The benefit is clearly that the experience will be good for both you and your puppy. If the schedule doesn't make it clear whether you can take him or not, you may need to contact the secretary organizing the show to check whether they allow young puppies to attend. Under the terms of their insurance, Kennel Club licensed shows cannot permit dogs or puppies to be present at shows without being disclosed in advance on the entry form.

RINGCRAFT

Although you can read books and magazines, look up articles on the internet or watch YouTube videos, there is no substitute for going to a good ringcraft training class to find out what goes on in the show ring and how to present your dog in the best possible way.

From as early an age as possible you should start to stand or stack your dog, and, if it applies to your breed, get him accustomed to standing on a table. He needs to get used to someone he doesn't know approaching him, looking in his mouth at his teeth and running their hands all over his body and, in the case of a dog, to check whether he has both testicles descended.

You'll get the help you need to do this at your local ringcraft class; these provide specific training for show dogs and handlers. It's useful to contact the society or club as soon as you know you're getting a puppy so that you can enrol him and be ready to start attending classes as soon as his course of vaccinations has been completed and he is able to go out and mix with other dogs.

Fig. 2.5   *Different breeds are presented in different ways. The Akita is shown stacked. 'Minoso's Bear Balinor at Worthysway'.*

Showing different breeds

Different breeds of dog are shown in different ways. Some are stacked, which means the handler places their feet and holds them in position to show the dog to his best advantage. Other breeds are free-standing and have to learn how to obey the handler's signals to shift their feet until they are set up correctly. Whichever method is used, dogs have to learn to hold this position for some time, and maintain the stance when the judge is going over them.

Ringcraft classes are often run by your local canine society, so you should be able to find one reasonably close to you. Classes are normally held weekly, and you can find a list of clubs on the Kennel Club website. Normally the cost of the weekly sessions varies from £1 to £2, with possibly an initial joining fee for the club (£2–£6). The trainers at ringcraft classes are experienced in many breeds of dogs, but before you go along it's an idea to view YouTube videos so you know how your dog is supposed to look when standing. The Breed Showing Information Guide at the back of this book gives a list of breeds and specifies whether they are stacked, free standing or presented on a table, as well as whether a particular type of show lead is recommended.

The trainers will act as judges, and run their hands over your dog to check how he's put together exactly as it happens at shows. This is useful practice as it will show you what your dog accepts and what he doesn't like, for example, having his teeth looked at, and you can work on this at home. There is no substitute for having experienced people offering their advice to help improve your chances when you're in a show ring for

Fig. 2.6   *A typical example of a ringcraft club where the 'judge' will go over the dog and give the handlers tips on how to stack, stand and move them.*

real. Older dogs are usually welcomed too. Ringcraft classes are sometimes open to non-pedigree as well as pedigree dogs.

Most people enjoy going to ringcraft. It's a chance to meet up with experienced people and novices alike, and an opportunity to share trials and tribulations. You should find your class very supportive. It is also a good place to pick up schedules for shows coming up in your area. Although most shows advertise online, there are still a number which issue paper schedules only.

TRAINING FOR THE SHOW RING

You cannot just rely on weekly training classes to prepare your dog for the show ring; you will also need to put in a lot of practice at home. Training your new puppy for the show ring might well have already begun by the time you collect him if you are buying from a breeder who specifically breeds pups to show. Often breeders will have started getting the pups used to being handled, and teaching them to stand. How much

training has been done will depend partly on the size of the litter – a breeder with a small litter will have far more time to devote to each, than one with a litter of fourteen or more!

Whether or not any pre-training has been done, if you are going to show your new puppy, it's never too

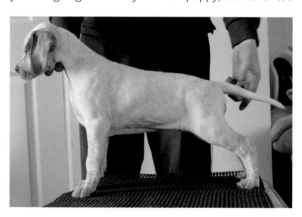

Fig. 2.7   *It's never too early to start practising! Pointer pup being stacked by breeder (Sharnphilly) at seven weeks old.*

early to start. The essentials are that your puppy will need to stand still and be able to concentrate on you while ignoring distractions.

Using bait

Bait is the word used in showing to describe the treats or titbits used in the show ring either to reward the dog for good behaviour, or to get his attention. In some breeds bait is thrown in the air to make the dog look up. Bait is a two-edged sword. It is useful for training, but some dogs become so fixated on the reward that they can think of nothing else, and don't offer the behaviour that they should be being rewarded for. If bait is used to try to make a dog move nicely beside the handler, there is the risk that, instead of moving nicely, he will run and constantly jump up to get the treat. Likewise, a dog taught to stand by chewing at a piece of bait may not want to stop nibbling and open his mouth for the judge to inspect his teeth.

Most people start by using bait in training, but it's good to be aware that as behaviour is learned, rewards

Fig. 2.9   Baiting Boxer 'Ch Faerdorn Dusted Over Tartarian', winning Bitch CC at the Scottish Kennel Club. (Photo: John Carnaby)

should start to become physical (i.e. fusses, stroking), rather than edible. You can still reward him with a treat, but less often. It will make life much easier in the ring if the dog expects a reward on exit from the ring, not all the time he is being judged. Throwing food around in the ring or using squeaky toys to get a dog's attention are activities which are not welcomed by other exhibitors. Whatever you choose to train with initially, work towards getting your dog's attention or rewarding him for the right behaviour without the use of any support items. Your life will be easier, and your fellow exhibitors will thank you for it.

Using a clicker

Clicker training has become very popular. The idea is that the click is a signal that identifies the behaviour

Fig. 2.8   Keeping a dog's attention with bait. Basset Fauve de Bretagne 'Ch Mochras Mahogany' winning BOB at Boston. (Photo: Ian Sexton)

you want, and he is rewarded for achieving it. An alternative to clicker training is to use a verbal cue, such as 'good', or 'good boy'. This is positive training, enabling the dog to understand what we want of him, and not punishing any behaviours we don't want. A dog does not want to be naughty (even though we might think at times that he's setting out to embarrass us) and misbehaviour normally comes from him not understanding what we are asking him to do.

If you are going to try clicker training, you must first teach your dog to connect the click with the reward. There are various methods to do this. One is to put some treats on the ground and click as the dog goes to eat them, or you can click and then just give him a treat. Once he associates the click with the treat, you can start to reward behaviours. Timing is essential. You must click precisely when he does the behaviour you want; for example, if you're training a sit, then it's important to click when he is actually sitting, not when he starts to get up again. The click tells him, 'Yes, that's what I want.' Treating should follow the click. A clicker is used as, with practice, it is a faster and more accurate signal than verbal praise. Clicker training is used by many people to achieve a correct stack or stand, and also to improve the gait. The emphasis is on training. Clickers should not be taken into the show ring (unless you want to make fellow exhibitors very unhappy), so you should not become dependent on the clicker for getting the behaviours you desire.

Some people swear by clicker training, but others don't get on with it.

Starting to stand your dog

Smaller dogs are placed on a table for judging, and this is a useful place to start with all puppies when

How dogs are presented to the judge

The majority of dogs are presented to the judge side-on, and most seem to face to the right. But some dogs (and handlers) are more comfortable facing to the left. Perhaps some dogs have a 'good' side that is better to present to the judge. The coat may have different patterning, for example, or perhaps you want to hide a trimming error! When it's time for the judge to go over the dog, most are presented facing to the right, but there are no penalties if your dog prefers to be different and will only stand the other way. Some dogs are presented face on to the judge, and some, like the Japanese Akita Inu, are presented at a 45 degree angle.

Fig. 2.10   *The majority of breeds are presented side-on to the judge, as demonstrated by this Tibetan Terrier 'Ch Gandaki Jin Tsin'.*

Fig. 2.11
The Japanese Akita Inu is presented at a 45 degree angle to the judge. 'BiSS/ Multi/Int/ Bel, Ger, Ir, Champion Tsoyu Amaya'.

they are little. Training sessions should be short as a young puppy has a very short attention span. Begin by getting your puppy to stand still for a few seconds, and then reward him with lots of fuss. A popular method of persuading a wriggly puppy to stand still is to use a tube of soft cheese as bait. This treat doesn't run out, and he can lick away while you are placing his feet. Say 'Stand' or whatever word you are going to use so he associates the action with the command. Practising a few times every day for a short time is far better than lengthy training sessions.

When he knows he has to stand still, you can start to move his feet into the correct position. The breeder is normally the best person to ask about the correct way to stand your dog, but there are other ways to find out. You can use Google, go to shows and watch YouTube videos to see how your breed should be presented. Normally front legs should be straight (at a 90 degree angle to the ground) and set beneath the shoulder blades. For some breeds the hind legs are extended behind the dog, and vertical from the hock to the foot, while others stand four square.

There are whole books and many articles about how to stack or free stand your dog, but there's not enough space in this book to give the subject the attention it deserves. It is also a hard feat to accomplish from just reading the written word. That's why it is essential to go to ringcraft classes to be shown how to do it properly. Unfortunately, while YouTube videos or articles with pictures can illustrate how to set your dog up, they sometimes forget that you've got a wriggly, squirming puppy who seems intent on doing anything except what you want him to do. He is also an individual who hasn't read the text books! You need to understand how he is developing, and that some things might be harder or easier as he grows and matures. Puppies may not be able to achieve or hold the adult show stance as their muscles are simply not strong enough.

Stacking and free standing

Stacking refers to the way in which, in many breeds, the handler places the dog's feet into position, and then holds the head (and in some breeds, the tail) to show

Fig. 2.12   Irish Setter 'Highclare Knight's Tail' ('Murlin') is a good example of a dog being stacked.

Fig. 2.13   The Miniature Pinscher is shown free standing. 'Ch Vardenais Show Fairy'.

him off to best advantage. The handler normally kneels or stands behind the dog.

In free standing, the handler does not hold the dog in position; the dog has to learn to walk into the stand himself. When free standing, the handler normally stands in front of the dog, and the dog's attention is on the handler.

In some breeds the handler stands behind the dog. Stacking or standing your dog well can mean the difference between winning the class, and going out of the ring without a rosette. It's often the case that an experienced handler can get a dog placed, while a novice won't. It's the same dog, I hear you say, and isn't this unfair?

You would be right in thinking that the conformation of the dog is the same whoever handles him. But in breeds where straightness from hock to floor is required, for example, a dog that is overstretched can look as though his conformation is wrong. If the dog's feet are not placed properly, his back can look roached (or rounded). A head held wrongly can take away the alert appearance, and make it look hunched and depressed. The presentation of the dog in the show ring shows off the stance of the dog as it looks its best, prepared and ready for the job it is to do. Think of a gundog who's on the scent and ready to flush out a bird: he's alert, poised and ready to work.

Fig. 2.15 The German Shepherd Dog has an individual way of being presented in the show ring, as demonstrated by 'Quattro von der Partnachklamm'. (Photo: Louis Cambridge Donald)

Fig. 2.14 Attending shows is the best way to fully understand how a breed is shown. The Siberian Husky stands four square, as demonstrated by 'Ch Rajarani Ezekiel'. (Photo: Krystyan Greenland)

Fig. 2.16 Belgian Shepherd Dogs, such as this Groenendael 'Grondemon Krusader', usually stand facing outwards to show alertness.

Fig. 2.17   The Border Collie can either be stacked or free standing, as shown by 'Miraje It Can't Be'.

Practice makes perfect! Experienced exhibitors often practise in front of a mirror so that they can see exactly how their dog looks. Repeating the stand time after time will make it automatic for both you and him, and placing his feet in the ring will become instinctive. At first you may only get him to stand for a second or two, but by practising you can build this up to the several minutes he will need to hold this position in the ring. Little and often is the best approach – ask him for one stand at a time, and reward him copiously when you get it. When stacking and moving his legs into position, always move the front legs from the elbow, and the back legs from above the hocks.

Table dogs

Dogs which are shown on the table are first stacked or stood in the ring. Only when the judge is going to examine them are they placed on the table. So it is equally important to ensure that your puppy can stand on both surfaces. From the time you get your puppy

Fig. 2.18   The stand with hind legs extended is a natural stance for many dogs, as demonstrated by this picture of a wolf. (Photo: the UK Wolf Conservation Trust)

Fig. 2.19   Practice makes perfect! This six-month-old labrador 'Oakhouse One For Joy at Serengoch' is practising the stand at home.

Fig. 2.20   Small dogs, such as the Shetland Sheepdog, are examined by the judge on a table. 'Mossvale Moonlight at Arcticfrost'.

Fig. 2.22   In the UK the Yorkshire Terrier is exhibited on a box covered in a red fabric, normally velvet. 'Ch Keriwell Dreamweaver'. (Photo: Keith Burgoyne Photography)

Fig. 2.21   Judge going over Basset Fauve de Bretagne 'Ch Brequest Bailee Basler'. (Photo: Geoff Baldwin)

Ramps

Bulldogs, Basset Hounds and Chow Chows are heavy dogs but low to the ground, making it difficult for judges to examine them. It has become increasingly popular in the USA and on the continent to use ramps so that these breeds can be shown at an elevated level. This means that the judge is able to make a more comprehensive examination, particularly of the eyes and skin. Ramps were used for the first time in 2014 for showing Bulldogs at Crufts and at the Scottish Kennel Club Championship Show. It is expected that it will become common practice, so these breeds may benefit from being trained to use a ramp. Exhibitors are not penalized for not using a ramp.

Fig. 2.23 *Ramps are becoming common for Bulldogs, Basset Hounds and Chow Chows. 'Andlares Summer Breeze'. (Photo: Andlare Bulldogs)*

Fig.2.24 *Originating abroad, ramps were used at Crufts for the first time in 2014. Here a ramp is used at an Italian dog show. (Photo: Andlare Bulldogs)*

make sure the table is a nice place to be. Don't just use it for grooming, nail trimming or training – make it a fun place. Feed him on it, fuss him on it. If he objects to nail trimming, you may choose to do this on a different surface. The last thing you want is to place your dog on the table in front of the judge and for him to get stressed as he's expecting something he doesn't like to happen!

GAIT

Gait is the word used to describe the way a dog moves around the show ring. Although different breeds move at different speeds and have different ways of moving, all are expected to trot in the show ring as the Kennel Club suggests this is the best movement to bring out a dog's virtues or to expose any faults. A dog moving well around the show ring with legs flowing freely, head up and alert and tail wagging is an absolute pleasure to watch. The judge may ask for exercises such as the triangle or straight up and down, perhaps continuing round to the back of the line, so that he can check if

Fig. 2.25   'Sh CH Sharnphilly Juici Cuture JW' winning Reserve Best in Show at the Scottish Kennel Club Championship Show. (Photo: Alan V. Walker)

the dog is running straight and with the correct movement for the breed. The correct gait for each breed is described in the breed standard. For small dogs the handler only needs to walk, but for larger breeds the handler needs to be fit and able to run at the speed best suited to the pace and action of the dog. Some exhibitors stack or stand their dogs themselves, but may ask other people to run their dogs if they have mobility problems.

In trot, the dog's legs on one side should meet together, with the front leg going back, and the back leg going forwards at the same time. Sometimes dogs will pace (both legs on one side moving forwards together), which is unacceptable for almost all breeds in the show ring – one exception being the Neapolitan Mastiff. Pacing gives a rather ambling, rolling look to the movement. It can result from a conformation fault, a tired dog, or simply because the handler is moving at the wrong speed for the dog.

Getting your dog to move nicely requires as much practice as the stand. You can practise in the garden, in your local park and, of course, at ringcraft, where you'll get advice on how your dog is looking. Have a command (such as 'Trot') so your dog knows it's time to get his nose off the ground and run beside you.

Keeping the dog's head up can be a problem at some shows, particularly if you are in the ring late in the day and food has been thrown around by the exhibitors before you. It's understandable that there will be desira-

Fig. 2.26   The Miniature Pinscher has a precise hackney action, as demonstrated by 'Ch Shotopa King of Arabia JW ShCM'.

Fig.2.28   *Spanish Water Dogs should have a powerful drive and their movement should be brisk, sound and athletic. 'Valentisimo's Castro'. (Photo: Allie Broome)*

Fig.2.27   *The English Toy Terrier should never have a hackney action, but instead has a flowing extended trot. 'Ch Witchstone Telling Tails'. (Photo: Alan Seymour)*

Fig. 2.29   *Miniature Bull Terriers should cover the ground smoothly with free easy strides and a jaunty air. 'Eng and Ir Ch Grascos Honky Tonky'. (Photo: Graham Peers)*

ble smells to sniff on the grass or matting, and your dog may be more interested in these than in running beside you. This is where your training comes in. Preparing in different environments with different distractions will help your dog to realize that when you ask him to move, he must ignore all the other things he'd prefer to be doing – at least for the short time he's in the ring.

When moving, make sure your show lead is kept neat and tidy in your hand – you want to present a smart picture to the judge. Some dogs run better on a loose lead, while other dogs have a slip lead pushed high on their neck behind their ears, with the handler holding the other end up over the head. This can give the impression of a dog being strung up, but this needn't be the case if the handler is just loosely holding the lead, rather than pulling the dog's head up. If the lead is held too tightly, the front legs will come off the ground and can make the dog look as if he's goose-stepping.

Figs 2.25, 2.26, 2.27, 2.28 and 2.29 show examples of how different breeds should move.

In the show ring the judge will often ask all the class to move together, and again the best place to practise this is at ringcraft. In a breed class most dogs will be moving at the same speed, but in an Any Variety class there will be a mixture of breeds and sizes. The small dogs should be together, either at the back or the front of the line, and should move separately but this may not always happen if the judge hasn't asked the steward to organize them that way. Look at the speed of the dog in front of you, whether it's the same breed or a different one, as you may find it's moving more slowly than you. When you start off, watch carefully to see where the judge or ringcraft trainer is looking, and remember he hasn't got eyes in the back of his head. If you need to, you can slow your pace when you are behind him to get a little space in front of you, and then speed up to allow your dog to do his best trot when he is in the judge's eye line! At ringcraft practise different positions, so your dog learns to move nicely whether he's at the front of the group, at the back or in the middle.

MATCH NIGHTS

Some ringcraft clubs run 'match nights'. These are like mini shows, but the competitors are all members of the club. Occasionally match nights involve a competition between two clubs. Match nights are informal in that you're amongst friends, but formal in that they have to be run to Kennel Club Show Regulations. A club cannot run more than twelve shows per year, so match nights are normally held monthly. Entry is limited to just sixty-four dogs, and dogs which have already won a Challenge Certificate or equivalent are not permitted to enter. Placed dogs may receive prize cards, rosettes or other prizes. Dogs can only be exhibited by the owner, and have to be registered with the Kennel Club.

Match nights are a good way to get experience of showing, with the added advantage that you will have the support and advice of trainers and experienced exhibitors. You may be able to enter your puppy from four months old.

Puppy walks

Ringcraft clubs often hold 'puppy walks' for puppies up to six months old, which are too young to compete in the match nights. Many experienced exhibitors go to ringcraft to take part in puppy walks as it's a good experience for a young puppy.

PUPPY OBEDIENCE TRAINING CLASSES

Showing takes up a day or so every weekend at most, and for the rest of the time your puppy will be living with you as part of your household. If he's not going to drive you up the wall, he needs to be a well adjusted,

Fig. 2.30   Puppies attending a training class to learn basic obedience and how to behave around other dogs.

trained and socialized dog. In addition to learning how to be a show dog, he will need basic obedience training, otherwise you will find him impossible to live with. No one likes a dog jumping up with muddy paws, no matter what size they are, and constantly being dragged up the street by a dog straining on the lead will soon become very tedious.

Puppy training classes are essential for all young dogs, and should be started as soon as possible after the course of vaccinations has been completed. This is where he will learn basic commands or build on what you've already taught him. It's an excellent opportunity for him to mix with other dogs and learn how to act appropriately around them. Beginner classes usually run for around six to eight weeks, and costs can vary from as little as £1.50 to about £10 a session. Look around for courses in your area, and don't be worried about contacting them early, even before you bring your puppy home. The best courses may be oversubscribed so putting your name down early will give you a better chance of getting on a course as soon as possible.

Many puppy training classes are held, and there are many different training methods. A course run by your local canine society may be a lot cheaper than one run by a private trainer, as the latter has to make a living. While you can listen to recommendations from friends, read reviews on websites or be swayed by a trainer's qualifications, the best way to find out if a class is for you is to visit without your puppy to watch a session taking place. There are some training methods which have become completely outdated, but unfortunately there are still some trainers around who believe in them, particularly the dominance theory. This takes the view that if you don't discipline your puppy by rough treatment, smacking or shaking, alpha rolls and taking his food away, etc., he will seize any opportunity to become pack leader and dominate you. Avoid these trainers like the plague! You need to find a trainer who practises positive training methods, which is reward-based training, rather than punishment-based training. A dog who does something because he wants to please you is far happier than one which obeys you out of fear. And in the case of show dogs, a dog cringing in the ring is unlikely to bring you any rewards.

The best courses will have a number of puppies starting at the same time, and completing the course together. Often you will be given a certificate at the end to show you've completed the class, which you can keep as your dog's first award. Some, however, have dogs starting every week, and training can become confused as the trainer tries to teach at different levels at the same time. So it's important to understand the training methods employed and how the class is taught to make sure you are going to be happy taking your puppy there.

At training classes it is you, the owner, who will be taught how to train your puppy. Your dog won't be trained for you. Training with your dog is an enjoyable activity and should be fun, resulting in a well behaved dog which is a real joy to live with. The basics will include the 'Sit', 'Down', 'Stand' and 'Stay', often a 'Watch me' (to make sure your dog has his attention on you), and of course, the all-important 'Recall'! You'll find it a good place to get advice and help with worries such as puppy nipping and toilet training, and meet people with puppies the same age facing the same problems.

Should a show dog be taught to sit?

There is a school of thought that says show dogs should not be taught to sit in case they sit in the show ring. The reasoning is that judges may glance round the dogs waiting in the ring and may prefer dogs which remain standing, rather than those which are slouching around or sitting. Be assured, dogs are capable of learning a number of commands, and even if you have taught your dog to sit, you can also teach him to stand. The sit command is very useful for everyday life – it's easier to wait for traffic to pass if your dog is sitting calmly at the kerbside, or if you want to wait for a horse or bicycle to go past on a bridleway.

Taking obedience further

Training is fun, and doesn't need to stop after you've finished your initial puppy training. You can take your puppy to more advanced classes, and think about gaining the Good Citizen's Award, working your way through Bronze and Silver, and ultimately to Gold. Show dogs, like any dogs, need to be obedient to their owner, and good members of society. Once you have a Good Citizen's award, you will be able to enter additional classes at some shows, including Crufts (although you will need to qualify for your breed class to be eligible).

COLLARS, LEASHES AND SHOW LEADS

Your puppy will need to get used to wearing a collar and walking nicely on a lead soon after you bring him home. When buying a collar for a show dog, think about the type of coat he has. Long-haired dogs should have a rolled leather collar to avoid leaving marks and indentations in their fur. It may be a good idea to take the collar off when in the house to avoid getting marks/indentations on the coat. Do be careful about leaving a collar on if you crate your puppy, as it has been known for collars to get caught and some dogs have even been strangled this way.

It is against the law for a dog to be out in public without an identity tag on his collar (or harness) that has the owner's name and address on it. When ordering a tag, it's a good idea to include your mobile number as well as your home phone number. If your dog gets lost out walking you'll want someone to be able to contact you as soon as possible.

Show dogs also need show leads. Some breeds use a particular type of lead, for others it's simply a matter of the exhibitor's personal preference. Suggested lead types for each breed (if any) are shown in the Breed Showing Information Guide at the back of this book, and a few of the more common leads are pictured here. When you practise standing and moving your puppy at home, or when you take him to ringcraft, get in the habit of using your show lead. He'll soon come to associate this lead with having to 'work'. Try not to use this lead at any other time.

Examples of show leads

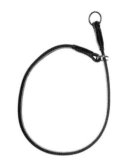

Fig.2.31   The American show collar – can be used as a slip or fixed collar.

Fig.2.32   A leather slip show collar.

Fig.2.33   A leather loop lead with swivel.

Fig.2.34   A leather slip lead.

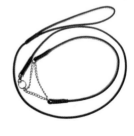

Fig.2.35   A half-check collar and lead.

Fig.2.36   A leather half-check show set with swivel.

Fig.2.37   Leads can come in a variety of colours and materials. (Figs 2.31–2.37 courtesy of The Show Dog Company: www. theshowdogcompany. co.uk)

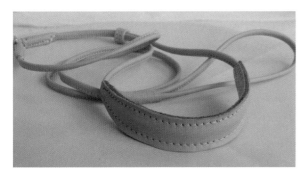

Fig.2.38   Lead with comfort collar. (Picture courtesy of Hides and Collars: www.hidesandcollars.co.uk)

GETTING YOUR DOG USED TO TRAVELLING

Although you might be intending just to do a few local shows, almost every show you go to will be out of town. Shows are normally held in sports centres, at county showgrounds or often at equestrian centres. Having a car, and a dog which is accustomed to travelling, is crucial for show dogs, even for the closest shows. If he's unhappy travelling, then he is not going to be eager to get in the car to go to a show, nor will he perform at his best once he is there.

Most dogs suffer some form of travel sickness during their first car journey, often on the way home from the breeder. It's quite normal for young puppies to suffer from motion sickness as the ear structures necessary for balance won't yet be fully developed. Most puppies grow out of being car-sick, but unfortunately some don't. Some dogs start to equate travelling in the car with being sick, and begin to get stressed even before

they've jumped in. Signs that your puppy is unhappy in the car can include listlessness, whining or excessive drooling, as well as actually vomiting. It's important to make travelling as stress-free and comfortable for him as possible, and essential to ensure that he is safe. If your dog suffers from motion sickness, having him secured in a seat harness on the back seat will help him face forwards and thus help minimize the effects of travelling. Alternatively, you can use a crate, which is probably the safest form of transportation. If you have trained him to feel secure in his crate at home, he may feel less stressed when he's in it in the car.

Fig.2.39   The Highway Code states that animals must be under control when travelling in a car. If they are travelling on the back seat, a harness is recommended.

Start taking your puppy for short car journeys as soon as you can, and always end up at a place he enjoys – a special walk, for example. Try to associate car travel with having fun. Open the window to equalize the inside and outside air pressures and use air conditioning to keep the car cool. Do not feed him before travelling, and do not have the radio on too loud. Sprays and collars (Adaptil, for example) are available that emit pheromones, which can have a calming effect. If all else fails, your vet can provide medications, but make sure these do not have a long-lasting sedative effect as you will need your dog to be bright and alert in the show ring.

When you venture out on longer journeys, remember to take frequent breaks so that he can stretch his legs and toilet.

Fig. 2.40   Car crates are available to fit most cars, and are probably the safest way to transport your dog.

Fig. 2.41 Rhodesian Ridgebacks 'Gunthwaite Diamond Heist' and 'Gunthwaite Flash Diamond' ('Kilo' and 'Rudi') show how to travel in style in their van fitted out with custom cages.

Fig.2.42   Make car journeys enjoyable by starting with short journeys to a favourite walk. Shetland Sheepdog 'Arcticfrost Alaskan Star'. (Photo: Arcticfrost)

START YOUR GROOMING REGIME EARLY

All dogs need to be groomed to some extent, even very short-haired dogs. Grooming is covered in more detail in Chapter 9, but it needs a quick word here as a puppy destined for the show ring will need to accept more pampering than a pet dog. A grooming table is useful for all but the largest breeds as it helps keep a young puppy from squirming as you brush him, de-mat him, or simply cut his nails. Do not leave it until the day before your first show to give him his first proper groom, as it may well result in a battle which won't set either of you up for your big day. So be sure to get your puppy used to being brushed from the day you bring him home.

SO NOW YOU'RE READY ...

You've taken your dog to ringcraft, you've given him his basic puppy training, you know he's familiar with all the different sights and sounds you could find, and you've got him used to travelling and grooming – so now it's time to start looking for your first show.

A word about breakdown cover

Travelling to shows often necessitates long journeys, so it is possible that your car might break down at some point, and you'll need the assistance of a breakdown recovery service. Before choosing, or renewing, your breakdown recovery policy, make sure you understand their policy on transporting animals. Some companies leave it to the individual driver's discretion as to whether he will transport your dog along with your broken-down car. This is not much use if you're stranded on the M1 with your show dog in the back and the driver sent to help you doesn't like dogs. Some companies insist on your dog being left in the car if it is towed, and on a hot summer's day this may not be practicable, as the engine of the towed car will not be running and the air conditioning will not be working. Some companies ask you to tell them if you've broken down with a dog, or dogs, in the car. They will then endeavour to find a driver who is not allergic to, nor afraid of, dogs to come to help you. This may mean a slightly longer wait, but will mean that your canine friend will be recovered too. So check the policy carefully, and make sure your dog/s will be recovered along with the vehicle, driver and passengers.

CHAPTER 3

TYPES OF DOG SHOW

There are literally thousands of dog shows held all over the country throughout the year. If you wanted to go to a show every weekend (and some weekdays), then as long as you had the time, money, energy and stamina you could do so. You may be lucky enough to find some shows very local to you, especially if you live near any of the major show grounds. But others you will definitely need to travel to, perhaps some distance, if you want to take up the sport seriously. Dog showing starts to become more expensive once you factor in fuel costs and entrance fees, and going to some shows may even necessitate an overnight stay. But one of the attractions of this sport is that you can show as little or as much as you want to, depending on your time available and your pocket.

There are three main categories of dog show – companion, open and championship shows – which are licensed by the Kennel Club, and thus are governed by the Kennel Club showing regulations. In addition, there are fun dog shows which are normally held to raise money for a local charity, and may well be run alongside a village fete.

WHICH SHOWS CAN YOU ENTER?

Cross-breed dogs (or unregistered pedigree dogs) can be shown at fun days and companion shows. Kennel Club-registered pedigree puppies and dogs can be entered at any fun, companion, open or championship show except for those which are limited to members of a particular club or a specific breed. Crufts is the only exception. To be eligible to enter Crufts you need to qualify your dog by being placed at a championship show. Which classes you need to be placed in, and which places qualify depend on your breed of dog and which stud book band he's in – see Chapter 6.

There is nothing to stop you entering a championship show with your six-month-old puppy without going to any other show, and some people are indeed lucky enough to gain a Crufts' qualification at their first attempt in the show ring. But showing your dog to his best does take practice, and most novices prefer to start with open and companion shows to gain some experience. Each type of show has different procedures for entering and varying entry fees.

Do you need to take your Kennel Club registration certificate?

Newcomers to showing often ask whether they need to take their Kennel Club registration certificate to shows, and the answer is no. Fun and companion shows are very informal, and you do not need any kind of identification to enter your dog. At these shows entry is normally under your dog's pet name on the day. To exhibit at open and championship shows entries must be made some time in advance and your dog's full details (Kennel Club registration number, breeder's name, names of sire and dam) must be written on the entry form.

A quick guide to shows you can enter

Fun Days and Companion Shows

Open Shows and Championship Shows

Crufts

- Open to all dogs whether cross breed or pedigree. Pedigree dogs do not need to be registered with the Kennel Club.
- May allow puppies under the age of six months to enter.

- Only pedigree dogs registered with the Kennel Club can enter.
- Puppies under the age of six months cannot be entered.

- Only open to dogs who have qualified.
- Puppies under the age of six months cannot be shown.

Fig. 3.1   Types of dog show.

HOW YOUR DOG WILL BE JUDGED (AND WHY YOU MIGHT NOT ALWAYS BE PLACED)

Before we discuss the shows themselves, it's useful to take a minute or two to consider how your dog will be

Fig. 3.2   The judge will assess how closely the dog meets the breed standard. Lancashire Heeler 'Lankeela Tracy's Quest'.

judged. At any type of show the judging will be carried out along the same lines, but one judge may like your dog and give him a high placing, while another may not place him at all. But remember, whatever your level of showing, you always take home the best dog regardless of the opinion of the judge!

Although dog showing is competitive, your dog is not directly judged against the other dogs, but against the 'breed standard'. The standard describes attributes such as appearance and temperament, as well as the ideal characteristics of the breed. The perfect dog is described in terms of head and skull, eyes, ears, mouth (correct 'bite' for the breed), neck, forequarters, body, hindquarters, feet, tail, coat, colour and size. It also paints a picture of how the dog should move. As you can see, the standard is fairly comprehensive.

Your dog will not meet the standard exactly – it's highly unlikely any dog ever could. The judge will be looking to award first place to the dog which, in their opinion, is the closest match to the breed standard. Some of the points where the dog deviates from the standard are taken more seriously than others, and these may be ones you can do nothing about. For example, it is impossible to know how a young puppy's adult teeth will grow through, and the showing career of some dogs comes to an abrupt end if their adult teeth do not grow through with the correct bite. On the other hand, some faults can be worked on. Your dog may have been having an 'off day' which affected the way

Fig.3.3   *A Chinese Crested stacked on the table for the judge. 'Annamac Perseus at Aucristae'. (Photo: Miss V High)*

Fig. 3.4   *The movement should be correct for the breed. Entlebucher Mountain Dog 'Torfheide Beethoven'. (Photo: Amy Scales)*

Fig. 3.5   *The dog should stand to show off his conformation in relation to the standard. Deerhound 'Tailormade for Kilbourne'.*

he moved, or you may not have run him at the correct speed or stood him properly.

Dog showing is not a beauty competition: the judge is looking as much at the inner construction of your dog as how well he looks in the ring. The judgements made have to be somewhat subjective; judges are only human, and each may have a slightly different interpretation of the breed standard. Some have a preference for one type of dog over another, or will put more weight on some features than others. You may find your dog is placed highly under one judge, and you optimistically enter your next show to find you're not even in the line-up. As you attend more and more shows you will get to know which judges might give you the best chance of success. Unless your dog is a very poor example of the breed you will always have a chance to get placed. This is what makes showing so addictive.

Some judges are breed specialists – that is, they only judge one breed – but others can judge more than one. So some may have more experience of judging your breed than others. This, too, may make a difference to which dogs are placed.

We'll discuss judges and the judging process in more detail in Chapter 5.

SHOWING REGULATIONS

Every time you enter a Kennel Club licensed show you are agreeing to abide by the showing regulations. There are some general points for you to be aware of, in addition to the more obvious qualifications for various classes and criteria for different awards.

General points

Firstly, when you enter your dog in a show you must take all reasonable steps to ensure his needs are met, and you must not put his health at risk. This means you must make sure he has water and is comfortable, and under no circumstances should you leave him in a car when he is likely to overheat. As an exhibitor, you must not handle your dog harshly, nor punish him at any time at the show, whether you are in the ring, the car park or any show caravan site. At all times your dog must be kept under proper control, which is specified as being on a lead. If you breach these rules, you could be reported to the Kennel Club. The mating of bitches anywhere in the environs of the show is prohibited. And though it's probably an archaic leftover, you are not allowed to use firearms or amplifiers or cooking stoves without the permission of the show management.

Dogs cannot exhibit at a show if they have had, are suffering from or have been exposed to a contagious or infectious disease in the three weeks preceding the show.

Keeping venues clean

Always clear up after your dog – this includes when he has fouled and any grooming waste. It is an unfortunate fact that venues are starting to refuse to hold dog shows because of the few inconsiderate people who leave their dog waste lying around for others to clean up. Bins and bags are always provided around the venue, and you should make sure you use these. Don't leave filled bags lying in the car park – there is no such thing as a poo-bag fairy!

TYPES OF SHOW

Fun days

Fun dog shows or novelty shows are often run in conjunction with a village or church fete, and are informal with low entry fees (usually just £1 or so) being taken on the day. They can be for both pedigree and non-pedigree dogs, so do check before going if you are specifically looking to enter a pedigree class. Typical classes on offer will include Prettiest Bitch or Most Handsome Dog, Best Rescue, Fancy Dress, Dog most like its Owner, Waggiest Tail and other such novelty classes. Pedigree classes, if offered, will probably be limited to Any Variety Puppy (any breed of puppy aged up to twelve months) and Any Variety Open (which any dog of any breed and age can enter). The classes may be split into sporting and non-sporting breeds.

Fig. 3.6   'Holly' having fun in the scurry.

Fig. 3.7 'McKenzie' showing off her agility skills.

Fig. 3.8 Any pedigree or cross-breed dog can take part in a fun or companion show.

Sporting dogs traditionally include Hounds, Gundogs and Terriers. These shows can be a lot of fun. Even if no pedigree classes are on offer, fun shows are a good place to socialize your puppy. You may even be able to enter a puppy before the age of six months, but you may need to ring the show secretary before the day to check.

Some fun shows can be quite large affairs, offering something for the whole family, and often there's a chance to try your hand at other dog activities, such as the Scurry, Flyball or Agility.

Fun shows are a good place to start if you've never shown a dog before, as it doesn't matter if your dog shows you up or if you're not quite sure what to do. However, people do like to win, and you might find the pedigree classes are taken a little more seriously than you expect. There may be a combination of complete newcomers giving it a go, and experienced exhibitors getting in a bit of extra practice with a new dog, or simply entering to support the charity. It wouldn't, however, be considered very sporting to exhibit a top winning dog at a fun show.

You'll find fun shows are normally advertised in the local paper, or on posters near the venue. Often places like pet shops will have leaflets you can collect. Sometimes a quick 'Google' search for 'fun dog shows near [your location]' will bring up some events which you can enter.

Fig.3.9 Tornjak 'Tacker Zlatna Sapa'. This breed is still working towards recognition in the UK, but in the meantime he can compete in companion shows. Here he is winning Best Puppy aged four months.

Companion dog shows

Companion dog shows are run under a Kennel Club licence and have to abide by the showing regulations, but they are open to all dogs of any breed, whether cross-breed or pedigree. They will have a range of novelty classes similar to the fun days, but will also have classes just for pedigree dogs. Pedigree dogs shown at companion dog shows do not have to be Kennel Club registered, but dogs who have won a Challenge Certificate (or equivalent award which counts towards the title of Champion, that is, an award gained overseas), a Reserve Challenge Certificate or a Junior Warrant are not permitted to enter.

Pedigree classes can simply be Any Variety Puppy, Junior, Open or Veteran classes, or they may be divided into the seven Kennel Club groupings, such as Any

Fig. 3.10 A pedigree puppy class at a companion show - the atmosphere is far more relaxed than at more formal shows.

Fig. 3.11   Dog shows aren't just for young dogs - older dogs can be exhibited too! 'Rue' winning Best Veteran in Show at a companion show.

Variety Hounds, or Any Variety of a combination of groups, or Any Variety Sporting or Non-Sporting Dogs. There may also be specific breed classes, although there cannot be more than two for each breed. The Kennel Club Groups are: Hounds, Gundogs, Terriers, Utility, Working, Toys and Pastoral. If you're not sure which Group your puppy comes under, check the Breed Showing Information Guide at the back of this book.

Puppy classes may be split for dogs aged either six to nine months or six to twelve months; Junior classes are for dogs aged up to eighteen months; and Veteran classes are for dogs over seven years of age. Any dog may enter an open class if it otherwise qualifies – for example, a puppy or veteran or anything in between can enter the Gundog Open class as long as it is a breed which comes under the Gundog Group.

Entry is on the day of the show, and it usually costs only a small amount to enter each class. Under the Kennel Club rules at least 50 per cent of the proceeds should be given to a charity.

Companion shows are often run by local dog clubs and canine societies. They are less formal than open or championship shows and as such are a great training ground for novice handlers and young dogs. You can experience competition in the show environment and have the chance of winning a rosette or prize. As at fun shows, you may find experienced exhibitors including

Fig. 3.12   Companion show winners.

companion shows in their normal show diary, particularly if they are local.

Once inside the ring you'll find that your ring-craft training comes in very handy as you will know how to stack or stand your dog, and what to expect when the judge goes over him. However, you will find the judge may be more understanding at a companion show if your dog is reluctant to behave, and you will be among other novice handlers who will be sympathetic if your dog gets excited and jumps round the ring on two legs, rather than four. Sometimes there can be a very high entry at companion shows, resulting in large numbers of dogs in the classes you enter, so don't be disappointed if you aren't placed. Remember, you have gone along for the practice and experience.

Judges at fun and companion shows will normally be all-rounders and there will probably only be one judge judging all breeds/classes on that day. Although they may not be an expert in your breed, they will be judging all dogs against a general conformation standard – that is, the bone and muscle structure, and how the dogs move.

Fun days and companion shows – which classes to enter?

As these shows are normally run to benefit a charity, multiple entries are encouraged, and there is nothing to stop you entering as many classes as you wish. Make sure, though, that you do not over-tire a young puppy.

OPEN SHOWS

Open shows are more formal and only Kennel Club registered pedigree dogs can enter. Through showing your dog at an open show you can really start to evaluate your dog against others as you'll hopefully find some classes just for your breed. These types of show are normally run by a local canine society or a breed club.

When you're starting out it's advisable to aim to go to at least a couple of open shows before going to your first championship show. Although more expensive than fun or companion shows, entry at open shows is normally a fifth of the fee of a championship show, the atmosphere is more relaxed and it is an ideal place to get used to being in a more formal show ring and handling your dog. Many people get nervous in front of the judge, but experience and practice should help steady those nerves. Cutting your teeth at open shows means you can assess whether your dog has sufficient potential to warrant the far greater investment involved in entering a championship show.

At the vast majority of open shows classes are mixed and dogs and bitches will be shown in the same ring at the same time. For this reason, while it is not a rule, bitches in season are very much discouraged from attending open shows as they will be a distraction for other dogs.

Different types of open show

There are five main types of open show: general, group (and sub-group), breed, limited and premier. The majority of open shows tend to be general open shows, which all breeds can enter. Some are restricted to one breed or group, or sub-groups (that is, one or more breeds which fall within that group).

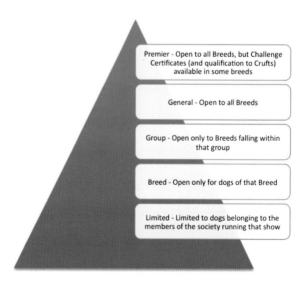

Fig. 3.13   Different types of open show.

Kennel Club groups

The 210 breeds currently recognized by the Kennel Club are divided into seven groups. The group into which your breed falls is shown in the Breed Showing Information Guide at the back of this book. This is a brief summary of each group:

- Hound Group: Originally hounds were bred for hunting. Examples of this group are Irish Wolfhounds, Beagles, Afghan Hounds and Basset Hounds.

- Gundog Group: Gundogs were bred to hunt with guns, and mainly hunt birds. Their names often describe the way they hunt, as in Retrievers, Pointers and Setters.

- Terrier Group: Originally terriers were bred to hunt vermin and tend to be smaller dogs. Their names often give them away, for example the Border Terrier.

- Utility Group: Nowadays the original purpose for which utility group dogs were developed has since disappeared, so mostly the dogs in this group do not fit anywhere else. They include Dalmatians, Schnauzers and Poodles.

- Pastoral Group: These are herding dogs bred to work with cattle and sheep, and include Sheepdogs, Collies and Corgis.

- Working Group: This group includes Dobermans, Great Danes, St Bernards, Mastiffs and other breeds bred to do a particular job.

- Toy Group: Originally, toy dogs were bred as lapdogs, but the group also now includes smaller versions of larger dogs. Examples include Chihuahuas, King Charles Spaniels and Yorkshire Terriers.

Fig. 3.14   A typical open show.

General open show

A general open show is normally run by a local canine society and is open to any breed of dog. The classes on offer vary from show to show. Some are quite big, with separate classes for many breeds, and some are smaller, with only a few breed classes on offer. But whatever dog you have, you'll be able to enter, even if your breed isn't listed in the schedule.

Breeds that can be expected to have a large entry at shows, such as Labradors and Golden Retrievers, are normally catered for with their own breed classes. But breeds which have a much lower entry will be grouped together in Any Variety Not Separately Classified (AVNSC) classes.

General open shows may be run on the group system, and separate AV (Any Variety) and AVNSC classes will be held for each group – see Chapter 4. Judging of the group system means there is an extra step for selecting the Best in Show. When each breed has been judged to find the Best of Breed, group judging then takes place. This is where all the best of breed winners in the group, together with the first placed dog in the AVNSC class, will be judged to select the group winner. The Best in Show will then be selected from all group winners.

Group and sub-group open shows

A group open show is run exactly like a general open show, except that entry is restricted to the breeds which fall within that group. Sometimes you will find there are shows that cater for two groups, for example Gundogs and Terriers. A sub-group show is one which is held for more than one breed within the group: Setters and Pointers, for example, form a common sub-group of the Gundog Group.

Breed open show

Most breeds have their own societies which hold their own open (and championship) shows. As a newcomer to showing, these shows offer a great opportunity to get to know other people in your breed, and the turnout is usually a lot higher than for the general open shows. Obviously entry is restricted to that breed, but you do not need to be a member of the society to exhibit. It is recommended that you join your breed society, or at least one of them (more popular breeds often have more than one breed club, sometimes split by region), as you will receive useful information and may have an opportunity to become more involved.

Fig. 3.15   Italian Greyhound 'Barnesmore Billy The Kid'. If there are no separate breed classes at open shows, such breeds will need to enter AVNSC.

Fig. 3.16   Less numerous breeds like the German Spitz Mittel 'Zephon Stormchasing' may not have their own breed clubs.

Limited open shows

Entry at limited open shows is restricted to members of the society who are running the show. Under Kennel Club regulations, there can be no more than seventy-five classes on offer at a limited show. Dogs who have won a Challenge Certificate (CC) are not permitted to compete.

Fig. 3.17   German Shorthaired Pointer 'Barleyarch Trumpeter' winning first place at a limited show. (Photo: Shel Coules)

Premier open shows

A premier open show is similar to a general open show, but because the society has been able to consistently attract a high entry of dogs in some breeds, the Kennel Club has awarded them special status. At these shows, in the breeds with the relevant number of classes, the Best of Breed winner can qualify for Crufts.

Entering an open show

Unlike companion shows, where you can sign up for the class on the day, open shows are more formal, and you will need to have submitted your entry at least three weeks beforehand. Nowadays the majority of shows have online entry, which brings the benefit of a later closing date and an email acknowledgement of your entry. Some shows are still paper entry-based, requiring you to complete an entry form by hand and post it to the secretary. Before you can think of entering a particular open or championship show, you will need to get hold of a schedule which will give you necessary information. In Chapter 4 we'll discuss in more detail where to get schedules, how to select which classes to enter, and how to complete the entry form.

If you want to enter your puppy into a show when he reaches six months of age, you will need to start looking for show schedules as early as possible.

Fig. 3.18 Championship shows are much bigger and busier than open shows. Terrier Day at the Welsh Kennel Club. (Photo: Graham Peers)

How much does it cost?

Entry into an open show is around £5 to £6 for the first class you enter, and usually £1 for each additional class. If you add on the purchase of a catalogue, then you are looking at around £10 to £11 per show that you enter.

CHAMPIONSHIP SHOWS

A championship show is run along the same lines as an open show but will be far bigger: at general shows for all breeds there will be literally thousands of dogs attending. General championship shows are normally run over three or four days, with different groups (or combinations of groups) being judged on different days. Some championship shows are specific to a breed or group, and are held on one day only. Championship shows are popular and attract a high entry as achieving certain places in some classes can qualify your dog for Crufts.

The entry fees at championship shows are a lot higher than for other types of show, averaging around £25 for the first class, and possibly £4 per additional class. Catalogues can be £5 or more. Championship shows may be held some way from where you live, and

Fig. 3.19   American Cocker Spaniel 'H'ozale Daphne of Anamericha Colour Dreams (IMP FRA)' at the East of England Championship Show.

you might need to find overnight accommodation as well. You may also need to pay for car parking, which at some venues can be as much as £10. Most general championship shows have space for caravans, and you can usually camp here for up to a week for around £40.

With some exceptions for shows restricted to one breed, you will receive an exhibitor's pass for championship shows. Check when entering whether passes will be available, and how many passes you will get. Sometimes only the registered owner, or owners, will be given free passes into the show and you might need to buy an extra ticket if someone else is going with you. (For couples, my advice is to register the dog in both your names, and then you will both always get free entry into the show.) If you are entering the show online, then your passes will usually either be emailed to you, or will be made available for download. If you have entered by post, your passes will normally be posted to you.

You will not easily be able to enter the show without your pass if one has been sent, so it is imperative that you remember to take it with you. You may also have to display or surrender your car park pass on arrival. If you do forget your pass, you should go to the secretary's office on arrival at the show.

Benching

The other difference at championship shows is that they are normally 'Benched' shows. The benches form

Removal pass

The most important piece of paper is your removal pass. This will have the number of dogs you are showing, and their breed(s). On leaving the show, you will only be able to exit with your dog(s) if you have this pass with you. So don't lose it and keep it handy. You may need to give it in at a pedestrian exit, or when leaving the car park. At some shows you will need to show your removal pass whenever you take your dog out of the building for a comfort break.

a long line of little wooden/metal cubicles where your dog should be kept unless he is being exercised or being shown in the ring. Most dogs entering a championship show will be allocated a bench, but sometimes the schedule will say that benches will not be provided for toy dogs. If this is the case you will need to take a crate with you. The benches will be numbered consecutively within breeds, and should be close to your show ring. Your bench number will be the same as the entry number shown for your dog on your show passes (often on the removal pass). When you arrive at the show just look for the bench with the same number on it. Dogs are benched by breed, and bench numbers are normally allocated in alphabetical order of exhibitors' surnames. If you are showing two (or more) dogs, it's useful to remember that different breeds are not benched together.

You can purchase a benching chain which fastens to the bench to keep your dog secure. Some people prefer to put crates on the bench, but these do need to be properly secured. Alternatively you can buy a bench front that can be adjusted to fit the different bench widths, and which can be locked. It really depends on your dog/breed how you secure him on the bench – if he is nervous or might snap at other dogs or people passing by, then a crate or bench front may be your best option.

He will need a comfortable blanket to lie on, and you should try to get him to settle. Dogs do need to get used to being benched, but once they are they can relax and sleep and take a break from the stress and excitement of the busy show. Do not leave a nervous, barking dog alone on a bench, as it can be a nuisance to other people.

You may prefer to keep your dog with you rather than benching him. When it is provided, benching should be used, but it is common practice to have your dog with you for at least some of the time. Dogs (or crates)

Fig. 3.20   Benching at a championship show.

should not be allowed to block gangways, nor distract other dogs in the show ring. If you are at the show on your own, you'll appreciate a dog which is used to staying on the bench as it allows you to pop to the loo or get a drink without worrying about him. As you make friends in the show world you'll usually find at least one person hovering around the benching area who'll keep an eye on him for you.

If you qualify for Crufts, you will have to use your bench. Apart from being in the rules of the show, there are just too many people milling around for you to be able to take your dog around with you. So getting him used to being benched as soon as you can will help you prepare for your big day on the green carpet.

If you wander around the benching area at a show you will see most dogs lying quietly or sleeping and ignoring what's going on around them. Dogs who learn to relax on a bench will be fresher, and less stressed, for their performance in the show ring.

Benching is a hot topic: some people like it, some people hate it. If you show abroad you'll find that shows on the continent do not use benching at all. The continued use of benching is currently under discussion and it's possible that it may be made optional, or not provided at all at some point in the future.

Now we've talked about the types of show that you might consider taking your dog along to, we'll move on to schedules and how to decide which classes to enter, and how to complete the entry form.

CHAPTER 4

ENTERING A SHOW

Entries have to be submitted at least three weeks before the show date, and sometimes a lot longer, so you need to organize your show diary well in advance. Of course, the first step is knowing what shows are on and when, and which classes you are eligible for and wish to enter. The way to do this is to get hold of a schedule.

THE SHOW SCHEDULE

The schedule will tell you important information about the show, not least where it is. This should be checked very carefully before you send off your entry. Although the name of the show might sound quite local to you, the actual event may be held at some distance from the location of the society running it. The Manchester Championship Show, for example, is currently held in Stafford. Shows held annually can also occasionally change venue, so it's very important to check where you are going so you don't end up in the wrong place. Also, many general championship shows rotate the days on which different groups are shown from year to year.

The next crucial part to look out for is the closing date for online and postal entries. You may want to make a note of this and put it on your planner if you are not going to send in your entry until nearer the time. Just be certain you're not going to miss it! Even experienced exhibitors often forget and miss putting in their entries. It is not possible to enter after the closing date (although sometimes online dates are moved backwards if the show wants to attract a higher entry). You might like to be organized by entering shows well in advance, but in some circumstances it may be better to wait, particularly if you have a bitch which may come into season just before the show date.

The schedule will specify the entry fees for that show. If you are a member of the society running the show you will be entitled to a slightly reduced entrance fee. The society may be one you would like to join, and you can do so on the entry form when you come to complete it. Unless it's a club for your breed of dog, or a local society you have connections with or want to support, it is not financially worthwhile to join just to get the reduction in fees.

Where to find schedules and show information

The Kennel Club has a comprehensive list of shows on its website but without hyperlinks, so you will need to do a bit of hunting around to find the schedules. The majority of shows are now listed online, have electronic copies of schedules to view and allow online entry. The websites you need to keep an eye on include Fossedata, Higham Press and Dog.Biz. But there are still a fair few shows which still have paper schedules only. At your ringcraft class or the secretary's table at shows you can often find a selection of paper schedules. You can also contact the secretary for a paper schedule if you can't find it anywhere else, or if you just prefer to have a paper copy. The website dogshowcentral.co.uk has a handy list of shows and links to schedules and online entry where available.

The schedule then lists the classes that will be judged at the show. If the show uses the group system, then breeds will be listed by group. For a Toy breed, for example, you'll need to look at the classes for the Toy Group. Smaller shows will only have classes for the more popular breeds, but there will usually be AVNSC (Any Variety Not Separately Classified) classes that you will be able to enter.

AVNSC and AV classes

It's important to understand the difference between AV and AVNSC classes so that you enter the right one, particularly now that changes have been brought in which allow you to enter only one of the classes catering for all breeds without entering a breed class first. You now have the option of entering a breed class AND an AV class (if your breed is catered for with separate classes), or just entering the AV class.

Choosing the right classes can influence how far you can go in the show. To become Best in Show or Best Puppy in Show you need to go through to the group judging. If you enter an adult dog in AV classes only, he will not be eligible to go through to the group judging even if he wins his classes.

Dogs aged over twelve months
If there is a breed class for your dog at open and limited shows, you cannot enter AVNSC but you can enter AV.

Under the changes brought in in 2015, you can enter the AV class without entering the breed class, but even if you win your class you will not be eligible to compete in the group.

If there isn't a specific breed class for your dog, you should enter the AVNSC class as this is only for dogs with no specific breed classes on offer. The first placed dog in the AVNSC class will be eligible to compete for the Best in Group title. You could also enter the AV classes, but there may be a larger entry there and you wouldn't be able to go forward and compete in the group with an adult dog, even if you won Best in AV.

Dogs aged between six and twelve months
If there are breed classes available for your breed, you can enter your puppy either in the breed class or in AV. If there are no breed classes, you can enter your puppy in AVNSC. If your puppy wins Best AV Puppy, or has ONLY entered an AV class and is only beaten by an adult dog (for example, if there were no puppy class and he entered the Junior class), he can go forward to compete for Best Puppy in Group.

Author's Note: the definition of AV and AVNSC classes given here incorporates the changes brought in by the two-year suspension of the beaten dog rule.

Breed classes on offer

The number of classes offered per breed depends on

AVNSC

- Any Variety Not Separately Classified classes can only be entered by dogs who do not have specific breed classes. Unbeaten dogs aged 6 - 12 months and unbeaten adult dogs can go forward to Group Judging.

AV

- Any breed of dog in that group (or any breed if the show is not run under the Group System) can enter Any Variety classes whether or not there is a specific breed class. Only unbeaten dogs aged 6 - 12 months can go forward to Group Judging.

Fig. 4.1 The difference between AVNSC and AV.

Fig. 4.2   *There may not be separate breed classes for the Japanese Spitz so this breed can enter AVNSC and could enter AV. 'Ch Newstart Hooza Starr'.*

Fig. 4.3   *If there are breed classes for the Boxer, then they can enter the breed class and/or AV classes, but not AVNSC. 'Ch Tartarian Kicks up a Dust'. (Photo: Tim Hutchings)*

the breed's popularity and the number of dogs likely to enter. Smaller shows will have less choice available. Larger and championship shows may have what at first seems a bewildering array of classes. We'll next look at the definitions of classes, and then talk about which you might want to enter when you first start showing, and the pros and cons of entering more than one class.

Checking you meet the criteria

Before you select the classes to enter at a particular show, read the criteria for each class in the schedule and make sure your dog (and possibly you) qualify to take part. Some societies have special classes for members, for example, and some may have a slightly different definition of classes from the norm. Classes which do not run strictly to the Kennel Club definitions should be marked 'Special'. It is particularly important to check the schedule carefully now that the Kennel Club has suspended the beaten dog rule.

Picking the right classes

At the end of the day, the best dog in that judge's opinion is going to win Best of Breed (or the Challenge Certificate), whichever class he is entered in. However, winning a class may gain you points towards a Junior Warrant, so it's important to maximize your chances to gain a first place. Even if you haven't got an award in mind, you'll want to be at least placed in the shows you attend. Entering the right class for the age and level of maturity of your dog will mean you have the best chance of going home with a rosette and/or prize card.

Age-restricted classes

If you are showing a puppy or dog under the age of two, then it is important to put him in the class most appropriate for his age as he'll be competing with other dogs of the same level of maturity. There is nothing to stop you putting him in the next class up as well (but see the information about entering more than one class below). One of the most common mistakes is entering too many classes at your first show.

Minor Puppy: This class is for puppies who are at least six months old, but no more than nine months.

Fig. 4.4   Picking the wrong class might mean you end up alongside an International Champion such as this Pyrenean Mountain Dog, 'BE, CH, LU and INT CH Jazanah Jaunty'. (Photo: D. Murphy)

What happens if my dog's birthday falls during the show?

The age restriction relates to the age of your dog on the day of the show. If it is a championship show being run over more than one day, then it is his age on the first day of the show. So if your dog's birthday is on the second, third or fourth day of the show, even if your group is showing on the last day, his eligibility to enter age-restricted classes depends on how old he is on the FIRST day, despite the fact his class may be held later.

Your puppy is eligible to enter this class if he is less than nine months old on the first day of the show. This is a useful beginner's class. If you have a bouncy pup who is still learning to behave in the show ring, you'll probably find you are in good company. The judge will make allowances (as far as possible) for puppy behaviour,

but if your puppy runs round on two legs or doesn't stand for the judge, he may not get the best placing simply because the judge won't be able to go over him properly or see his movement. If this happens to you, chalk it up to experience. You'll probably get a lot of sympathy from the ringside spectators. Minor puppy classes are usually only held at the bigger breed or championship shows.

Puppy: Puppy classes are slightly more common than Minor Puppy classes, and are for pups aged at least six and no more than twelve months. Again, puppy behaviour will be tolerated, and some allowances made.

Fig. 4.5   If you have a puppy, you should enter him into a puppy class. Puppy Basset Fauve de Bretagne 'Mochras Casper'. (Photo: Tim Arnold)

Junior: This is the most common class at open shows, and mops up all dogs aged between at least six and eighteen months. You may find your young puppy is up against much more mature dogs, but it is still worth entering as he may be eligible for Best Puppy if such a competition is listed in the schedule.

Yearling: This is the last age-restricted class for young dogs. To enter Yearling your dog must be at least twelve months of age, but not more than twenty-four months. There can be quite a difference between dogs at the upper and lower ranges of this scale, so although you might be tempted to enter this class with your twelve-month-old puppy, remember you will be up against

Summary of classes where entry is restricted by the age of your dog

Class	Age of Dog				
	Six months but less than nine months	Nine months but less than twelve months	Twelve months but less than eighteen months	Eighteen months but less than twenty-four months	Seven years plus
Minor Puppy	✓				
Puppy	✓	✓			
Junior	✓	✓	✓		
Yearling			✓	✓	
Veteran					✓

Note: Remember that the age restriction relates to the age of the dog on the FIRST day of the show irrespective of which day you are showing on.

dogs which are a lot more mature. This class is not normally an option at most open shows, so once your dog is over the age of eighteen months he will normally need to compete in the classes for dogs of all ages. If your puppy is a larger breed (which tend to mature later), you may be at a disadvantage until he has finished growing.

Veteran: The last class with age restrictions is Veteran, which is for dogs which are at least seven years old on the first day of the show.

Classes for dogs with a limited number of first prizes

Once you've paid for entering your first class, entering another class doesn't add much to the cost of the show as subsequent entries are a lot cheaper. There are pros and cons to entering more than one class, and here we'll discuss the classes you might consider. Of course, if there is no applicable age-related class for your puppy or young dog, then these will be your only options.

The classes in this section are open to dogs of all ages which meet the criteria. If you're considering showing a youngster in them, you will almost certainly be competing against dogs which are more developed in body shape than your dog and much more experienced. However, entry to these classes is limited by the number of first places won at open or championship shows, which means you can select classes where you won't find yourself up against Champions, or dogs well on their way to becoming one.

Awards for Best Puppy when no puppy classes are available

Where shows do not have puppy classes listed for your breed, but do have awards for the Best Puppy in Breed, Best Puppy in Group and Best Puppy in Show, the judge will award the place to the best puppy who is less than twelve months of age, regardless of whether he has been beaten by an older dog in the actual class(es) he was shown in. So even if there isn't a minor puppy or puppy class, it is still worth entering a six-month-old puppy in the junior class.

Fig. 4.6   *You will need to keep records of results. It's useful to include the name of the judge as well. Canadian Eskimo Dog 'Akna Marluk'.*

Fig.4.7   *You can enter any class for which you qualify, but it's best to enter into the first class for which you qualify. Dogue de Bordeaux 'Furzeydrong Thundercloud at Emberez'.*

Winning awards after you've submitted your entry form

It is important to make a note of all your first place awards so you know if you can still enter a class. As shows are entered some weeks beforehand, a dog may qualify for a class at the time of entry, but become ineligible due to a win after the closing date for entry to the show. Wins up to a week before the closing date are not counted, and therefore do not disqualify a dog from entering that class. For example, you can still enter a Maiden class even if you have subsequently won a first prize, unless that placing was gained more than a week before the closing date. If you get a place that means you are no longer eligible to take place in a class, you should alter your entry if you have applied online, or contact the club secretary if you have submitted an entry by post.

Challenge Certificates or 'tickets'

This is probably a good time to introduce the Challenge Certificate. These are won by the best dog and/or the best bitch of the breed at a championship show. You'll find CCs are also referred to as 'tickets'. At championship shows there may be some breeds where CCs are not being awarded, especially with the less numerous breeds. Some classes do not count first prizes won at championship shows, where CCs were not on offer for your breed, as wins at championship shows; instead they are treated as wins at open shows. So make a separate note of these if this applies to your dog.

Not all the classes described below are available at all shows. Check the criteria in the show schedule as

Fig. 4.8   Winner of Dog CC and Best of Breed at the Welsh Kennel Club 2010. Dandie Dinmont Terrier 'Cassencarrie James Blonde'. (Photo: Graham Peers)

sometimes the class conditions may vary slightly. You will note that most classes do not count wins in puppy classes (i.e. Minor Puppy or Puppy), so even if you have been placed first in these classes you can ignore them when submitting your entry. Also note that for the purpose of assessing your eligibility for classes with restrictions on the number of wins you can have, the reference to a Challenge Certificate includes awards that may have been won abroad; for example, if you have won a Green Star, CAC or a CACIB you must count this as equivalent to a Challenge Certificate.

Beginners: This class is sometimes called Special Beginners. If you are new to dog showing, this is a good class to enter, as neither handler nor dog nor owner can have won a first prize at an open or championship show.

Maiden: This class is for dogs which have not won a first prize or a CC other than in puppy classes at an open or championship show.

Debutant: For dogs which have not been placed first at a championship show other than in puppy classes.

Tyro Only for dogs that have not won a CC or have been placed first five or more times at Open or Championship Shows other than in puppy classes.

Novice: Open to dogs which have not won three or more first prizes at an open or championship show (except in puppy classes), or which have not won a CC.

Undergraduate: This class is only open to dogs which have not won a CC, or three first prizes at a championship show where CCs were on offer for the breed. (As stated above, if CCs were not on offer for your breed, your first prizes will not exclude you from this class).

Graduate: Open to dogs which have not won four or more first prizes in the following classes at championship shows: Post Graduate, Minor Limit, Mid Limit and Open.

Post Graduate: For dogs which have not won five or more first prizes in the following classes at championship shows: Post Graduate, Minor Limit, Mid Limit and Open.

Minor Limit: For dogs which have not won three CCs or three or more first prizes in Minor Limit or Mid Limit at championship shows, or three or more first prizes in open classes at open or championship shows.

Mid Limit: For dogs which have not won three CCs or five or more first prizes in Minor Limit or Mid Limit at championship shows, or five or more first prizes in open classes at open or championship shows.

Limit: For dogs which have not won three CCs or seven or more first prizes in Minor Limit or Mid Limit at championship shows, or seven or more first prizes in open classes at open or championship shows.

Open: This is for any dog of the breed or breeds which the class is provided for. Any dog can enter, whatever his age or number of first prizes won. Open classes will attract entries from dogs which have won their way out of all the other classes. Unless you have an exceptional dog, it is probably not worth entering a youngster in the open class, unless there is no other class available, as you may be up against dogs which have already gained Champion status.

Classes limited by number of first prizes

The tables below show the number of wins that will disqualify you from entering a particular class. Except for the Beginner, Maiden, Novice and Tyro classes at championship or open shows, first places at open shows do not count. However, if you are entering a limited show, first places at open shows do count. So make sure you read the schedule carefully. Dogs which have won Challenge Certificates cannot enter limited shows.

Only wins in breed classes count; you do not need to count your wins in AV or stakes classes.

1. Championship and open shows only

	First prizes at open shows	First prizes at champ shows	Challenge Certificates*	Notes
Beginners	None	None	None	Owner, handler and dog not to have won a prize at any show
Maiden	None	None	None	Puppy class wins not counted
Novice	Not more than three in total	Not more than three in total	None	Puppy class wins not counted
Tyro	Not more than five in total	Not more than five in total	None	Puppy class wins not counted
Debutant	N/A	None	None	Puppy class wins not counted
Undergraduate	N/A	Three	None	Puppy class wins not counted
Graduate	N/A	Four	None	Only first prizes in the following count: Graduate, Post Graduate, Minor Limit, Mid Limit, Limit and Open
Post Graduate	N/A	Five	None	Only first prizes in the following count: Post Graduate, Minor Limit, Mid Limit, Limit and Open
Minor Limit	N/A	Three	Two	Only first prizes in the following count: Minor Limit, Mid Limit, Limit and Open
Mid Limit	N/A	Five	Three	Only first prizes in the following count: Mid Limit, Limit and Open. A Champion cannot enter
Limit	N/A	Seven	Three	Only first prizes in the following count: Limit and Open. A Champion cannot enter
Open	Any dogs can compete regardless of how many awards they have won			
Champion	For dogs which have become Champions			

* A CAC, CACIB or Irish Green Star counts as equivalent to a Challenge Certificate.

2. Limited shows only – no dog which has won a Challenge Certificate can compete.

	First prizes at open shows	First prizes at champ shows	Notes
Beginners	None	None	Owner, handler and dog not to have won a prize at any show
Maiden	None	None	Puppy class wins not counted
Novice	Not more than three in total from both shows	Note more than three in total from both shows	Puppy class wins not counted
Tyro	Not more than five in total from both shows	Not more than five in total from both shows	Puppy class wins not counted
Debutant	None	None	Puppy class wins not counted
Undergraduate	Three	Three	Puppy class wins not counted
Graduate	Four	Four	Only first prizes in the following count: Graduate, Post Graduate, Minor Limit, Mid Limit, Limit and Open
Post Graduate	Five	Five	Only first prizes in the following count: Post Graduate, Minor Limit, Mid Limit, Limit and Open
Minor Limit	Three	Three	Only first prizes in the following count: Minor Limit, Mid Limit, Limit and Open
Mid Limit	Five	Five	Only first prizes in the following count: Mid Limit, Limit and Open. A Champion cannot enter
Limit	Seven	Seven	Only first prizes in the following count: Limit and Open. A Champion cannot enter
Open	Any dog which has not won a Challenge Certificate can compete		

Stakes classes

Some shows offer stakes classes. These are for any breed of dog, and sometimes have prize money on offer.

At open shows they are usually held after breed classes, or when a ring becomes free, while at championship shows they can run throughout the day. This may mean that if your breed class is running late, you may miss the stakes class you have entered. Entries can be high for stakes classes, but this can be very good experience if your breed classes tend to be small.

Wins in these classes do not count towards points for a Junior Warrant or Show Certificate of Merit.

The two-year trial introduced in January 2015 means that you can enter a stakes class without

Fig. 4.9 The open class is where you will find dogs which are already Champions. Gordon Setter 'Sh CH Lourdace Fulcrum JW'. (Photo: Horler)

Other Classes at Shows

Class	Qualification
Brace	One handler showing two dogs (two males or two females, or a mixed pair) of the same breed. The aim is for the dogs to look and move as one. Both dogs must also have been entered and shown in breed classes.
Team	One handler showing three dogs (all males or all females, or a mixed trio) of the same breed. The aim is for the dogs to look and move as one. All dogs must also have been entered and shown in breed classes.
Stud Dog/ Brood Bitch	These classes are for stud dogs or brood bitches and at least two of their progeny. The stud dog or brood bitch need not have been exhibited in a breed class, but the progeny must have been. There are different handlers for each of the dogs, but the stud dog or brood bitch owner pays for the class and completes the entry form.
Progeny	This class is for a stud dog or brood bitch along with at least three of its progeny. As above, the dog or bitch does not need to have been shown in a breed class, but all the progeny must have been.
Breeders	For dogs bred by the exhibitor. This class is more commonly found at single-breed shows (or included in the breed classifications at multi-breed shows) and are for one dog bred by the exhibitor. This is generally the first entry for that dog unless the breeders' class is held after Best in Show, when the exhibitor might then enter this as their second class. The schedule will show any other conditions pertinent to that show.
Champion	This class is for dogs which are confirmed Champions, Show Champions or Field Trial Champions. Only one class is held, for dogs of all breeds.
Field Trial and Working Trial	For dogs which have won an award in competition in a field trial held under Kennel Club or Irish Kennel Club regulations, or in a Bloodhound working trial or a Kennel Club licensed working trial.

Fig. 4.10 Ben Moore competing in the junior handlers class with Whippet 'Barnesmore El Bandito'.

entering a breed class as well. Or, of course, you can still enter both. If you are Best of Breed but are beaten in a stakes class, you are no longer counted as a beaten dog, and can continue to compete in the group.

Other classes

Other classes include the Brace, Stud Dog, Brood Bitch, Progeny, etc., as the table shows. Note that these classes continue to have the constraint that you

Fig. 4.11 Irish Red and White Setters in a brace class. (Photo: Jane May)

must have entered and shown the dogs in their breed classes first.

In addition, there may also be special classes for members of the particular society running the show, or additional AV classes; for example, a Bred by Exhibitor class is sometimes held at some open and championship shows. At some shows large businesses may sponsor classes, such as the Puppy of the Year stakes. These classes are listed at the end of the schedule. Be sure to read the special criteria and make sure you qualify before submitting an entry.

If the word 'special' appears in front of a class name, then the definition will be different from the normal classes described above.

ENTERING MORE THAN ONE CLASS

If you've started out showing at companion or fun shows, you will probably have entered every class you were eligible for – and you would have been encouraged to do so, as the money goes to charity and the more entries the better. But when you enter the more formal world of dog showing, you need to think a little tactically about which classes you should enter. Open shows and championship shows will be tiring, for both you and your dog. So don't enter too many classes, even if you think you qualify for them. As a newcomer, you need to gain experience in handling your dog, and if he is young, he will need practice to show at his best

Handling

Shows usually have handling classes, either for junior handlers or adults. These classes judge the handler's ability, not the dog, but to enter a handling class the dog may still have to have been entered in a breed class first. Sometimes these classes are for Young Kennel Club (YKC) members only, and some are run by the Junior Handlers Association. The classes often serve as qualifiers for national finals held at the end of the year. Wins in these classes do NOT affect other competitions as it is the handling that is being judged, not the dog.

Fig. 4.12   Welsh Springer Spaniel 'Bushwacker Gregory's Girl at Highclare', winner of a heat of an AV puppy stakes at the East of England Championship Show 2014.

in the ring. It can be extremely discouraging if you keep going to shows without being placed, and part of doing well is selecting the most appropriate class to enter.

At open shows you may well find there are only two or three classes for your breed, and the normal maximum is five, even for the most popular breeds. The most common classes at open shows are Junior and Open. If your dog is less than eighteen months old, then enter him in Junior, but don't bother about the Open class as you'll be up against stiff competition. There will probably be an AV class, either a general one, or one

for your group. If you want to enter a second class, the AV class would probably be a better bet. Obviously, if your dog is over eighteen months you will have to go into the Open class, but make sure you look at the AV classes as well, as there might be one which is more appropriate to the age of your dog and which you can enter in addition to, or instead of, your breed class.

Seen dogs

Unless you find a 'mentor' who can talk you through everything to do with dog showing, some things which happen in the ring seem a bit mystifying at first, and one of these is what happens when you're a 'seen dog'.

When you enter your first breed class the judge will go over your dog thoroughly and watch him move. If you subsequently enter a second class with the same judge, your dog will be a 'seen dog' and the judge will not need to go over him again. He will probably want to see you move again, so you may be asked to do another 'up and down' or run round the ring. But if your second class is an AV class you will be under a different judge, and he will need to examine your dog as he won't have seen it before.

If you are a 'seen dog', when you go into the ring for your second or subsequent classes, the steward will direct you to a corner of the ring. If there are other 'seen dogs', then the steward will line you up together, normally in the order that you, and the others, were placed in the earlier class(es). If the first five dogs in your first class also enter your second, and you were placed fifth in that class, it is extremely unlikely you will be able to get higher than fifth place in this one.

And most probably you will not get placed at all, as the unseen dogs, that is, the dogs for whom this particular class is their first class, may take some or all of the places.

This does make sense: if the judge thought another dog better than yours in a previous class, then he will not change his mind in the next class. The only time you may feel this is unfair is if your dog played up first time round, and wouldn't allow the judge to go over him properly. But unfortunately this is the way of things, and your first chance is your only chance to make a good impression on the judge.

This is something to bear in mind when entering multiple classes. It can be demoralizing if you have not been placed in your first class, and then have to stand in the corner of the ring for your subsequent classes knowing the dogs in front of you will take all the places! But, on the other hand, if your dog has won or been highly placed in his earlier class, then you'll be in a good position to be placed in your subsequent classes. If you are aiming for your Junior Warrant, then getting a first place in more than one breed class will help you build up your points quickly.

Until you have started showing and have entered classes, you will not know if you have an outstanding dog which will easily be placed in most shows, or if your dog needs time to mature, or your handling skills need more work to show him off to best advantage. So take care not to enter too many classes on your first outings.

Fig. 4.13   Samoyed 'Fairvilla Imperial Isabella'.

To maximize your chances, enter the breed class that is most appropriate to your dog. If there is no age-specific class for your dog, and you have not won any (or have won a limited number of) first prizes, you should enter your dog in the class which reflects your number of wins. As a beginner, you can enter the Maiden, Novice or Undergraduate classes. It is completely up to you how many classes you enter, but most people enter just one or perhaps two in their breed, and then enter AV classes and/or stakes classes for extra experience as these will be under a different judge and your dog will be gone over again and asked to move afresh.

COMPLETING AN ENTRY FORM

When you enter a companion or fun dog show, you complete a simple entry form on the day, normally only putting down your dog's pet name. As you step up to open and championship shows, however, things are done quite differently. All dogs entered into the breed shows must be clearly identified. At the end of the day the dog may end up a Champion, so it is important that any wins are awarded to the correct dog.

You need to enter your dog's registered name on the entry form. This is the full kennel name given on your Kennel Club registration certificate. Other details include your dog's breed, date of birth, breeder's name and the names of his sire and dam, as well as the classes you wish to enter. If you enter online you'll be able to save these details so you do not need to type them in every time you fill in an entry form – a great advantage of online entry! The form also has space for the Authority to Compete (ATC) number if applicable. The ATC number is only relevant for exhibitors from overseas as these dogs will not be registered with the UK Kennel Club. If you are from overseas and wish to compete in UK shows, you will need to apply to the Kennel Club for an ATC. You will then be assigned a number to put on the form. You cannot enter a UK Kennel Club show unless you have an ATC number or have applied for it, in which case you can use the acronym NAF ('Name Applied For').

When selecting the classes to enter, always check the schedule to make sure you are eligible for them. When entering online, the systems will filter out

LOCAL CANINE SOCIETY

235 Class Unbenched **OPEN SHOW**

(Judged on the Group System)
(held under Kennel Club Limited Rules & Regulations)

LOCATION AND ADDRESS OF SHOW

on **SUNDAY, 20 MARCH**

Postal entries close: Wednesday, **17** February   (Postmark)
On-line entries can be made up until midnight on Wednesday, **24** February

ENTRY FEES:

Members First Entry per dog @ £5.00	£	
Members each Subsequent Entry £1.00 with same dog	£	
Non-Members First Entry per dog @ £5.75	£	
Non-Members each Subsequent Entry £1.25 with same dog	£	
Not For Competition @ £1.00 per dog (over 6 months)	£	
Junior/Adult Handling @ £1.00 per class	£	
Catalogue @ £3.00 pre-paid (none for sale on the day)	£	
Membership @ £1.00 Single; £1.50 Joint; 30p Junior	£	
General Rosette Donation - thank you	£	
Breed Rosette Donation @ £2.50 - thank you	£	
Enclosed cheque/postal order for payable to:	£	

Please Note: A Charge will be made for all dishonoured cheques
ON NO ACCOUNT WILL ENTRIES BE ACCEPTED WITHOUT FEES

This form must be used by one person only (or partnership). Writing must be in INK or INDELIBLE PENCIL. Use one line only for each dog. The name of the dog and all the details as recorded with the Kennel Club must be given on this entry form. If an error is made the dog may be disqualified by the Committee of the Kennel Club. All dogs must be REGISTERED at the Kennel Club in the name of the exhibitor. If the registration or transfer of ownership has not been confirmed it must be applied for before the closing date of entries. In case of dispute proof of postage of such applications may be required by the Kennel Club. Puppies under 6 months of age on the first day of the Show cannot be entered for competition. On no account will entries be accepted after its name. Please put classes in numerical order and USE BLOCK CAPITALS throughout when completing this entry form "the Kennel Club Authority to Compete number (for dogs registered and resident outside the UK) must be stated or the entry will be returned. PLEASE CHECK ALL DETAILS BEFORE POSTING.

JUNIOR/ADULT HANDLING Entries will **NOT** be taken on the day.
Fee: £1.00 per class. Put class number alongside other classes for the dog.

Name of Handler .... Age ....

You may enter all your Breeds on one Entry Form
Enter on-line at www.fossedata.co.uk

REGISTERED NAME OF DOG (and ATC Number if applicable)	BREED	SEX D or B	Full Date of Birth	Breeder (if owner put Exh)	Sire (Block Letters Please)	Dam (Block Letters Please)	To be entered in classes
*KC ATC No.							
*KC ATC No.							
*KC ATC No.							
*KC ATC No.							

Only undocked dogs and legally docked dogs may be entered for exhibition at this show

DECLARATION I/We agree to submit to and be bound by Kennel Club Limited Rules and Regulations in their present form or as they may be amended from time to time in relation to all canine matters with which the Kennel Club is concerned and that this entry is made upon the basis that all current single or joint registered owners of this dog(s) have authorised/consented to this entry. I/We also undertake to abide by the Regulations of this Show and not to bring to the Show any dog which has contracted or been knowingly exposed to any infectious or contagious disease during the 21 days prior to the Show, or which is suffering from a visible condition which adversely affects its health or welfare, or to bring any dog which has been prepared for exhibition contrary to Kennel Club Regulations for the Preparation of Dogs for Exhibition F (Annex B). I/We agree without reservation that any Veterinary Surgeon operating on any of my/our dogs in such a way that the operation alters the natural conformation of the dog or part thereof may report such operations to the Kennel Club. I/We declare that where any alteration has been made to the natural conformation of the dog(s) the relevant permission to show has been granted by the Kennel Club.

I/We further declare that I believe, to the best of my knowledge, that the dogs are not liable to disqualification under Kennel Club Show Regulations.

Usual Signature of Owner(s) .... Date ....

NOTE Dogs entered in breach of Kennel Club Show Regulations are liable to disqualification whether or not the owner was aware of the breach

Fosse Data Systems Ltd., Newton, Rugby, Warwickshire CV23 0TB. Tel: 01788 860960

In the case of joint registered ownership the name of every owner must be given here

Name(s) .... (MR/MRS/MISS/MS)
Address ....
Postcode .... Phone No ....
E-Mail Address ....

Your address will appear in the Catalogue unless you tick here [ ]

All entries and fees which must be pre-paid to be sent to:
Hon. Secretary:

Fig. 4.14   An example of an entry form. (Reproduced courtesy of Fosse Data)

Judges you cannot show under

There are a number of circumstances where you might have an unfair advantage if you showed under a particular judge, and for this reason the regulations make clear the circumstances where you cannot enter classes at a particular show. You cannot show under a judge if they are the breeder of your dog, if they have handled or prepared your dog for show, or have boarded him, or owned or registered him within the last twelve months. You can, however, show under the owner of your dog's sire (as long as the sire is not owned by the breeder). If you are unable to enter breed classes because of the judge, you should look to enter the AV classes as this will be a different judge. To be fair to other competitors, you should avoid competing under a judge if you are a particular friend of theirs and they know your dog well outside the show ring. Judges can also not enter their own dogs at shows where they are judging, even if they are handled by somebody else.

some classes that you cannot enter, for example, puppy classes will not be available to select for a dog over the age of twelve months. Be aware that wins are not recorded, however, so the systems will continue to offer you any other classes which appear to be available to you, even though, for example, you might already have gained too many first places to enter the Novice class.

The catalogue

You can choose on the entry form whether to purchase a catalogue. The catalogue is a list of all competitors at the show, and gives the names and numbers of dogs in each class. Against your name will be a number – this is your ring number, and it's useful (but not essential) to know it before entering the ring. If it is a benched show, this number will also be the number of your bench. You do not need to purchase a catalogue, and many people don't as it is a way of saving money. But if you are showing seriously, it is useful to buy and keep catalogues for future reference. As you go to more shows

and learn the names of your competitors and their dogs, you will be able to assess the competition before you enter the ring. If you do not order a catalogue when entering, you may be able to buy one on the day of the show, but this is usually more expensive and you should not rely on any being available for purchase as they do get sold out. It's probably advisable to pre-order a catalogue at least for your first couple of shows; once you've met a few people you'll find there will usually be someone with a familiar face standing around with one in their hand that you can borrow!

Other purchases

The entry form may also include options to join the particular society running the show, and to make a donation towards rosettes if you wish to do so. At championship shows there may be other purchases to make, such as car parking, entry passes for people going with you, and parking for caravans. You will be given one pass for each dog unless it is owned in

Fig. 4.15   At most general championship shows there will be a caravan site where you can stay for up to a week for around £40. This is a good way to get to know other exhibitors.

partnership, when you will get an additional pass. If you are showing three or more dogs, you will also get an additional pass.

Check carefully for options to pay in advance for the car park. You may find it more expensive to pay on the day.

If you want to take a dog to the show but not actually enter it into any classes, you may be able to do so if the society allows dogs 'Not for Competition' (NFC). If so, it will say so in the schedule, and there'll be space to enter the details on the entry form. A small fee will normally be charged. Some societies allow puppies from the age of four months to be entered as NFC. Some societies may allow 'spectator' dogs and do not charge for these, but they must be kept under proper control. If it is not clear from the schedule, contact the secretary to confirm whether or not you are allowed to take a dog you are not showing with you.

If you are sending a postal entry, add up the total you need to pay and write a cheque. Make sure you make it payable to the correct person. If you enter online, then the website will do the sums for you, and your payment will be by credit or debit card.

Your address will be printed in the catalogue unless you tick the box to say you don't want it to appear.

Sign the declaration (or check the tick box online) and then you're done!

Proof of entry

Make sure you get your entry in on time! If you post your entry, you will not receive an acknowledgement of it unless you enclose an SAE, so it's useful to check that your cheque has been cashed, and take evidence of this when you go to the show as mistakes can be made. Likewise, take with you the email acknowledgement if you've entered online. The last thing you want is to turn up at a show some distance away to find you've been missed off the catalogue. If you do not have proof that you entered on time, you will still be allowed to show your dog, but your claim will be checked by the Kennel Club. It is rare that an entry is missed off the catalogue, but it certainly has been known!

WHAT NEXT?

So you've sent in your entries, and the big day is looming. In the next chapter we'll look at what you can expect at the show itself.

CHAPTER 5

AT THE SHOW

WHAT TO WEAR AND WHAT TO TAKE

Dress code

One of the most common questions asked by newcomers to dog showing is what they should wear to various shows. You'll have probably spent time bathing and preparing your dog to look his best, so don't forget to take some care about your appearance too. The judge's first impressions will be formed by the overall picture of you and your dog in the ring. Basically he shouldn't really notice you, his focus should be on your dog. So you should be thinking about wearing colours that make your dog stand out. If you are wearing black clothes while showing a Doberman, his outline is going to be lost against the dark background. So for a dark-coloured dog, wear light clothes, and vice versa.

You don't want to present any distractions for the judge. So ladies should not have too much cleavage on show, nor wear too short a skirt so that underwear is on display! The 'bending over' test is a good one when deciding on your show clothes!

The dress code can really be summed up as smart/casual with the emphasis moving more towards the smart end as you move up through championship shows to Crufts. For open shows jeans are acceptable, as long as they are smart and clean, but for championship shows many people (both sexes) wear suits. One

Fig. 5.2   The judge's attention should be drawn to the dog, not the handler. Cavalier King Charles Spaniel 'Ch Leogem Minuet JW'.

Fig. 5.1 The handler and dog should present a nice overall picture to the judge. Dobermann 'Mianna's Cracklin Rose at Luftez JW'.

Fig. 5.3   Smart attire for men at a championship show - Bullmastiff 'Ch Copperfield Cicero'. (Photo: courtesy of Dog World)

Fig. 5.4   Crufts - smart attire is the order of the day! (Photo: © Kennel Club Picture Library)

common piece of advice is always to wear the same or very similar clothes – it makes you more recognizable and people will remember who you are. A jacket always looks smart, but make sure you button it up so it doesn't flap around when you run.

Don't leave choosing your show clothes until the day of your first show. Never wear shorts; if it is a hot day wear a lighter pair of trousers or skirt with a shirt or blouse, and for men a short-sleeved shirt and tie, or possibly a waistcoat instead of a jacket. Don't wear clothes that are going to flap about or skirts that will fly up with the wind: remember, you may well be outdoors. Flat, comfortable shoes are a must for running round the ring and for walking around the show.

Whatever you wear, it is against the regulations to wear or carry anything, or display anything on your dog, which would identify you, your handler (if someone else) or your dog. Judging should be completely impartial and not influenced by any display of kennel names or previous wins. If you've won a previous class, do NOT wear your rosette into the next class.

Weather, seating and crates

Most of the open, breed and limited shows in the UK

are held in indoor venues – sports centres, larger village halls, equestrian centres – but some are held outdoors and have few, if any, indoor rings. The schedule will tell you if there are outdoor rings only, so you can dress appropriately if rain is expected or if it is very cold. Championship shows often have outdoor rings which are used if the weather is good, but normally have an alternative indoors for wet weather.

Seating is not generally available, so it is a good idea to take your own folding chairs if you are going to want to sit down. It can be a long day.

Schedules for open shows will say 'unbenched' on the front, which means benching is not provided. You can either keep your dog with you, leave him in the car (but NOT if the weather is warm or sunny), or take a crate. If you take a crate, make sure you set it up away from gangways and rings so that it is not in the way, and your dog cannot be disruptive. Do not leave your dog unattended for longer than absolutely necessary. It is a requirement by the Kennel Club that any crate, cage or container taken to a show must have identification on it so that show organizers can contact the owner should their dog become distressed. The simplest form of identification will normally be the ring number, but at open and other shows, where the ring number is not known in advance, alternative information (name, mobile number) can be provided.

What to take

It is useful to keep a bag packed with the essentials so you don't need to rush around finding everything early on the show day. How much you need to take depends on your breed of dog: a short-haired dog, for example, will need less in the way of grooming kit than a long-haired breed. Suggested items are:

- Show lead
- Ring clip or armband to hold your ring number. (Ring clips can range from plain and simple to special ones for your breed. If you choose an armband make sure it's not loose so that it will slip down your arm as you move. You can find clips online or purchase them at some shows.)
- Treats or bait if you use them in the ring
- Slobber cloth (if you have a breed likely to drool)
- Grooming kit and wet wipes
- Poo bags (always keep one handy in your pocket in case of accidents in the ring)
- Schedule and map
- Proof of entry
- Water and water bowl for your dog
- Blanket and benching chain for benched shows

Fig. 5.5   On a very hot day you will need to consider how to keep your dog cool at outdoor venues. These Hungarian Viszlas are modelling their cooling coats.

- Crate, cage or carrying box if you are using one, plus identification label
- Trolley (if you have a lot to carry)
- Dog toy (to keep him amused but not a squeaky one as it may annoy other exhibitors)
- Wet weather gear for you and your dog (essential if the venue is outdoors, but don't forget you may have a long way to walk from the car park to the show venue even if it is being held indoors)
- Umbrella for shade on hot days
- Copy of your dog's pedigree (in case someone asks)
- Refreshments for you (normally there will be somewhere to buy food and drink, though it may be expensive)

And finally, don't forget your dog! Yes, it has been done – or exhibitors owning more than one dog have taken the one they've not entered!

ORDER OF JUDGING

At least the day before, or possibly earlier, you should be able to find out the proposed order of judging for a show. Sometimes it will be printed in the schedule, so you'll be aware long in advance. For championship shows it may be announced on the Fosse Data, Higham Press or Dog.Biz websites, or for open shows on the website of the society holding the show. The order of judging allows you to estimate when you need to arrive at the show and helps you plan your travel arrangements.

For championship shows, if your breed is not first in the ring you will often be given a suggested time to arrive; in part this is to try to avoid congestion in the car park. For open shows you will only know the order of the breeds to be judged in the different rings. Unless you've been explicitly told a different arrival time, while you are a novice you should aim to be there at the latest when the judging starts. Some breeds have very low entries, and there may be only a handful of dogs in the classes before you. Or sometimes shows clash, and only a few dogs turn up for a class you expected to have a high entry. Occasionally some shows do publish the number of dogs entered per breed beforehand, but it is still quite tricky to be able to estimate exactly when you need to be ready to go in the ring. Some judges are extremely polished and quick at their trade – some seem to take an inordinate amount of time examining each dog and making up their minds which to place. There is nothing worse than arriving just after the class you should have been in has finished, and it's not much better to arrive only minutes before, as neither you nor your dog will be settled.

Fig. 5.6 Schipperke 'Zeena'. (Photo: Wagtail Art)

Make sure you know when judging commences. Judging may start earlier than the main start time for different breeds, and will vary from show to show. Sometimes the proposed start times for championship shows are altered from that printed in the schedule if there is a higher entry than expected. This information should be sent with your show passes.

ARRIVING AT THE VENUE

At open shows you will probably find the car park isn't too far from the show venue, but at championship shows (and particularly at Crufts) parking can be a long walk from the show rings. If your breed is one of the first in the ring, you may find you'll be queuing at the entry to the car park as everyone will be turning up at

Arriving late

One short piece of advice – do NOT arrive late! The regulations specify that you could be disqualified at the discretion of the Kennel Club if you have not exhibited in all the classes you have entered. If you arrive late and miss the first breed class that you entered, you cannot transfer to another class or AV.

You can continue to exhibit in the other classes which you have entered, for example, another breed class, AV, stakes or handling, but any award you win will need to be ratified by the Kennel Club. A report will be sent to them after the show and the reason why your initial classes were missed will be investigated. If the reason proves unacceptable, you may be liable to lose any award gained at the show.

Normally, exhibitors who miss their first class would not exhibit in further classes, and just accept they should have got up earlier, or considered their travel plans more carefully. It is worth knowing this, however, in case there was a genuine emergency that delayed you getting to the show. Frivolous reasons are not likely to be considered, and in most cases any wins would be disqualified.

Sometimes there is a major delay on a main route leading to the show ground. In these circumstances the starting time of the show might be delayed for everyone so that those people caught in the hold-ups have a chance to get there. If this happens, it's still worth heading to the show, even if you know you're going to be late. But do try to check the travel news before setting out, and make sure you leave in good time.

the same time. Always allow extra time to park your car and walk to the venue, particularly at the larger, more crowded shows, which may also have members of the public trying to get in and park as well.

On the way from the car park to the venue take the

opportunity to make sure that your dog has relieved himself before going inside. Collect any mess in bags and dispose of it in the bins which will be available.

Appointment of an emergency judge

If it is known in advance that the scheduled judge will not be able to attend a show, a message is normally posted on the online site from where you obtained your schedule. However, in certain cases the judge may have been taken ill, or have had another emergency on the day of the show. If you turn up to find the judge who is now judging your breed classes is a judge you cannot normally show under, in this circumstance you can continue to show in the breed class, or withdraw and just show in an AV class without entering the breed class first. However, you will not be able to transfer to an AV class if you did not enter it on your entry form.

Fig. 5.7   *Watch the exhibitors in front of you so you can see what they are doing. Kerry Blue Terrier 'Int-Multi Ch Dandy Black and Blue Rokoko'. (Photo: Graham Peers)*

AT OPEN SHOWS

If you have ordered a catalogue, go to the secretary's table to collect it. Ask for it by surname. Check your catalogue to find your number. There should be a list either at the secretary's desk or at the entrance to the venue indicating which breeds are in which ring. Each ring should have a large number displayed, usually near the steward's table. Once you've found where your ring is, you can relax and take in your surroundings. If you can't see what ring your breed is in, don't be afraid to ask!

If you've arrived before the judging has started and the rings are still empty, seize the opportunity to take your dog in and have a quick practice at stacking/standing and moving him; this will give him a chance to get used to the new surroundings. If it is your first show, then the more time you can spend getting him used to the busy atmosphere the better.

Make sure you watch the classes before you, particu-larly if it is the same judge who will be judging your dog, so you know what you'll be expected to do. Although most judges will ask you to do a triangle, and then run straight up and down, some vary this a bit. Some dismiss you to just go back to the end of the line, others will ask you to run round to the back, and will continue watching you move your dog until you have rejoined the rest of the competitors.

There is generally somewhere to get refreshments, even if it's only a van selling tea, coffee and snacks, and normally a few stands where you can pick up dog treats, toys, collars and leads. So it's useful to take some money with you. And don't forget about your dog: showing is thirsty work and he'll need water throughout the day.

Showing nerves

While some people seem to have an innate confidence, it is completely normal, particularly for first timers, to have an attack of nerves at a show. Unfortunately, your

Getting your ring number at open shows

At open shows you will be given your ring number card by the steward when you go into the ring for your first class. It must be attached to your clothing with a ring clip or armband so that it is clearly on display. Your ring number is unique to you on that day for that show, and you'll use the same number whatever classes you enter, unless you are showing more than one dog, when you'll have a different number for each. If you are very nervous, you may well find your hands are shaking and you fumble to attach your ring number. Don't worry, and take your time. If you have an excited young dog who is liable to jump up to grab the number, then either wear an armband or, if you have a clip, pin it to your waistband and cover it with your jumper or shirt.

nervousness can travel down the lead to your dog and affect his behaviour in the ring. As with anything, the more you expose yourself to a new situation, the easier you will feel and with practice those nerves will get better. Tips to help are to be positive, and visualize a positive outcome – your dog is the best in his class and is going to win first prize. There are some herbal remedies which supposedly help reduce anxiety, or you could have a stiff drink beforehand!

A misbehaving puppy in the ring is one cause of nerves. Be assured that judges are very accustomed to puppies and younger dogs who play up in the ring, and will make allowances for this type of behaviour. Even experienced exhibitors' dogs can embarrass their handlers on occasion! People watching will be sympathetic – there won't be many who haven't been in the same situation themselves!

AT CHAMPIONSHIP SHOWS

Breed championship shows can be fairly small, depending on how popular your breed is, and are run very much along the lines of open shows, and at similar venues. Benching is normally provided.

A general championship show is just a bigger general open show, but there are some differences. Unless stated otherwise in the schedule, you will be sent admission passes about a fortnight prior to the show date. These will either arrive in the post, be emailed to you or be available to download online depending on how and where you have entered. As these shows are run over two, three or four days, make sure you go on the right day for your breed.

Along with your pass, you are likely to receive a map of the venue, showing where you should park and where the rings are. You may be sent a proposed order of judging, along with the number of dogs entered by breed, or you may need to visit the website where you submitted your online entry to find this information. You'll also usually be able to find which ring you are in, and the benching for your breed will be situated close by.

Getting your ring number at championship shows

If you have been sent a pass, your bench number will be printed on it, often on the removal pass slip. If passes have not been sent out, on arrival at the show go and collect your catalogue as you will find your number there. If you haven't ordered a catalogue, then ask for your number at the catalogue collection point or the secretary's office. At championship shows your ring number card will be on your bench, or at some shows it will be placed on a table outside the ring shortly before your class.

Larger general championship shows are usually held at county show grounds, and must have both outdoor and alternative rings under cover for wet weather. Breed club championship shows, open and limited shows are not required to have wet weather rings. While a vast number are held in indoor venues, some only have rings outside with limited or no wet weather accommodation, so be prepared for wet or cold weather if a restriction is noted on the schedule. Although you may have been sent a show map with your pass(es), these venues, as well as being further from the car park, can still be bewildering and large, so do leave yourself enough time to find your bench and ring without getting into a panic as any stress will increase those show nerves.

There will be numerous vans selling refreshments, ice creams, burgers and hot dogs, and a vast array of trade stands selling everything from herbal remedies to dog food. You can often pick up a few bargains, so make sure you go with enough money to buy that irresistible dog coat. (Or with only enough to buy a couple of cups of tea if you don't want to be tempted!) Shows are good places to see new show leads, and to buy slobber flannels and brushes for the ring.

WHAT HAPPENS IN THE SHOW RING?

Whether you are entering a ring at an open show or a large championship show, the procedure will be virtually the same. There will be a steward's table in the corner at which the judge will probably be sitting, possibly writing up notes from a previous class. The steward will come forward and check your ring number (or give it to you at an open show), and mark you off on his copy of the catalogue.

When you enter the ring, you may find the judge is still making notes about the winner of the previous class. Use the extra time to get your dog into position in the line and then set him up as best you can – it might mean the difference between winning a red rosette or coming home with nothing. Experienced exhibitors know how they want to position themselves in the ring; some, for example, know their dog performs best when he is first in line, others like to be nearer the end.

At your first show, try not to be at the front. Although your ringcraft training should have prepared you, it will be different when you are in your first proper class. You and your dog may need time to relax, and by not being first you'll be able to watch what the person in

Fig. 5.8 In the UK exhibitors can choose the position they take in the ring. Some prefer to be seen first, others like to give their dog more time to settle.

Fig. 5.10   Pekingese 'Yakee Celebrity Status' stacked in the ring.

Fig. 5.9   When you've positioned yourself in the ring, take time to stand or stack your dog. Keeshond 'Ricara Rose'. (Photo: Bodrhanyn Photography)

front does. If it is a large class, you may not want to be last in the line as your dog may get bored, and you'll also have to stand your dog in a hurry after moving him.

Once you've been along to a few shows you will have a better idea of where your dog does best; he may be fresher if he's the first to be seen, or may benefit from being the last as he'll be calmer.

You'll quickly find that dog showing is competitive, and people will try a few tricks to show their dog in a better light than yours. Old hands may manoeuvre you so that you end up in a corner, or stand a little forward so that your dog ends up behind them – both these actions make it harder for the judge to get a good view of your dog. You should aim to position yourself so that

the judge can see your dog straight on. If you get boxed in, then don't be afraid to move. If the judge hasn't got a clear view, then your dog won't stand out from the competition.

When you have got into position in the line of exhibitors, you will be expected to stand your dog. This might mean free standing or stacking, dependent on the breed, and in some cases on the individual dog. First impressions are important, and the judge will form an opinion of your dog when he runs his preliminary glance around all the dogs stacked and standing in the ring. A dog poorly stacked or stood at the start of the judging will have a lot of ground to make up if he is going to change the judge's initial opinion of him. Even if you're feeling nervous, try to appear confident as if you're showing the potential Best in Show!

Some judges like to see all the dogs moving round the ring after they have had their first glance at them, while others want to get on with the individual examinations; in this case the steward will wave the first dog in line forward to be stood either in front of the steward's table or on the table if it is a small breed. Occasionally a judge may want to see on the table a breed that is normally gone over on the ground. If this happens to you, don't argue with the judge, just go along with it. This tends to occur more often with an unusual breed, or one with which the judge is less familiar.

If you are in an AV class, then small dogs who are shown on the table will usually be put at the front of the line, and will be gone over first, but do make sure you listen to what the steward is asking as sometimes table dogs are seen last.

While the dog in front of you is finishing moving around the ring, you should move forwards and start setting your own dog up for the judge so that judging can continue without delay. Often the steward will be directing people forwards at the correct time. Don't try to start a conversation with the judge. He may say a pleasantry such as 'Good morning', to which you can respond, but his only other question may be to ask the age of your dog.

The judge will expect you to present your dog free standing or stacked as appropriate. He will look at him from the side to see whether he is the correct shape for the breed, and whether he appears balanced. He will then move round to the front, and look at the set of the forelegs, checking they are straight and set at the correct width. He will look at his expression, at his eyes to make sure they are the correct colour, size and shape, and check that the ears are the correct shape and length, and set in the right position on the head.

The muzzle will be checked to ensure it is in the right proportions.

The judge will want to look at your dog's teeth and you should have prepared him well so he doesn't object to a stranger looking into his mouth. He will be checking that the bite is correct for the breed. If the dog has facial wrinkles, he will check that the folds of skin are clean. In some breeds the judge will expect you to show him the teeth, rather than opening your dog's mouth himself.

Now the judge will get very hands on. In some breeds the musculature is quite easy to see, but in long-haired or thick-coated breeds it is only by really feeling how the dog is made up that the judge can evaluate how good his frame is. He will look at the proportions of various measurements and the degree of angulation of major joints, and the depth of chest. He will check that the spine and tail are straight and not kinked, and look at the set of the tail. Muscles on the hind legs should be firm and hard. If the dog is an entire male there should be two normal descended testes. When the judge has finished his hands-on examination, he will take into account the texture and length of the coat, and also whether it is an accepted colour for the breed.

This sounds like the judge must spend an inordinate amount of time on each dog, but in reality it takes place very quickly as he knows what he is looking for.

You will then be asked to move your dog so that the judge can assess his gait. The first movement is normally a triangle to assess his movement from the

Fig. 5.11   A judge taking her first look at the dogs standing in the ring.

Fig. 5.13   Checking the front assembly.

Fig. 5.12   Start preparing your dog for the judge to go over him when the dog before you is finishing moving. Havanese 'Ch Blevwil Cast a Glimpse at Berrywood'.

side. Always make sure your dog is on your inside as the judge wants to see him, not your legs! He will then ask you to move your dog 'up and down', which may be to the other side of the ring, or to a corner and back. This time he will be assessing how straight the dog moves, both going away and coming towards him. Some judges just ask for an up and down and then ask you to run round the ring to join the back of the line. Ensure you listen to what the judge is asking. When you return from the 'up and down', pay attention to where the judge is and aim directly towards him.

Fig. 5.14   Checking the shoulders.

When you have finished moving your dog (unless he's told you to just join the line), you may be asked to stand him again. You need not stack him at this stage, but just let the judge see his natural stand. Remember that you remain on show when moving back to join the line: the judge may well still have his eye on you, so don't relax just yet.

It is a shame that some rings are too small for larger breeds to properly step out. If the ring is small and you are worried your dog won't get into his stride before he hits the corner, turn him in a small circle before starting on your triangle or other exercise the judge has asked you to do. With a young dog you may find he thinks that moving round the ring is very exciting. He may jump up at you, try to grab the lead, or pull

Fig. 5.15   Checking the back end.

away to get back to the other dogs in the line. If he starts misbehaving, you are quite within your rights to go back to your starting point and begin the exercise again. Remember, you've paid your money to take part in the show, and you deserve a chance to show your dog to his best. Sometimes, if your dog is playing up, the judge may suggest you repeat the exercise as he cannot be assessed unless he has four feet on the ground! Don't worry or feel embarrassed; judges know that young dogs in particular can become over-excited in the ring and will give them some leeway. At the end of the day, though, the judge will find it very difficult to judge a dog who will not stand, or who plays about as he runs around the ring, and you may lose out in being placed. If this happens, resolve to put in more practice.

Fig. 5.16   After going over the dog, the judge will want to see him move. Pyrenean Mountain Dog 'BE, CH, LU and INT CH Jazanah Jaunty'. (Photo: C. Tesseron)

Fig. 5.17   This Siberian Husky demonstrates an effortless trot on a loose lead. 'Ch Rajarani Ezekiel'. (Photo: Krystyan Greenland)

Once the judge has gone over all the dogs and seen them move, all the dogs will be stood again and he will cast his eye over the line once more. He may walk down and check some aspect, such as the eyes of a particular dog, or perhaps feel the hindquarters or shoulders. At this stage he will be determining which, in his opinion, best meets the breed standard. Make sure that you are looking at the judge; not only does this show the judge you are confident in your dog, but it will make sure that you don't miss a slight wave of the hand calling you forward to take a place. Dogs have been known to lose their places if the judge's signal is ignored.

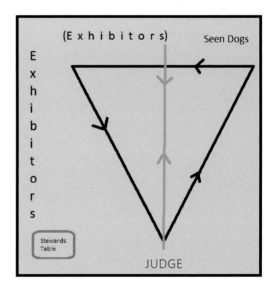

Fig. 5.18   Typical layout of a show ring. Exhibitors normally stand on the left, but in big classes may also extend round the back of the ring, or even up the other side. 'Seen dogs' will be asked to stand in the corner. The judge will usually ask first for a triangle – this is normally completed in the direction shown by the arrows, with your dog on your left hand side, but if you prefer running your dog on your right you can complete the triangle in the other direction. You will then be asked to do an 'up and down'. Occasionally you may be asked to run to the corner and back instead, particularly if the ring is small. Always keep your eye on where the judge is standing and make sure you are running directly towards the judge on your way back.

Just two minutes . . .

It will have taken far longer for you to read about how the judge goes over a dog than it actually takes in practice. You've spent good money on your entry fee, and possibly fuel costs to get to the show, and then you'll find your time in the limelight seems to be very short indeed! The Kennel Club recommends that judges should only spend two minutes on each dog. Although to newcomers it may seem that they are rushing things, the reason for this is to enable the judge to get through all the dogs in his class and not hold up the next class. An experienced judge can assess a dog both accurately and very quickly.

The judge may not find it an easy decision to make, and might ask the whole class to run round the ring again, or ask to see each dog move individually once more – usually just an up and down. In a large class he might choose a group of dogs he wants to consider further, and dismiss those he knows will not be placed. To 'make the cut' can be something to be proud of in a big class, even if you are not eventually placed. When the judge is left with five or so dogs in the ring, he may still shift them around before he is happy with his decision. He will then point to the dogs and ask them to line up in the centre of the ring, with the first placed dog to the right (the judge's left).

The judge will normally place up to five dogs: first to third, reserve (fourth place) and VHC (Very Highly Commended). In some classes at larger shows a sixth place is sometimes awarded, known as HC (Highly Commended), or even a seventh (Commended). If there are only five (or six or seven where relevant) dogs in a class then normally all will get placed, but the judge does not have to place a dog if he does not think it is worthy of it. He does not even need to award first place if he doesn't think a dog is potentially worthy of becoming a Champion. So even if there are only a few dogs being shown in your class, and you come, for example, third out of three, you should still consider this as a good result! The judge need only have awarded two places.

The steward will then hand out the prize cards and announce the ring numbers of the placed dogs. At most open and breed shows you will either be given a rosette in the ring with, or in place of, your prize card, or you will be able to collect a rosette from the secre-

Fig. 5.19   Saluki 'Ch Glenoak Kiyan JW'.

tary's table. Rosettes are not yet given out at general championship shows; instead you will just be given a prize card. A lot of people find this disappointing as they want to commemorate their win, especially if it's a special one. You can get a rosette, but you will need to purchase it from one of the trade stands at the show. Some will even print your dog's name on it for you!

JUDGING CONFORMATION – A QUICK GUIDE

Dogs are judged not against each other, but against their individual breed standard, and it is therefore impossible to present accurate diagrams of ideal conformation without many permutations relating to different breeds. The underlying skeleton and body parts, however, are the same for every breed, albeit some might have deeper chests than others or other differences such as a level or sloping topline.

Figs 5.20 and 5.21 use a Welsh Springer Spaniel to illustrate a typical dog. The judge will have an in-depth knowledge of canine construction, and how it relates to the breed. When he goes over your dog, he will be feeling that the shoulder and stifle joints, for example, are at the correct angle. The judge gets his first impression of how well each exhibit matches the breed standard when the dogs are presented in the line-up. The diagrams show the level of detail that up-and-coming judges should know before they go to their breed specific seminars.

Figs 5.22 to 5.28 give a highly simplified view of what the judge is looking at when he looks at your dog from the front and the rear, and are reproduced here not as a guide to judging but to illustrate some obvious faults. As we've discussed before, some pedigree dogs do not do well in the show world as they deviate too far from the standard. Some of the faults shown below are congenital and, unfortunately, if a dog is born with a fault, there is nothing that can be done about it. A dog presenting poor conformation will have a severely limited showing career. But in some cases, the novice handling skills of inexperienced exhibitors may spoil the overall look of a very good dog.

These diagrams, drawn by Virge Neary, are intended to help you present your dog to its best in the show ring.

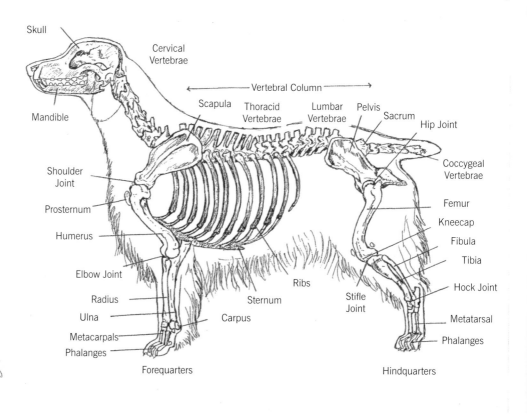

Fig. 5.20   The skeleton of the dog. (Permission kindly provided to reproduce this drawing by the Estate of Angela Begg)

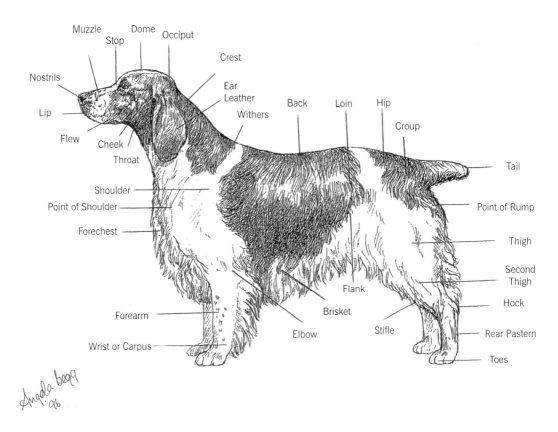

Fig. 5.21 Points of the dog. (Permission kindly provided to reproduce this drawing by the Estate of Angela Begg)

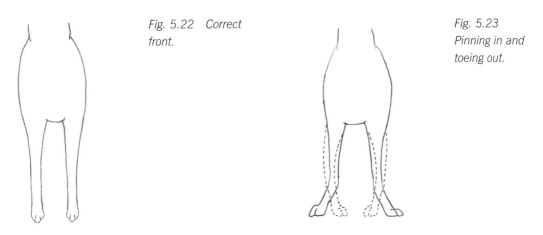

Fig. 5.22 Correct front.

Fig. 5.23 Pinning in and toeing out.

A correct front should show the front legs set square beneath the chest. The front feet should be level. Dogs sometimes fidget when you are stacking them, so double check the position of the front legs after you have moved the hind legs into position. With a free stand, you may need to walk your dog round and into the stand again to make sure he is standing square.

Feet that turn in (pinning in) or out (toeing out) are considered faults. Both can be an inherent conformation fault, but it's also possible that he is just standing awkwardly. When stacking your dog, or training him to stand, make sure that his feet are placed directly under his shoulders and are pointing forwards, not in or out.

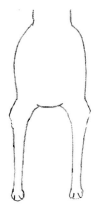

Fig. 5.24   Elbows turning out.

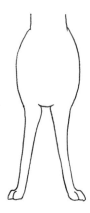

Fig. 5.25   Tied elbows.

Elbows that turn out or are tied in are normally due to the physical make-up of the dog.

Fig. 5.26   Correct hindquarters.

Correct hindquarters should be square, with a good covering of muscle, and hocks to feet should be straight. Most breeds stand with the back legs parallel (one exception is the German Shepherd). Having stood or stacked your dog, keep a close eye on what he is doing as it is easy for him to move a foot out of place without you noticing, causing what should be a good back end to look poor.

Fig. 5.27   Weedy or mean hindquarters.

Mean or weedy hindquarters lacking muscle are undesirable. In this case extra exercise could help strengthen those muscles and give your dog a better chance in the show ring.

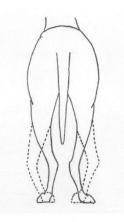

Fig. 5.28   Bowed or cow hocks.

Hocks should not turn in (bowed hocks) or out (cow hocks). While these can be congenital faults, it may look like he has these problems if you have not stacked him properly or he has not walked properly into his stand, or even if the ground is uneven. Make sure his

Fig. 5.29 Irish Setter 'Highclare Knights Tail' showing perfect straightness when moving as his back legs are obscured by the front.

feet are straight and that he keeps them that way while the judge has his eye on him.

Judging conformation on the move

The judge will hold in his head a mental image of your breed, and will be comparing this to the profile of the dog in front of him. When he assesses a dog on the move, he checks to see that the dog is balanced and moving straight coming towards him, and has the correct gait and action for the breed from the side.

Fig. 5.30 Rottweiler 'Javladare The One at Rivaz' presenting a perfect sideways view to the judge.

SHOW ETIQUETTE

We all like to win, but obviously not everyone can. We've already talked about the fact that judges can, and do, have preferences for certain types of dog and each interprets the breed standard a little differently. Dogs can be Best of Breed at one show and yet be unplaced at another under a different judge and with different dogs. That's what keeps us going to show after show: you can never predict how you will do.

If you don't get placed, don't be a sore loser. Congratulate the winners, and, even if you think it was unfair, keep your thoughts to yourself unless you feel you have real grounds for complaint. Dog showing has a reputation for being 'facey', where exhibitors who have been around a long time and have a well known kennel name always seem to win all the major prizes. But then, they might have better dogs, and will undoubtedly be better handlers than someone new to the sport. Sometimes other exhibitors will tell you which dogs are going to be placed *before the judging*. They may well be right, but again, the dogs could be well deserving of their places. There may be instances where judges don't seem to give high places to unknown dogs, but it's best to keep your grumbles and thoughts to yourself. The majority of judges are fair.

Even if you haven't been placed, remember to praise your dog. He did his best for you, and if you feel he didn't then it was probably down to your handling! Resolve to keep practising and enter a few more shows.

There will be another judge, another day, and you will definitely gain from your experience.

Handling and handlers

If you handle your own dog, you will get a great sense of achievement when you win your awards, but some people cannot cope with being in the ring due to nerves or are unable to move their dogs themselves as they have mobility issues. It is perfectly permissible to get someone else to act as the handler. You can ask them to do everything, or you could stand or stack your dog yourself and the other person can just be the 'runner'. An experienced handler may be able to get the most out of your dog, being more skilful at stacking or standing him, and moving him in a more competent way round the ring.

When you commence showing you probably want to do all the handling yourself, but as you get closer and closer to a Challenge Certificate, you might choose to get someone else's help. You can use the services of a professional handler, but clearly you would have to pay. Or you may find someone who is starting out as a handler and is willing help you out. As you show more, you will make friends in your breed, and you may find someone at shows to help you.

Making a complaint

If you really feel you have genuine cause for complaint,

Double handling

You may go to your first show with your partner, friend, or co-owner of your dog. Excitedly, they stand beside the ring, perhaps with camera at the ready. As a newcomer, you may well find their presence is a distraction. Your dog will try to stand facing them, or tear across the ring towards them, and drag his feet when moving back to the judge! But the opposite could also be true: your dog is well aware of their presence and stands with ears pricked watching them, or moves with a spring in his step as he runs towards them. Some exhibitors deliberately place someone outside the ring to enhance their dog's performance. This is known as double handling and it is strictly against Kennel Club regulations for obvious reasons. To avoid falling foul of the rules, or (more likely) having your dog play up as he wants to go and see his friend, ask any companion to stand behind other spectators, and to move further away if they can see your dog's attention is on them and not you.

Fig. 5.31 Papillon 'Toot Sweet's Charming Casanova at Ancojo IMP' winning Group 4. (Photo: Follyrose Photography)

you must follow the Kennel Club's objections procedure. There are three categories of grounds for making an objection: the first is that a dog is suffering from a contagious or infectious disease; the second is that he has had an operation which has altered his natural conformation; and the third is a contravention of the Kennel Club showing regulations. The latter, all-encompassing category covers everything to do with judging, from the conduct of exhibitors to that of judges and stewards, and the health and behaviour of the dogs themselves.

Anyone can make an objection under the first and third grounds, but only the owner or handler of a dog competing in the same breed or class can object on the second. Any objection must be made to the show secretary before the show closes, so unfortunately you cannot go home and consider your options. The complaint must be made in writing, and the current fee for making an objection is £35. The refund of this after a successful complaint is discretionary.

Obviously, raising an objection is a serious matter and it should not be undertaken lightly. Unless it is something which is clearly apparent, such as a dog which is ill, it is probably best to seek support from other people who may have noticed the same thing. Complaints have been raised and upheld, for example, against judges who didn't seem to be taking their role seriously, and paid scant attention to the exhibits.

Exclusions from the ring

If a dog is obviously unfit or unwell, then the judge can exclude him from the ring on the spot. Likewise, a vicious dog may be sent out. A dog excluded by the judge cannot compete in any other class in that show, be it another breed class or an AV or stakes class. The judge will make a report which will be forwarded by the show secretary to the Kennel Club, which will consider the circumstances and decide what, if any, sanction should be made. For example, a dog which bites another dog in the ring might face a six-month ban from showing, or be prohibited from ever exhibiting again if the offence was serious. Under the Kennel Club showing regulations, dogs of a vicious disposition are not permitted to take part in licensed shows.

Disqualification

There are two types of disqualification: one for the owner/handler, and the other for the dog. A person who contravenes Kennel Club rules can be disqualified or suspended and is unable to take part in any Kennel Club licensed show for the duration of the disqualification.

A dog may be disqualified for a number of reasons and have any award won at the show taken away. It may not, for example, have been exhibited in all the classes entered, or prohibited grooming products may have been used on his coat, or perhaps a complaint has been upheld. The dog is only disqualified from that show, not from any others.

Critiques

As already mentioned, handlers cannot speak to the judge in the ring, so it's hard to know what the judge's impression was of your dog if you were not highly placed. Some judges, but not all, are happy to talk to exhibitors after they have finished judging for the day. If you approach a judge, make sure you ask for his opinion on your dog, and don't sound critical of his decision on the placings. This is your opportunity to get that judge's opinion, and perhaps pick up some tips on your handling, or what you can do to improve your dog's chances. The judge may, for example, have thought he was carrying too much weight. It may simply be that he was up against dogs of a very high standard.

For dogs placed first or second in a class at a championship or open breed club show, or first in a general open show, the judge is required to write a critique. This critique justifies the judge's decision in placing the dogs as he did. Each critique is short – around thirty words in total – so don't expect a lengthy description. Despite their brevity, critiques are very useful to read for the shows you have exhibited at, or even those you didn't. Even if your dog does not merit one himself, reading that of the winning dog will give you some pointers about what the judge particularly liked or was looking for. Critiques are normally printed in the dog press, such as Our Dogs or Dog World, or online at Higham Press, and sometimes breed clubs publish them.

KEEPING RECORDS

As you attend more shows you'll find you come across the same people time and time again, and you will soon make friends in the showing world. When you ask them if they will be attending a particular show, you might well get the response, 'No, that judge isn't for me.'

Keep a record of the shows you attend, the name of the judge and where you were placed. When you first set out, you probably won't come across the same judge for a second time for many months, if not years, but when you eventually do, you'll be able to check back and see whether it's worth attending the show if your dog was obviously not that judge's 'type'.

Recording your wins is very important as it's the only way you'll know whether you have won too many first places to be able to enter particular classes; no database is currently kept of the results of all shows. As we'll see shortly, you'll also need to keep a record of your wins if you wish to aim for a Junior Warrant or Show Certificate of Merit award.

WHAT QUALIFICATIONS DOES A JUDGE HAVE?

When you are watching the judge looking at the dogs in the ring, you may wonder what qualifications he has to be there. Does he really know what he is looking for? How does he know to place one dog first, and not place another at all?

The first thing to say is that judges are not people pulled in off the street. You can be confident, even if you do not agree with his decision, that he will have a wealth of experience and training to draw on when assessing the dogs in front of him.

A judge is appointed because of his in-depth knowledge of the breed. He will normally be a standing member of the appropriate breed clubs, be an experienced (and successful) exhibitor/handler of the breed with at least five years' experience, and generally a breeder who has himself produced winning dogs. He will also have a deep interest and detailed knowledge of the various bloodlines within the particular breed.

As well as being involved in exhibiting, a potential judge will probably have spent time in the ring

Fig. 5.32   Bulldog 'Triarder Dreamseem at Andlare' waiting for the judge to start her inspection at Crufts.

as a steward, and may have participated in ringcraft training. Many judges start judging at match nights, and at companion shows run by their local canine society. Judges should also have attended the Kennel Club's judges' training programme, as well as breed seminars.

Judges cannot advertise their availability; instead they must be invited to judge a particular show. Their first formal judging appointment will be an open show and will normally be to judge a breed that has up to three classes (such as Junior, Post Graduate and Open), unless their breed is in Stud Book Band E. This band normally attracts a higher entry, so new judges can judge up to five classes.

Judges for open and limited shows (and at championship shows where Challenge Certificates are not available for that breed) do not have to be approved by the Kennel Club, but they do have to be on the breed judging lists. Each breed club keeps judging lists A–C, which comprise both breed and non-breed specialists depending on their level of experience, including the number of classes and dogs judged. The numbers on these lists can be determined by the individual breed clubs. For championship shows where Challenge Certificates are awarded, judges have to be approved by the Kennel Club and for this they require one year's notice before the show. The appointment of judges is taken very seriously. There are currently over 10,000 approved judges in the UK.

Championship show judges will either be breed specialists, or non-breed specialists if they are to award Challenge Certificates. To be a breed specialist, a judge needs at least seven years' judging experience in that breed, must have attended mandatory seminars and have successfully passed assessments. The subjects studied include conformation and movement, breed-specific judging, Kennel Club regulations and judging procedures. Except under exceptional circumstances, they also need to have owned at least three dogs which have gained their Stud Book number, and have acted as a steward at shows for a minimum of twelve days. After they have awarded Challenge Certificates in one breed, if they have five years' experience of judging another breed, they can become a non-breed specialist.

It's a long journey to become a judge! Judges are chosen carefully by show committees, and the right judge can attract a higher entry. An unpopular judge may mean exhibitors stay away.

The vast majority of judges receive no payment for their services, although occasionally they may be offered expenses. There are a few professional judges who judge at championship shows and who do get paid, as spending four days away every other week or so means they would not be able to hold down a day job as well. Judging, however, is not a particularly lucrative career, and most perform their services for free due to a love of their breed(s) and the enjoyment of the sport. Judges cannot exhibit their own dogs at shows where they are judging.

The Kennel Club has a framework document listing the criteria for breed clubs to compile their judging lists and this should be consulted for further information.

Code of Practice for judges

The Kennel Club has produced a Code of Practice which all judges should abide by. It covers how to treat dogs in the ring and the need to be courteous to exhibitors (but not enter into conversation). Overall judges should 'act at all times with honesty, integrity and impartiality'. Judges must take into account the health and welfare of the dogs they are judging, considering whether they are 'fit for function, fit for life', and when they award a Challenge Certificate they should be confident that that dog is worthy of becoming a Champion.

STEWARDS

The other official in the show ring will be the ring steward. He supports the judge by making sure the right dogs are in the ring for each class, and hands out ring numbers (at open shows). The steward will consult with the judge on what he wants the exhibitors to do, and will direct you to where you should stand, particularly in the case of 'seen' dogs. This is the person you should speak to if you are unclear on where you should be.

Stewards make a huge contribution towards the smooth running of the classes in the ring, and it is also their job to announce the names of the winners and hand out rosettes and/or prize cards. The steward also helps the judge with administration tasks, leaving him free to get on with the process of judging. At the end of the breed classes, the steward will make sure the correct unbeaten dogs come into the ring to compete for Best of Breed.

Becoming a steward is a good way of getting involved in showing, and show committees are often looking for people to help out in this way. If you are new to stewarding, you may be paired with an experienced steward to learn the ropes. Stewards need to have a good knowledge of the showing regulations.

This chapter has explained what happens at a show, and how you'll be judged. Now we'll move on to what you are there for: winning!

Fig. 5.33. Greyhound 'INT/BEL/UK Ch Windspiel Northern Steel for Alouann' winning the group.

CHAPTER 6

ROSETTES, AWARDS AND CHAMPIONS

When you first dip your toe into the world of dog show-ing, you'll probably be over the moon if you come home with a rosette, whatever colour it is. But there's more to showing than winning a class or two at each show. First, there are the obvious awards which can be won at most shows, such as Best of Breed (BOB), Best Puppy in Show (BPIS) and the ultimate Best in Show (BIS). But wins at shows can also gain you points that accumulate towards a Junior Warrant (JW) or a Show Certificate of Merit (ShCM), or you can collect Chal-lenge Certificates to become a Champion (CH) or Show Champion (ShCH). Gaining these awards entitles you to add the letters of the abbreviations to your dog's official name. And while not gaining honorifics for your dog, an important achievement to aim for is to qualify to exhibit at Crufts.

In this chapter we'll be looking at the awards you could achieve, and will introduce the Stud Book and Stud Book bands.

Fig. 6.2 Chinese Crested 'Kojiki's Little Lion Man of Aucristae' winning Best in Show.

Fig. 6.1 It's always good to be placed first! Irish Setter 'Sh CH Bardonhill Floating Moon into Glenlaine JW' winning his class at the East of England Championship Show.

ROSETTES AND PRIZES

If you win a place at an open show or a breed cham-pionship show you will normally be presented with a prize card and rosette. It will say in the schedule

Claiming your award

We've already mentioned the need for record keeping as records of most wins are not kept by the Kennel Club. Some wins gain points towards awards and it's up to you to record your wins, count up your points and then submit a claim to the Kennel Club to ratify your award. The only computerized records kept are the Stud Book qualifying awards at championship shows where CCs are on offer. If you haven't kept records but need to check your results, you can contact the show secretaries of the various shows you have attended, who should have the catalogues and may be able to help you.

how many places rosettes are awarded for – sometimes prize cards are given out to, say, fifth place, with rosettes only given for the first three. The colours of the rosettes are standard:

- First – red
- Second – blue
- Third – yellow
- Fourth – green
- VHC – white

At some shows prize cards are given out to seventh place if there is a high entry.

UNBEATEN DOGS AND THE 'UNBEATEN DOG' RULE

An 'unbeaten dog' is one which has come first in the classes he has entered, and has not been beaten in a subsequent class. All unbeaten dogs are eligible to go forward to compete for Best of Breed or Best AVNSC (Any Variety Not Separately Classified). You cannot withdraw from subsequent breed classes to remain an unbeaten dog. If you are beaten in a stakes or AV class, you are not counted as a beaten dog in your breed classes.

Unbeaten dog rule changes, 2015–2017

Prior to January 2015, if you had won all your breed classes and became Best of Breed, but were subsequently beaten in an AV or stakes class, you would have been considered a beaten dog and would not have been allowed to take part in the group judging. From January 2015, for a two-year trial period, the Kennel Club is suspending this rule. When you complete your entry form check the schedule carefully; if there are further changes within the trial period, the criteria for the classes should reflect this. Up-to-date information should also appear on the Kennel Club website, or you can check at www.trishhaill.co.uk.

If you've come second ...

If you've come second in any class, it is worth staying around and keeping an eye on who is being placed in subsequent classes. If you end up having been placed second only to the dog winning Best of Breed, then you may be called back into the ring to compete for the reserve place if there is one.

WITHDRAWING FROM CLASSES

If you have entered a breed class, you are expected to turn up to it. A dog which is not exhibited in the entered classes can be disqualified. There are only limited circumstances in which you can withdraw from a breed class, and the first of these is if an emergency judge has been appointed and he is one that you cannot show under. In this case, you should tell the show secretary before the judging. If you turn up late and miss your first breed class, you can still exhibit in the other classes you have entered, but a report will be submitted to the Kennel Club, and unless there was a very good reason for you to miss the first class, you may be disqualified and any award you have won is likely to be taken away.

If you have entered more than one class but after

your first one you feel you do not wish to continue in the other classes you have entered – perhaps your dog did not show well in his first class and you see little point in continuing, or perhaps you feel ill – then in these circumstances you can withdraw from subsequent classes. It is a matter of courtesy to tell the steward, as technically you need permission from the judge. You will not able to compete in any other class (a subsequent breed class, AV or stakes) if you withdraw from a breed class.

You can, however, withdraw from AV or stakes classes without effecting exhibiting in your breed classes. Sometimes at championship shows stakes classes will clash with your breed class, making it impossible to do both.

BEST OF BREED

Mixed judging

Where bitches and dogs are judged together in the breed classes, all unbeaten dogs of either sex are called into the ring to be judged for Best of Breed. If an exhibit has only been beaten by the dog declared Best of Breed, he may be called back into the ring to compete for Reserve Best of Breed (RBOB) if that award is on offer at that particular show.

Dogs and bitches judged separately

Where dogs and bitches are judged separately, the Best Dog and Best Bitch will be selected from the unbeaten dogs in the breed classes. The Best of Breed will then be judged from the Best Bitch and the Best Dog. If there were different judges for dogs and bitches, both judges will take part in the Best of Breed judging, and a referee will be brought in if the judges can't agree.

There may be a Best Opposite Sex award, which will be given to the other dog or bitch, depending on which sex won Best of Breed.

If there is a Reserve Best of Breed award, the dog which was beaten only by the Best of Breed is judged against the Best Opposite Sex. Occasionally, and more commonly in breed shows, the dog who was second to the Best Opposite Sex will also be called back into the ring to challenge for Reserve Best of Breed.

GROUP JUDGING AND BEST IN SHOW

If the show is being judged on the group system, all the Best of Breed winners in each group (including the AVNSC for that group) will compete for the Best in Group title. The judge judging the group will not have already judged one of the breeds. You may get a little confused when you first start hearing the results of the group judging. Instead of being called first, second, third, etc., the first four places in the group are called Group 1 to Group 4 (so Gundog Group 4, for example, will be the dog who was placed fourth in the Gundog Group).

Fig.6.3   Siberian Husky 'Ch Siberiaskey Brite Borealis of Pelenrise JW ShCM' winning Group 3 at Bath Championship Show. (Photo: Jenny Manley)

All dogs placed Group 1 (first in group) will then go forward to the Best in Show challenge. Once the Best in Show is awarded, the Reserve Best is Show is then chosen from the remaining Group 1 dogs.

Fig.6.5   Pointer 'Sh CH Shamphilly Juici Cuture JW' winning Reserve Best in Show at the Scottish Kennel Club Championship Show. (Photo: Alan V. Walker)

Fig.6.4   Boxer 'Ch Tartaria Gold Dust' winning Best in Show at Leeds Championship Show. (Photo: John Jackson)

SHOWS NOT JUDGED ON THE GROUP SYSTEM

If the show is not judged on the group system, then all dogs awarded Best of Breed, Best AVNSC or any 'Best of' title (for example, Best AV Junior, even if beaten in a subsequent class) will compete to be Best in Show. This can mean it is a very large class. The Reserve Best in Show is then selected from the remaining unbeaten dogs. Most shows not judged on the group system are limited shows.

BEST PUPPY IN SHOW

Where there is an award on offer for Best Puppy in Show (BPIS), the competition is held even for breeds which do not have specific puppy classes listed in the schedule. The judge will award 'Best Puppy in Breed' to the best dog aged between six and twelve months, whichever breed class they entered. Where the Best of Breed is a puppy, it will automatically be Best Puppy in Breed. Likewise with the group judging, where if the Best in Group is a puppy, he will also be the Best Puppy in Group.

This puppy will then compete for Best in Show, along with all the other Best of Group winners. If he then takes Best in Show, he automatically becomes the Best Puppy in Show as well. There may still be a Best Puppy competition, but in this case it will be to find the Reserve Best Puppy.

The Best Puppy in Breed competition is held after the Best of Breed judging, and so on for Best in Group and ultimately Best in Show. The judging for Best Puppy in Breed, Group or Show therefore always takes place after the judging for Best of Breed, Group or Show.

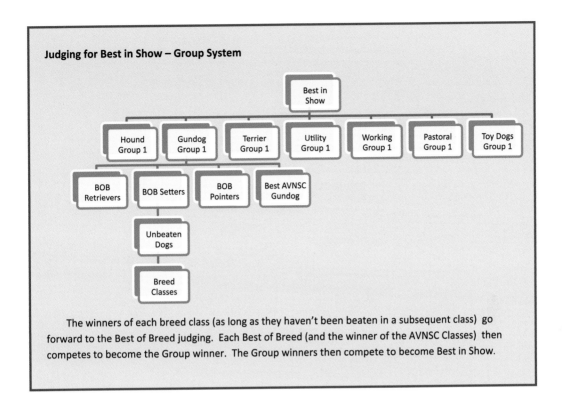

Judging for Best in Show – Group System

The winners of each breed class (as long as they haven't been beaten in a subsequent class) go forward to the Best of Breed judging. Each Best of Breed (and the winner of the AVNSC Classes) then competes to become the Group winner. The Group winners then compete to become Best in Show.

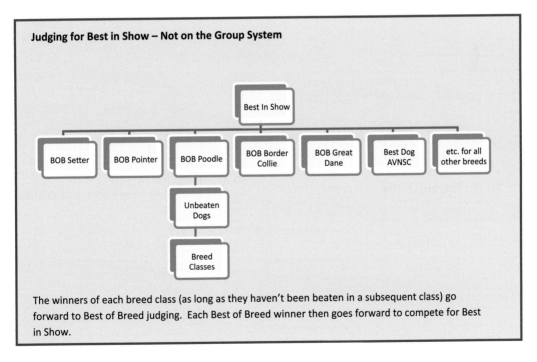

Judging for Best in Show – Not on the Group System

The winners of each breed class (as long as they haven't been beaten in a subsequent class) go forward to Best of Breed judging. Each Best of Breed winner then goes forward to compete for Best in Show.

Fig. 6.6   How to become Best in Show.

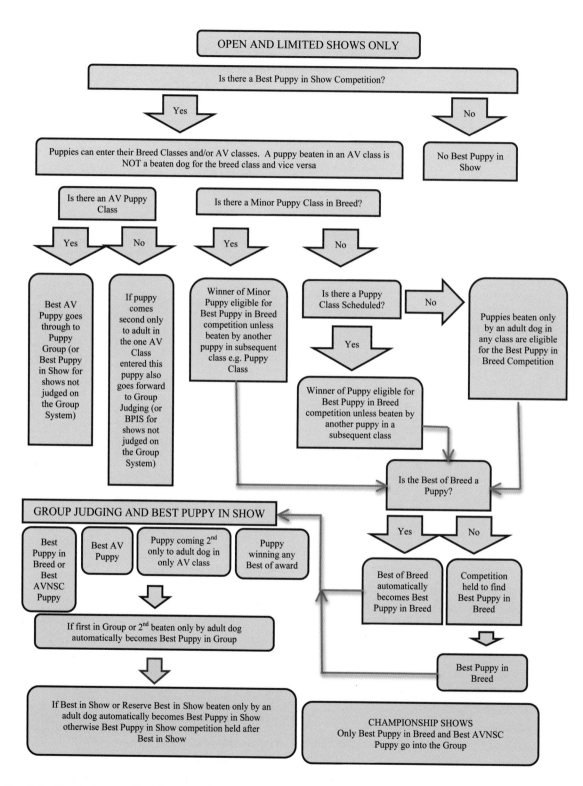

Fig. 6.7   How to become Best Puppy in Show.

Judging for Best Puppy

Points to note:

- The Best Puppy in Breed competition will be held after the Best of Breed judging and the Best Puppy will be selected from the winners of the Best Minor Puppy or Best Puppy (if both classes are scheduled), or if there is just one puppy class, the winner of that class will be Best Puppy. If no puppy classes are scheduled, then the Best Puppy will be the best dog aged between six and twelve months, even if it did not win a place in the class in which it was entered.
- If the Best of Breed is a puppy, he will automatically be Best Puppy in Breed.
- If there is a Reserve Best Puppy in Breed award, the competition will take place after the Best of Breed judging.
- If the Best of Breed is a puppy, he will go forward to the group competition. If he wins his group, he will become both Best of Group AND Best Puppy in Group.
- If he wins Best in Show, he will automatically also be Best Puppy in Show. The Best Puppy in Show competition takes place after Best in Show for this reason, and may only be needed to select the Reserve Best Puppy in Show.
- Technically, it is possible to change between routes if the group judge is different from the breed judge, as he may choose to select the Best Puppy in Breed to become Best of Group ahead of the Best of Breed.
- At open and limited shows all Best Puppies in Breed will be eligible to compete for Best Puppy in Group, along with the Best AV Puppy, even if the latter was beaten by the Best Puppy in its breed, or was beaten in a subsequent AV class. Any puppy winning a 'Best of' award, or any puppy which has entered just one AV class (for example, Junior) and was only beaten by an adult dog, will also be able to compete in the group. Thus you could potentially end up with the winning puppy not being the Best Puppy in Breed as the group judge will be a different person, with a different interpretation of the breed standard.

- At championship shows the Best Puppies in Breed and Best AVNSC Puppies will compete for Best Puppy in Group and thereafter Best Puppy in Show.
- Fig. 6.7 shows, on the left, how a puppy can become Best Puppy in Show, either by winning Best of Breed or Best AVNSC, or coming through via the AV route, and Best in Group.
- The alternative route on the right shows how a puppy can become Best Puppy in Show when he is only beaten by an adult dog. If the puppy wins Reserve Best of Breed and the Best of Breed is an adult dog, then the puppy automatically becomes Best Puppy in Breed. Likewise, if he is beaten only by an adult in the group and becomes Reserve Best in Group, he will also automatically become Best Puppy in Group and Best Puppy in Breed respectively.

If you are awarded Best in Show or Best Puppy in Show, you cannot compete in any further classes at that show, for example any stakes classes you have entered.

CHALLENGE CERTIFICATES (CC)

Challenge Certificates (often referred to as 'tickets') are significant awards and are on offer at championship shows but not necessarily for every breed. The Kennel Club assigns the number of CCs to each breed club annually, and the breed club decides how they should be allocated across the various championship and premier open shows. There may be one CC for the Best of Breed, or one each for the Best Dog and Best Bitch. CCs will not normally be available if it is expected there will be a low entry for breeds at a particular show. Some popular breeds can expect to be able to compete for CCs at almost every general championship show, while less numerous breeds may only have a couple of general shows where they are able to collect CCs each year.

It is worth noting that when awarding a Challenge Certificate (or Reserve Challenge Certificate), the judge must believe that the dog is worthy of becoming a Champion. The award, or indeed any place at a show, can be withheld if the judge does not believe the dog,

Fig. 6.8   Before he was famous! The (now) Sh CH 'Rutilus Esuberante for Hundwith' winning Best Puppy in Show.

which may be the best specimen in the class, does not sufficiently merit the top prize. If the judge decides not to award the Challenge Certificate, the Reserve Ticket will not be awarded either.

Currently, four all-breed championship shows offer CCs in all breeds: Crufts, the Birmingham Dog Show, the Scottish Kennel Club and the Welsh Kennel Club. From January 2015 other shows that agree to certain criteria will be able to follow suit.

In January 2015 the Kennel Club introduced new rules allowing a general championship show and a breed championship show, both awarding CCs, to be held at the same venue on the same day. This saves costs and travel for exhibitors who have a chance to enter both shows and may potentially end up with two CCs on the same day.

CHAMPIONS AND SHOW CHAMPIONS

The accolade of Champion is the highest award show dogs can achieve in the UK and entitles you to put the letters CH (or Sh CH) before your dog's name on entry forms and catalogues, and, of course, in the pedigree of any progeny. To become a Champion your dog needs to gain three Challenge Certificates, each awarded by a different judge. At least one Challenge Certificate must be won after the dog is twelve months of age.

The schedule for a championship show will tell you if, and how many, Challenge Certificates are on offer for your breed. For breeds with a higher entry there will normally be two tickets, one each for Best Dog and Best Bitch. If only one is on offer, it will be awarded to the dog or bitch which wins Best of Breed.

Becoming a Champion or Show Champion qualifies the dog for Crufts for life.

Show Champion

If your dog is a gundog breed or a Border Collie, he will not be entitled to be called a full Champion even with three Challenge Certificates as he will also need to prove himself in working trials. For these breeds the title of Show Champion is awarded (Sh Ch), to show the requisite number of Challenge Certificates have been won.

It is considered that a full Champion of these breeds

Fig. 6.9   Judge presenting a Challenge Certificate.

should not only be an outstanding example of the breed as proven in the show ring, but also be able to prove he can do the work he is supposed to do. Unfortunately, in many breeds nowadays there is a big split between 'show types' and 'working types', and many Field Trial Champions either lack the conformation to win Challenge Certificates in the show ring, or their owners lack the inclination to exhibit them. Likewise, many show dog owners lack the will to undertake the separate discipline of field trials.

Fig. 6.10 Champion Basset Fauve de Bretagne 'Ch Brequest Bailee Basler'.

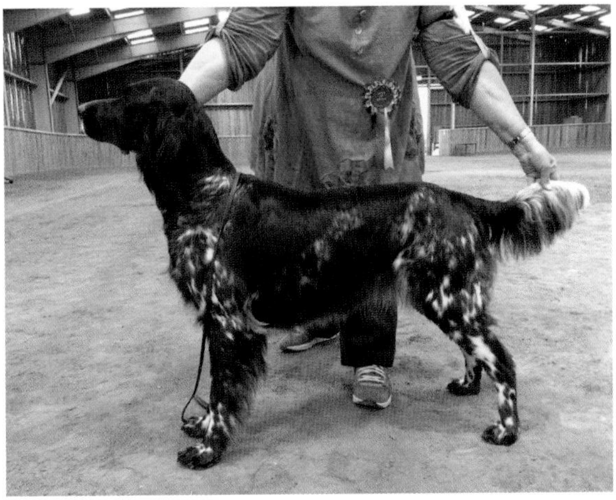

Fig. 6.12 Large Munsterlander 'Sh CH Rayaris Freya'.

To become a Champion (Ch), gundogs need to gain the Show Gundog Working Certificate, or win an award at a field trial, as well as achieving three tickets. Collies have to take a Show Border Collie Herding Test or be placed at a sheepdog trial.

Fig. 6.11 Champion Newfoundland 'Ch Zentaur Tee Tea Effen JW ShCM'. (Photo: Paul Dodd)

Fig. 6.13 Pointer 'Ch Fowington Five Bob Note JW'. (Photo: Susan Stone)

Dual Champion

If a gundog is both a Show Champion and has a working Champion title (most commonly as a Field Trial Champion), then he gains the title of Dual Champion, and can use the letters Dual Ch in front of his name.

Fig. 6.14   The only Border Collie that is currently a Full Champion, 'Ch Littlehorn Colt at Tobermory JW/SBCHT/ Beg Ex' ('Woody'), is owned, trained and handled in all disciplines by Rachel Spencer. (Photo: LW Canine Photography)

Fig. 6.15   'Woody' showing he is a working dog as well as excelling in the show ring.

Gaining this title is a considerable achievement and is quite rare.

Fig. 6.16   Dual Champion 'Fowington Slezak' got his full title in 1995 and is the only pointer to have done so since 'Ben of Bobbin' in the 1920s. (Photo: Nick Prior Designs)

WHEN NO CHALLENGE CERTIFICATES ARE ON OFFER FOR THE BREED

At championship shows where no Challenge Certificates are on offer for the breed, and where entries are few, dogs and bitches will still be able to compete for Best Dog and Best Bitch, even if the classes are mixed. The Best Dog and Best Bitch will then compete for Best of Breed, and Best Opposite Sex (if that award is on offer).

COLLECTING POINTS FOR AWARDS

Although at every show it can be exciting to be competing to be Best of Breed, etc., certain wins can gain you points towards two other awards that entitle you to put letters after your dog's name. These awards are the Junior Warrant and the Show Certificate of Merit. Both are achieved via a rather complicated points system, and unfortunately, as already noted, wins are not recorded in a central database and you will need to keep your own records of points gained. Once you have collected sufficient points, you can apply to the Kennel Club for the award. The Kennel Club will check your wins with the club secretaries who keep records of individual shows.

A Junior Warrant is particularly sought-after as a dog which gains it is qualified for Crufts for life, and is given a Stud Book number. The Show Certificate of Merit was introduced in 2004 to try to encourage greater attendance at open shows. Prior to that date entries were falling; you could go along to win a rosette, or even Best in Show, but with no Challenge Certificates on offer there wasn't much motivation for people to support open shows, and exhibitors would concentrate on championship shows instead. Achieving a Show Certificate of Merit allows you to put ShCM after your dog's name, but it does not qualify your dog for Crufts, nor count towards becoming a Champion. It is, however, a recognition of achievement and one to be proud of.

Show Certificate of Merit

You can only gain points for the Show Certificate of Merit from general open shows that are open to breeds from all groups, or from Group Open Shows. You cannot count wins at championship shows, breed or limited shows.

The points system is not the easiest to understand! You can pick up more than one set of points at one show, and it does not matter how many (or rather how few) dogs there were in the class. It's worth noting that as long as the other criteria are satisfied, you can also put the same wins towards a claim for a Junior Warrant.

Twenty-five points must be won to claim the Show Certificate of Merit, and five must have been won in group competitions (so you'll need to be placed in at least two group competitions to collect the right number of points).

There is no time limit to building up points to gain the Show Certificate of Merit, but any wins prior to 2003 cannot be counted, and the points system changed slightly on 1 January 2011 affecting the Best in Show and Reserve Best in Show at shows not judged on the group system. The maximum numbers of such wins prior to that date that can be claimed are five Best in Show awards and three Reserve Best in Show awards respectively.

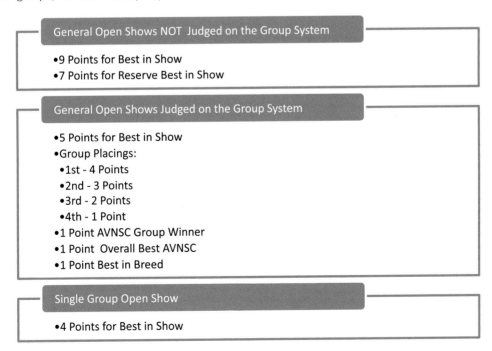

General Open Shows NOT Judged on the Group System

- 9 Points for Best in Show
- 7 Points for Reserve Best in Show

General Open Shows Judged on the Group System

- 5 Points for Best in Show
- Group Placings:
  - 1st - 4 Points
  - 2nd - 3 Points
  - 3rd - 2 Points
  - 4th - 1 Point
- 1 Point AVNSC Group Winner
- 1 Point Overall Best AVNSC
- 1 Point Best in Breed

Single Group Open Show

- 4 Points for Best in Show

Fig. 6.17   Show Certificate of Merit points that can be won at different shows.

Fig. 6.18   Gaining a Show Certificate of Merit is a major achievement. Keeshond 'Kichigai Ups a Daisy ShCM'.

Fig. 6.19   Any Champion awards go at the front of the name, and the Show Certificate of Merit award at the end. Brittany 'Sh CH Highclare Flaming Nora ShCM'.

Junior Warrant	Championship Shows with CCs on offer for Breed	3 Points for each 1st Prize for a Breed Class
		3 points for BOB UNLESS JW Points already won by winning a Breed Class(es)
		3 Points for Best Puppy in Breed if JW points not already earned by winning a Breed Class AND where the Best Opposite Sex Puppy has gained 1 or more points by winning a Breed Class(es)
	Championship Shows without CCs on offer for Breed and Open Shows	1 Point for each 1st Prize for a Breed Class
		1 Point for BOB UNLESS JW Points already won by winning a Breed Class(es)
		1 Point for Best Puppy in Breed if JW points not already earned by winning a Breed Class AND where the Best Opposite Sex Puppy has gained 1 or more points by winning a Breed Class(es)

Fig. 6.20   Junior Warrant points.

Junior Warrant

When you begin to show in puppy classes, you may hear people talking about getting points for a Junior Warrant. As the name implies, dogs achieve this award when they are young – before the age of eighteen months. To qualify dogs must earn a certain number of points, and these must be gained at both open and championship shows. To achieve a Junior Warrant you do need to be fairly serious about showing, and attend a sufficient number of shows to collect enough points. If your puppy consistently achieves first places in the ring, then a Junior Warrant could be within your reach.

A Junior Warrant is a major achievement, and means that your dog gains his Stud Book number (SBN) and is qualified for Crufts for life. He will also be able to use the letters JW after his name in show catalogues. Gaining a Junior Warrant is quite hard work, as you have just twelve months in which to accomplish it. You cannot start showing a puppy until he is six months old, and sufficient points must be earned before he is eighteen months old.

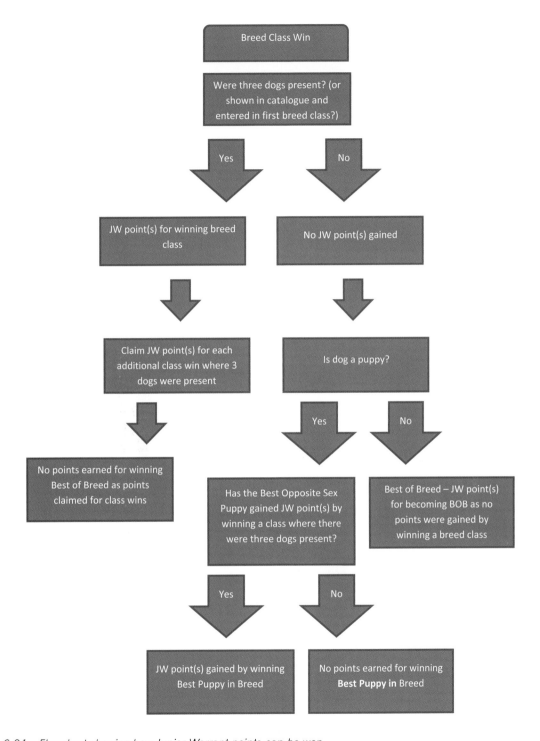

Fig. 6.21 Flowchart showing how Junior Warrant points can be won.

Note 1: Junior Warrant Points cannot be won if there are fewer than three dogs of the breed present. A dog may be counted as being present if it was entered in that class and was present in its first class for the breed in that Show, even if it doesn't subsequently turn up to that class.

Note 2: If the dog has gained points for being Best Puppy in Breed and Best in Breed, only one claim can be made.

A Junior Warrant requires a total of twenty-five points. A minimum of three points must be earned from championship shows where CCs were on offer or from open shows or championship shows where CCs were not on offer – this means you cannot claim more than twenty-two points from just one type of show.

Junior Warrant points cannot be won if there are fewer than three dogs of the breed present in a class. If the catalogue shows there should be three or more dogs in the class, and if a dog was present in his first breed class, but subsequently does not turn up to the class you're exhibiting in, that dog can be counted as having been present in that class. Therefore, in these circumstances a Junior Warrant point can still be gained even if there is only one dog actually present for judging. Another point to note is that even if the dog has gained points for being Best Puppy in Breed and Best of Breed, only one claim can be made.

Fig. 6.21 should simplify how you earn JW points having won a breed class.

Achieving a Junior Warrant is not easy. It necessitates attending a number of shows, and trying to pick shows that can be predicted to have a good attendance, and therefore the qualifying numbers in the classes. It can be very demoralizing to attend a show when your dog is quickly reaching that eighteen-month mark, and you're chasing that last point, to find there are only two dogs entered in the class!

Fig. 6.22   On the way to winning her Junior Warrant, Dobermann 'Mianna's Cracklin Rose at Luftez JW' won four first prizes and Best Puppy in Show, earning her a bunch of rosettes as well as quite a haul of dog food!

Can any dog gain a Junior Warrant?

Not all dogs will be able to come close to gaining the points required for a Junior Warrant. Many medium and larger breeds continue developing and maturing up to twenty-four or even thirty-six months. An older dog which did not achieve a JW is not necessarily a worse example of the breed than a dog which did achieve one. If you are considering a dog which gained a Stud Book number via the JW route for breeding, his wins as an adult should also be taken into account. It is possible that as the dog matured he did not achieve the potential shown as a youngster, and although he has a lifelong qualification for Crufts, he may not have won any major awards since.

STUD BOOK NUMBERS

The Victorians' early attempts at record keeping were poor which is why, only a year after its formation, the Kennel Club published the first Stud Book in 1874. This recorded the results of all dog shows and field trials from 1859 to 1873, and also included rules for running shows. As there were no rules about the naming of dogs, many pet names appeared with significant duplications. Fraud and substitution were rife at shows, so the Kennel Club embarked on a registration system allowing dogs to be uniquely identified, and from 1880 a monthly register of dog names was published in the *Kennel Gazette*. From this point on there were no registered dogs with the same name, and every dog could be ascribed to the right owner. Although now renamed the *Kennel Club Journal*, this monthly publication continues, albeit it is currently only available online.

How to get a Stud Book number

There are several ways to get a Stud Book number. If your dog achieves a Junior Warrant or receives a Challenge Certificate or Reserve Challenge Certificate, he qualifies for a Stud Book number irrespective of breed.

The Stud Book

The Stud Book is a record of achievement for the top winning dogs, and has been produced annually since its first edition. It records the top winners of all championship shows, field trials, obedience, agility and other activities, and all dogs named in the book will have gained their Stud Book number. The Stud Book is used as a reference for breeding because all dogs with Stud Book numbers have shown themselves to be exceptional examples of the breed. Gaining a Stud Book number qualifies a dog for entry to Crufts for life.

Stud Book numbers can also be gained from winning first, second, third or fourth awards or Certificates of Merit at the dog's first field trial.

Neutered dogs can gain a Stud Book number, but the letters NEUT will appear after their name in the Stud Book.

Fig. 6.23   Australian Terrier 'Ch Silhill Sweet Pea' obtained her Stud Book number after winning her first CC. (Photo: Graham Peers)

Changing a dog's name after gaining a Stud Book number

If your dog achieves a Stud Book number, then you cannot change his name if more than thirty days have elapsed since he qualified. If you want to add your kennel name as an affix, you must do so as soon as he qualifies.

STUD BOOK BANDS

Now the system becomes a little more complicated, and we have to look at Stud Book bands. Some breeds are more popular than others, and have a greater attendance at shows. Breeds are allocated a Stud Book band depending on how numerous a breed is. This band indicates which classes and which places at championship shows are Crufts qualifiers or qualify them for a Stud Book number.

The popularity of breeds waxes and wanes over time, so the Stud Book bands are revised annually. All exhibitors should be aware of the band for their breed, and check it regularly. The Stud Book bands are to be found on the Kennel Club website, and are also published online in the monthly *Kennel Club Journal*.

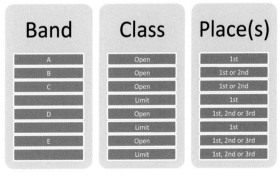

Band	Class	Place(s)
A	Open	1st
B	Open	1st or 2nd
C	Open	1st or 2nd
	Limit	1st
D	Open	1st, 2nd or 3rd
	Limit	1st
E	Open	1st, 2nd or 3rd
	Limit	1st, 2nd or 3rd

Fig. 6.24   Which places gain a Stud Book number in the various Stud Book bands.

As you can see from Fig. 6.24, for a breed in Band A only one winning dog will gain a Stud Book number from a championship show, but for a breed in Band E six dogs will achieve that honour.

EXAMPLES OF BREEDS IN THE STUD BOOK BANDS (2014)

Fig. 6.25 The Manchester Terrier is in Stud Book Band A. 'Rattustrap Maid Marian'.

Fig. 6.27 The Saluki is in Stud Book Band C. 'Ch Glenoak Ishaara JW'.

Fig. 6.26 The Chow Chow is in Stud Book Band B. 'Ch Towmena In the Frame'.

Fig. 6.28 The Shetland Sheepdog is in Stud Book Band D. 'Mossvale Moonlight at Arcticfrost'.

Fig. 6.29 *The Cavalier King Charles Spaniel is in Stud Book Band E. 'Ch Leogem Rhapsody'.*

OTHER PRIZES

Ringcraft club competitions

You might think that achieving any of the higher awards is beyond you at the present time, but it's still worth making a note of your wins and other places. If you belong to a ringcraft club, you may need to tell them about any prizes you have won as you may find you're eligible for a prize or cup at the end of the year.

Prize Money

Dog showing isn't something that you do to make money; even if you do win a cash prize at a show, it's unlikely even to pay for the petrol you used to get there! But it's always nice to have some recognition. Any prize money will be shown on the show schedule, but most exhibitors simply look on this as a bonus.

Special Award classes

Sometimes you may find Special Award classes at open, limited or championship shows. These classes are held separately from the main show (often during the lunch break) and will not have a class number. Instead, they will be denoted by a letter in the catalogue to make it clear they are different. Only three such classes can

be scheduled per show. At open and championship shows one class might be a Champions' class. These classes are intended to give less experienced judges the chance to judge. Prize cards up to four places can be awarded, and at the discretion of the show there may be prize money on offer.

Only dogs already entered in the main breed classes can take part, and dogs are not 'beaten' for the purposes of the main show if they do not come first in the Special Award class they have entered.

Trophies

Many clubs and societies award trophies – cups or plates – to winners of various breeds and Best in Show. You may well see a table laden with them when walking in. You normally need to be a member of that society or club to be able to take the trophy home, however, and even then you will only have it in your possession for up to a year. You may also get a prize for winning a stakes class, and this might be yours to keep.

SHOWING FOR CHILDREN AND YOUNG ADULTS

People of any age can start showing and it's a fun activity where children can take part alongside their parents. Many young exhibitors start by showing their pet dogs at fun days and companion shows, and it's not too big a step, if they have a pedigree dog, for them to begin attending formal shows as well. They can either show their dog in the main classes, or enter the special classes for young handlers.

To encourage children and young adults to enter the show scene, the Kennel Club has set up the Young Kennel Club (YKC). It is open to people between the ages of six and twenty-four, and it currently costs just £15 per year. The YKC is open to anyone in that age group who has a dog, whether cross-breed or pedigree, and even to people without a dog who want to become more involved in canine activities. The YKC holds special events and classes in dog agility, field trials, flyball, grooming, handling, heelwork to music, jumping, obedience and breed showing stakes. Young people can qualify to compete at Crufts via qualifying classes in all the disciplines. Many activities are run for YKC members, including a summer dog training camp.

Fig. 6.30 A junior judge judging a junior handler.

YKC stakes classes

At many open and championship shows there are special YKC stakes classes. These classes are similar to breed classes, but only YKC members can enter. Some stakes classes are judged on the conformation of the dog, just like the main breed classes. Other classes are to judge the handling ability of the young handler, rather than judging the dog against the breed standard. To compete in the YKC handling classes, the dog must be a pedigree registered with the Kennel Club. If a YKC member is showing a dog in a YKC breed showing stakes class, there is a further restriction in that the dog must be registered in the YKC member's name, or in the name of someone in the family who must be resident at the same address as the YKC member. Entries must be made on the entry form, and cannot be taken on the day.

YKC handlers can collect points from the stakes

classes at companion, limited, open and championship shows. Showing points books are available free from the Kennel Club in which a record can be kept of the points won. A total of 150 points is required to win a handling badge.

Stakes classes are divided into three age groups, namely six to eleven years, twelve to sixteen years and seventeen to twenty-four years. Gaining a first place means that the young handler has qualified for Crufts – but only if they were a fully paid-up YKC member at the time of the show.

YKC members are encouraged to play a wider role in the show world if they wish to do so, and have the opportunity to train for stewarding qualifications, and can help out at shows (partnered with adult stewards) to enable them to gain experience.

Junior Handling Association

In the 1970s an organization emerged which offered youngsters between the ages of six and sixteen the opportunity to compete for the title of UK Junior Handler of the Year, and from there to represent their country in the International Junior Handler competition at Crufts. The competition is held in conjunction with *Dog World*.

Throughout the year, at a number of open or championship shows, there are junior handling classes. Some of these will be marked in the schedule as qualifiers for the semi-finals. The classes are divided into two age groups, six to eleven years and twelve to sixteen years. Handlers gaining a first, second or third place qualify to take part in a semi-final. As in the YKC classes, any dog handled must be a Kennel Club registered pedigree dog. The dog does not need to belong to the handler. Please see the schedule to check whether the dog needs to have been entered in another class at the same show.

Up to 2014 there was only one venue for the semi-finals, which were always held at the Richmond Championship Show. To try to make it easier for people to attend and compete, a pilot scheme is being trialled from the end of 2014. There will now be six venues where young people who have qualified can enter. These are spread over the year (starting in the preced-

Shows at which junior handling semi-finals are held

Name of Show and approximate Date	Classes
British Utility Breeds Association (December)	Utility 6–11 Utility 12–16
UK Toy (March)	Toy 6–11 Toy 12–16
National Terrier (April)	Terrier 6–11 Terrier 12–16
National Working and Pastoral Breeds Dog Society (July)	Working 6–11 Working 12–16 Pastoral 6–11 Pastoral 12–16
Hound Association (August)	Hound 6–11 Hound 12–16
National Gundog (August)	Gundog 6–11 Gundog 12–16

ing December), one for each of the groups. People who come first in the semi-final will not compete again. However, there is nothing to stop a youngster, once qualified, from showing off their handling skills with another breed from another group at a subsequent show, and making a second, or even third, attempt to become a semi-finalist.

Junior handlers need to qualify in the twelve months preceding the closing date of entry for each show, so the qualifying dates will be different for each of the shows.

Two finalists at the semi-finals (one for each age band) for each group will then compete in the final at Discover Dogs, currently held in October at Excel.

Apart from the class entry fee as per the schedule, junior handlers can take part at any qualifying show without paying a subscription to the JHA. If they qualify for the semi-final, however, they will need to become a member of the association. At the current time the annual subscription is £4.

These proposed changes are being brought in for 2015. Any future alterations to the pilot scheme can be found on the Junior Handling Association website at www.juniorhandling.co.uk.

Fig. 6.31 *Winning one of the last JHA semi-finals held at Richmond with Greyhound 'Int/Bel/UK Ch Windspiel Northern Steel for Alouan'. (Photo: Emily Guy)*

CHAPTER 7

BREED WATCH – BREEDING FOR HEALTH AND FITNESS

BREEDING PEDIGREE/ PUREBRED DOGS

When buying a puppy to show, you need to have a purebred dog that's registered with the Kennel Club. But out of the millions of pedigree dogs which fulfil these criteria, very few end up as show dogs – either because the owners have no wish to show them or, more often, because they don't make the grade. Pedigree dogs eligible to be registered might just be the offspring of Fred's dog, which mated with his friend Joe's bitch, which just happened to be the same breed, with no thought given to the compatibility of the sire and dam and no regard to any underlying genetic health issues or the knowledge of the original breeding lines these dogs have come from. The pups, however, would still be pedigree, and would be eligible to be registered with the Kennel Club.

So what's wrong with this scenario? This is largely how humans find a partner. But in the same way that humans can inherit traits, looks, behaviour or health problems that can be attributed back to their parents, grandparents or even further, and just as offspring from the same family can have very different looks and characteristics, so it is with dogs. But with our canines we have more tools at our disposal so that we can minimize any surprises in the progeny by arranging matings carefully, taking into account results of health testing, what we know of the temperament going back generations, and what we want to bring into (or out of) the lines in relation to how well they meet the breed standard.

Rather than the indiscriminate breeding in the Fred and Joe scenario, at the heart of the showing world is the identification and selection of the best stock for breeding. If you become seriously involved in showing with an excellent show dog, you may want to consider breeding at some point yourself. But even if you just want to have some fun in the sport, you'll still need to understand what goes into producing good show puppies in order to select the best prospect for you to bring on. Even someone just wanting to buy a dog as a pet should take as much care over the selection of their puppy as someone planning to exhibit, and ensure that they support only ethical breeding practices. Everyone who owns a dog deserves a well-bred healthy pet, and our dogs deserve happy, healthy lives.

HEALTH AND WELFARE

So here we'll talk a bit about the health and welfare of pedigree dogs, and in particular about the high profile breeds, what is being done about them, and what you need to be aware of if one of these breeds attracts your attention and is one you wish to own.

It would be difficult for anyone involved in showing or breeding pedigree dogs not to be aware of the controversy surrounding them. It cannot be denied that in the past, particularly in some breeds, breeders went over the top and in trying to produce the best specimens certain features became exaggerated – for example, over-long ears that tripped the dog up, excessive folds of skin that could harbour infections, and shortened noses that affected breathing. The breeders were not even trying to produce animals that matched the breed standard, but were simply catering for buyers who liked the look of these dogs, creating a market for animals that were unhealthy not because of any genetic predisposition but simply because fashion demanded it. The origins of breeding purely for looks goes back to the Victorian era when canine welfare wasn't on the agenda, and dogs had evolved as companions, meaning their working abilities no longer needed to be tested.

Over the last few decades, and as our concern for animal health and welfare grew, people began to believe that all pedigree dogs were unhealthy, and that showing was cruel as it perpetuated breeding for aesthetic reasons rather than health.

HIGH PROFILE BREEDS

It's probable that the majority of exhibitors enjoying their turn round the show ring do not realize how close the sport came to being phased out, and the breeding (and selling) of certain breeds being banned.

Publicly, this came to a head in August 2008 when the BBC screened a programme highlighting some of the most exaggerated breeds, and as a result of public pressure subsequently pulled out of televising Crufts. However, the real story started long before the public became involved. Much earlier than the famous television exposure, international concerns about the breeding and showing of pedigree dogs led to the European Convention for the Protection of Pet Animals (ECPPA) in 1987. This convention resulted in the banning of docking, and other surgical alterations to pet animals such as ear cropping or cosmetic surgery for aesthetic reasons. It also highlighted the responsibility of breeders to take care in selecting animals for breeding with respect to health and welfare. In 1995 there was a review of the convention, in which attention turned to the breed standards, and breed clubs were encouraged to review the standards 'to amend those which can cause potential welfare problems'. This was all good stuff, but hidden in the Appendix was the comment that 'if these measures are not sufficient, to consider the possibility of prohibiting the breeding and for phasing out the exhibition and selling of certain types or breeds when characteristics of these animals corre-

spond to harmful defects...'. The convention clarifies that the harmful defects which should be taken into account when revising the standards include references to maximum and minimum weights to avoid skeleton and joint disorders, very short legs, shortness of nose and skull that can cause breathing difficulties, problems with giving birth naturally, very long ears and excessive skin folds.

These recommendations appear reasonable, but the Appendix cited examples of more than forty breeds of dogs that were considered to have health issues, and bore the obvious threat that if the problems were not able to be resolved, these breeds would need to disappear from our lives.

In response to the seriousness of this situation, the Kennel Club set up the Dog Health Group with the aim of raising the standards of dog breeding and dog health. One result was the revision of all breed standards in 2009 to ensure there was no requirement for exaggerated features which would affect a dog's quality of life. The Dog Health Group worked to reduce the convention's Appendix down to a list of fifteen dogs, successfully arguing that there was no material basis for the

Fig. 7.1   Previously known as a High Profile Breed, the Pug remains on the Breed Watch Category 3 list.

inclusion of the rest. These fifteen breeds became known as the High Profile Breeds.

For the first time at Crufts in 2012 the Best of Breed winners of these fifteen breeds of dog were required to undergo a veterinary check, with the result that six were unable to proceed to the group judging as they were deemed not fit for function. Such vet checks are now in place at all championship shows, and dogs awarded Best of Breed in any of the High Profile Breeds may not take part in the group or Best in Show judging if they do not pass the examination.

BREED WATCH

As part of its 'Fit for function, fit for life' campaign, the Kennel Club has established Breed Watch, the purpose of which is to identify any problems with breeds at an early stage. From 2014 Breed Watch started to put a greater responsibility onto judges regarding the monitoring of and reporting on breeds with recognized issues, and an obligation to carefully watch all breeds to ensure problems don't develop. All breeds have now been categorized into the three groups described below. You can see which category your breed falls into in the Breed Showing Information Guide at the back of this book.

Category 1: there are no current points of concern. However, judges may complete an optional health report if they have concerns about any condition or exaggerated features.

Category 2: there are points of concern. These may include features that may not be described in the breed standard. For each breed under scrutiny, judges have to pay special attention to the list of points of concern and have to complete a health monitoring form after judging.

Category 3: there are points of concern. At general and group championship shows judges must complete a monitoring form, and Best of Breed winners must undergo a veterinary health check before being allowed to compete in the group. This category includes the High Profile Breeds discussed above.

High Profile Breeds (Category 3)
Basset Hound
Bloodhound
Bulldog
Chow Chow
Dogue de Bordeaux
German Shepherd Dog
Mastiff
Neopolitan Mastiff
Pekingese
Pug
Shar Pei
St Bernard

Fig. 7.2   High Profile/Category 3 Breeds.

Breeds can change category if the points of concern have been remedied within the breed. Examples include the French Bulldog, Clumber Spaniel and Chinese Crested, all of which have been moved from Category 3 to Category 2. This means they are still under scrutiny, but the compulsory health checks are no longer required.

Twelve breeds, however, do remain in Category 3.

The public, vets, animal welfare organizations and breed clubs can notify the Kennel Club of any breeds of concern so that all breeders can work towards breeding healthy dogs which are, in the words of the Kennel Club Campaign, 'Fit for function, fit for life'.

Fig. 7.3   The Chow Chow is currently on the Category 3 List. 'Jdlinchow chang Peng'.

Fig. 7.4   Also on the Category 3 List is the Mastiff. 'Ch Fearnought George Formby', Top Mastiff 2011. (Photo: Alan V. Walker)

Show breeders are working hard to meet the revised breed standards and it is as a result of their efforts that breeds are coming off the high profile breeds list. Although Bulldogs remain on the list, they are a good example of where improvements are happening. Bulldogs used to regularly need a Caesarean section when whelping, but selective breeding for smaller heads means they are now more likely to be able to give birth naturally.

Fig. 7.5   Bulldogs are on the Category 3 list as their oversize heads led to birthing problems, and their excessive skin folds could harbour infections.

DISREPUTABLE BREEDING PRACTICES

While the show world is making progress, there are some breeders out there who are still breeding to satisfy the public demand for dogs which look the way they want them to look, instead of considering the effect on a dog's quality of life. It should be remembered that only around 2 per cent of pedigree dogs are actually shown, and the vast majority of purebred dogs are kept solely as pets. While the demand continues, some breeders not involved in showing will ignore, or be ignorant of, any breed standard, and will continue to breed as they always have done. Puppy farmers will produce what their market wants in order to maximize their profits, as will pet owners who think breeding offers easy money. Although fingers remain pointed at the show world, it is only because it is a visible and

Fig. 7.6   Due to the diligence of good breeders, bulldogs are now being bred with smaller heads and less wrinkling, as shown by 'Odinschild Frigg Odin's Wife for Saxoncrown'.

Fig. 7.7   Cheap puppies are often illegally imported from abroad and kept in atrocious conditions. A litter of puppies in a suitcase. (Photo: Insp. Bell, RSPCA Photolibrary)

easy target. And the problem is further compounded when pedigree puppies are shipped in from abroad and offered for sale in the UK, often at a much lower cost than a pup of that breed produced by more scrupulous breeders in the UK.

An example of the public's unhealthy demand for designer dogs is the current craze for 'tea cup' dogs. A puppy which is born small would be described by an ethical breeder as the 'runt' of the litter, and may well have an endorsement that prevents him being bred from. An unethical breeder will advertise small puppies as 'tea cup' varieties, and then breed from the smallest, trying to create ever-more miniature varieties with no regard to any health problems that may ensue. No pedigree breed has a 'tea cup' version, and it is unfortunate that these small dogs are gaining in popularity.

Ethical breeders can only go so far in breeding healthy stock; anyone buying a puppy should do their homework so that the demand for dogs purchased for looks, rather than health, can be reduced, and unethical breeders put out of business. The Kennel Club is

Fig. 7.8   A well bred litter of Clumber puppies. The Clumber Spaniel came off the Category 3 list and moved to Category 2 in 2014, showing how improvements have been made in the breed.

Owning a Category 3 High Profile Breed

If you own a dog of a breed in Category 3 which has not been bred to the revised standards, you may find it affects how far you can go in the showing world. If your dog has exaggerated features and fails the vet test, you have the responsibility to ensure that you do not take a litter from such a bitch or use such a dog as a stud.

If you are considering buying a puppy from one of these breeds it is even more important that you understand the breed standard; look carefully at the dam and sire, and any previous progeny, and remember that Best of Group and Best in Show wins prior to 2012 did not need a veterinary check before being given the award.

working towards educating puppy buyers by running events such as Discover Dogs and establishing the Assured Breeders Scheme.

The measures that the Kennel Club is putting in place will hopefully ensure that we will be able to keep the vast variety of pedigree dog breeds that we currently have.

BREEDING HEALTHY DOGS

Principled breeders are keen to make sure they produce healthy dogs, and research carried out over the decades has shown us that some illnesses and conditions can be inherited; some of these can be avoided by health screening prior to breeding from particular individuals. In many breeds hip and elbow dysplasia have been shown to be caused primarily by hereditary factors.

By only using dogs with very good hips and elbows as breeding stock, the puppies will have a better chance of living happy, healthy lives. Likewise, some forms of blindness and heart or breathing problems can be prevented by DNA testing to identify dogs carrying the gene(s) responsible. In producing dogs with the potential to win top honours, good breeders nowadays are looking to eradicate genetic health problems within their lines. An example of this is the research continuing across a number of breeds to identify whether certain forms of epilepsy, for example, are carried by a particular gene. Most breeders who know there is epilepsy in their lines will not continue to breed from affected dogs in case they pass it on to their offspring.

The various breed clubs and the show fraternity are

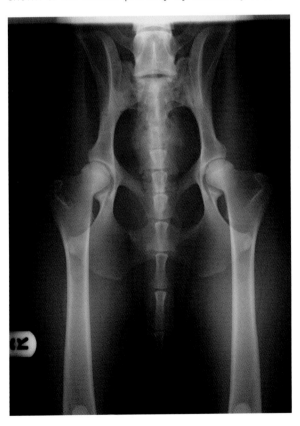

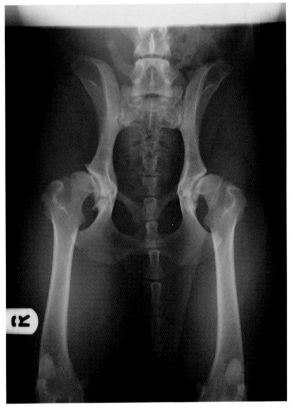

Fig. 7.9 X-ray picture of good hips. When considering breeding from a dog or bitch, their hip scores should be below the mean average for the breed. (Photo: Southern Canine Imaging)

Fig. 7.10 Bad hips. This dog should not be bred from as there would be a high risk of the puppies developing Hip Dysplasia. (Photo: Southern Canine Imaging)

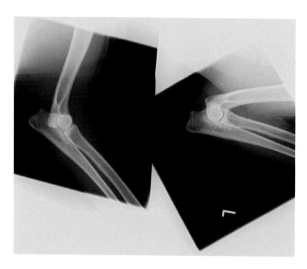

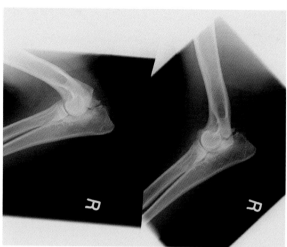

Fig. 7.11   *Good elbows. To avoid elbow dysplasia, only dogs or bitches with scores of 0 should be bred from. (Photo: Southern Canine Imaging)*

Fig. 7.12   *An example of bad elbows. Poor elbows can affect the quality of a dog's life. (Photo: Southern Canine Imaging)*

working together to improve the health and well-being of dogs in general, despite rumours to the contrary. If we didn't show dogs, analyse and know their pedigrees and backgrounds, and instead indiscriminately mated our bitch with the dog next door – whether or not he was of the same breed – then health problems would probably multiply. Cross-bred dogs are not necessarily healthier than pedigree dogs. Although mating two different breeds might counteract some of the weaknesses or hereditary problems in one, it also means that in many common 'designer' crosses the resultant offspring end up with the health problems of both parent breeds. A healthy cross-breed dog can be produced if the breeder investigates and tests for all known conditions inherent in all the breeds in the mix but in practice this is extremely uncommon.

CHAPTER 8

BUYING A PUPPY TO SHOW

DECIDING ON YOUR BREED

Buying a puppy with the intention of showing him is more complicated than simply buying a puppy as a pet and comes with no guarantee of success. No one, not even a top breeder, can guarantee that a puppy will turn out to have the potential to become Best in Show at Crufts, or indeed at any show. A promising looking puppy may not mature to fulfil his expected potential, and faults may develop which will limit his success in the show ring. Breeders often keep back for themselves what they think is the best prospect from a litter, and off the top of my head I can think of two instances where the puppy kept didn't end up with a show career, even though these were very experienced breeders. One puppy's adult teeth came through badly set, and with the other it was obvious by the age of seven months that his head shape was wrong.

But despite this, buying the best puppy that you can afford, from a breeder with a good reputation and a successful career in the show ring will give you a better chance of success. You should also find that this

Fig. 8.1 Dogs come in different sizes with different requirements. This Great Dane is only ten months old and still has some growing to do! (Photo: Graham Peers)

Fitting in with your lifestyle

Considering that your new puppy may or may not fulfil his early promise, it is vital when you make your purchase that you choose a breed you will be happy to share your home with for up to fifteen (or even more) years to come. Dogs should not be considered disposable assets; they are living, sentient beings, and whatever his performance in the show ring, he will be first and foremost a family pet. It's imperative that you choose a breed that fits in with your household and lifestyle, and not necessarily the one you like for its looks. A large breed will obviously cost more to keep – vet and food bills will be higher than for a toy breed, as will the cost of insurance. As well as premiums rising in line with the size of the dog, some breeds are known for being more susceptible to certain health problems than others.

Fig. 8.3   *Your taste might run to a Newfoundland, but taking on such a large breed needs a lot of thought and consideration. 'Ch Eragon Des Oursons De Svalbard ShCM'. (Photo: Paul Dodd)*

Fig. 8.2   *The Lancashire Heeler is a much smaller breed and will cost less to keep in terms of food and insurance. 'Ch Littlehive Daisychain Around Lankeela ShCM'.*

type of breeder will support, advise and encourage you along the way.

Finding out about different breeds

Selective breeding over the centuries has meant that we have cows that produce a higher yield of milk, hens that lay eggs every day, and, in the canine world, dogs that have been bred to perform specific functions. Although Dalmatians no longer run behind our carriages, they were originally bred to be able to run all day. In the gundog group, different breeds point, flush or retrieve game, and herding breeds were bred to round up cattle or sheep. Even if we're keeping these breeds as pets, they may still retain an innate instinct to do the job they were originally bred for. You may well find your Collie rounding up your children, or your Labrador retrieving your slippers! Not all dogs are the same and different breeds may need more or less stimulation and exercise. Knowing the traits of the breed you are considering will help you assess whether you can

Fig. 8.4   *Toy breeds, such as the Havanese, obviously take up less house room, but many need a lot of grooming to keep them looking good in the show ring. 'Georgie Girl by Labayamesa'.*

provide an environment in which your new companion can thrive.

There are a number of ways to find out about breeds you are considering. From the comfort of your home you can read about different breeds on the internet, and join Facebook groups or online forums where you

Fig. 8.5   Discover Dogs at Crufts: an ideal opportunity to find out about different breeds. (© Kennel Club Picture Library)

can ask owners what it's actually like to share your home with that particular breed.

A good place to find information is at a Kennel Club's Discover Dogs event. This is held annually alongside Crufts, as well as at other venues around the country throughout the year. Visiting a Discover Dogs event is a great starting point for your research – at the bigger shows up to 200 breeds of dogs may be present, along with knowledgeable enthusiasts. You can pick up information about the breed's exercise needs and other requirements such as grooming and feeding.

If you're looking to exhibit, the recommended start-ing point is to visit a show. You will find most exhibitors are more than happy to talk about their breed, and it can be a good place to make contact with breed-ers who have litters planned. Of course, once you've decided that you want to buy a dog to show, it's only human nature to want to get a puppy immediately. But patience here, as in most things, is a virtue. Good breeders may well have waiting lists for their puppies, even for those which haven't been conceived yet. Wait-ing for the right puppy from the right breeder may well take time, and may be measured in months (or even years), rather than weeks.

Fig. 8.7   The Golden Retriever is an example of a breed where there is a split between the working lines and show lines, as illustrated here by 'Ardyle King Lear' ('Flyte'), who is very much a working dog. (Photo: Peter Fisher)

Fig. 8.6   The German Long Haired Pointer is more commonly seen as a working gundog than in the show ring. 'Questor Eros at Swifthouse'. (Photo: Nick Ridley)

Working and show lines

Some breeds, notably in the gundog group and pastoral breeds, have a split between working and show lines. Show lines may have longer coats, for example, which would be impractical for retrieving in undergrowth, or have evolved a different body shape. Cocker Spaniels and Springer Spaniels are excellent examples. There can be serious rifts between people who breed and own the different types, with working dogs being set as the epitome of how an active, healthy dog should look and behave. In many cases a dog bred for the show ring is perfectly capable of doing a day's work in the field, and gundogs and Border Collies have to prove it in order to become full Champions. Dogs bred from working stock, however, may be unlikely to win in the show ring, as they have been bred away from the breed standard as working ability has been given preference over looks and even conformation. When buying a puppy to show make sure that you are buying a puppy from showing stock, rather than working.

Fig. 8.8   An example of a Golden Retriever which has been very successful in the show ring. 'Sh CH Shardanell Talk O' The Town at Ipcress JW'. (Photo: Lesley Durrant)

Fig. 8.10   A show English Springer Spaniel 'Sh CH Trimere Trading Places at Sheledams'.

Fig. 8.9   'Millrowan Adar' ('Skye') is a working bred English Springer Spaniel. The working strain of the breed has moved away from the breed standard, most noticeably with less feathering. (Photo: Peter Fisher)

Fig. 8.11   This Large Munsterlander excels in the show ring, but can also do a day's work! 'Sh CH Raycris Freya'.

Popular versus less common breeds

When you visit a show, you will soon see that some breeds have a far greater entry than others, and the less numerous breeds might tempt you as the number of dogs in each class is far lower, and thus the chances of getting placed in a class seem higher.

It is true that if you choose a popular breed of dog (Golden Retrievers, for example), the class sizes can be quite large. But you'll also find that there are normally specific breed classes at most general shows, and within these a greater range of classes will be on offer in order to limit the number of dogs in the ring at any one time. At some open shows, the more popular breeds may even have separate bitch and dog judging. You will also find that Challenge Certificates are on offer for each sex at most (if not all) championship shows. If you decide that one of the more common breeds is for you, there are likely to be a greater number of breeders for you to choose from.

Fig. 8.13   Breeds like the Brittany will not have classes at every show, nor will CCs be available at all championship shows. 'Highclare Hold Your Horses at Bremalyn JW'.

Fig. 8.12   The Irish Terrier is one of the less numerous breeds. 'Montelle Royal Leader'. (Photo: John Kenyon)

As a novice to showing, you may feel that you would have a greater chance of winning a rosette by being in a ring with only a few other dogs, and thus you may

believe a less common breed would be a better bet. But life is never simple, and there are definitely some drawbacks to having a breed which is less popular. You may find it harder to find shows with specific breed classes, and you will therefore need to enter the AVNSC (Any Variety Not Separately Classified) classes instead. You may find there are fewer judges with specialist knowledge of your breed. When shows do run breed classes, the number of classes on offer may be just two or three at most. In order for wins to be counted towards a Junior Warrant, there need to be at least three dogs present (including you) in the class that you win, so having a less numerous breed may mean that you come home with a lot of rosettes, but you don't end up with any serious awards as you've been the only exhibitor in your class. Many championship shows will not offer Challenge Certificates for your breed, or may just have the one, which both the Best Dog and the Best Bitch will need to compete for. Becoming a Champion will not be easier than for a more popular breed.

Popular breeds aren't just those that you see out and about around your neighbourhood. Some breeds

Fig. 8.14 The Labrador Retriever is a popular breed. 'Ludalor Kohaku'.

Fig. 8.16 Whippets have a large attendance at shows. 'Barnesmore Peter Pan'. (Photo: Robert Moore)

Fig. 8.15 Cocker Spaniels are also plentiful around the show ring. 'Int Ch, Bel Ch, Sh CH Joaldy Mandolin Wind JW ShCM'. (Photo: Tracey Morgan)

have a higher representation at shows than you might think: Whippets and Irish Setters, for example. To get an indicative idea of how many dogs are entered for each of the breeds you are considering, visit Fosse Data or Higham Press, which will list the entries per breed at championship shows.

There isn't a scientific formula to help you choose the right breed for success in the show ring. The best advice is to go with your heart and select a breed that's compatible with your temperament, your lifestyle, your activity levels and your pocket.

FINDING A BREEDER

Pedigree puppies are expensive, and you should avoid trying to get a bargain. If you are paying less than the going price for your breed, there will be a reason why. Although it may appear that breeders can make a good living from selling their puppies, when all the costs are added together many reputable breeders would probably be seen to make an overall loss. Cutting corners on buying the right puppy may eventually cost you much more than you have initially saved in vet bills going forwards, and may also not help to further your showing hobby.

Everyone who breeds a dog – even just once – is a breeder, and they should take lifelong responsibility for the offspring they produce, agreeing to take a puppy back should the new owner's circumstances change drastically. But just because there is a clause in the

Fig. 8.17   Dogue de Bordeaux puppies (Emberez).

contract stipulating this, the puppy buyer should not take home their new pet on a whim. From the moment you agree to purchase your puppy, you are making a long-term commitment – whether or not your puppy does well in the show ring.

Cheap puppies

As with anything in life, if a puppy looks like it's a bargain, then it will be too good to be true.

It is quite common for dogs to be bred by a pet owner with all the best intentions, but without the knowledge or experience to produce show-quality puppies. If neither the dam nor the sire has been shown, then there is no guarantee that any of the puppies will be successful as a show dog, no matter how many Champions there are in the pedigree. Often, a person owning

a bitch will use a famous sire for their pups, but if the bitch herself has not been shown, then she may be carrying faults that will cancel out any of the benefits of using a Champion sire. It may be possible to end up with a lovely dog from such a mating, and indeed even one which could become a Crufts Champion, but it is rare.

People breeding from a pet dog are often ignorant about health testing. They may take their bitch to the vet for a 'vet check' to ensure that she's fit enough to go through a pregnancy, but they don't undertake the expensive health tests that will show if she is likely to pass on any hereditary problems, increasing the chances that the puppies may be unhealthy.

Breeders who have a number of puppies of different breeds available should also be looked upon with suspicion; it is possible that they are ethical breed-

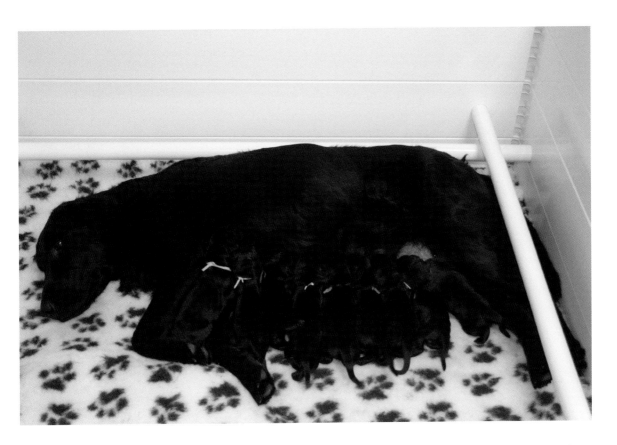

Fig. 8.18 Although you won't be able to see the puppies at this age, the breeder may send you photos if you ask. This lovely Flat Coated Retriever is happily caring for her puppies in a purpose-made whelping box.

ers, but the majority will be puppy farmers or selling imported puppies.

With the advent of pet passports and the permitted import of dogs from abroad, there has been a large increase in the number of pedigree puppies being imported illegally from abroad with forged documentation regarding their vaccinations and pedigrees, and often too young to travel. Such puppies can become sickly and die, and there is no guarantee of their parentage, however good the paperwork looks.

Puppy farmers abound, unfortunately. These unscrupulous people often have numerous breeds available at one time, particularly small breeds and especially Chihuahuas and popular cross-breeds. It's quite possible to buy a puppy over the internet, which may satisfy some 'I want it now' people. Although the parents at puppy farms will normally be pedigrees of the same breed, there is no guarantee that they are. The breeding dogs are kept in atrocious conditions, puppies can be very unhealthy, and the breeding animals will probably not be of show quality unless they were stolen. NEVER buy a puppy unless you can see him with his mother and check the conditions in which he was raised, but be careful: puppy farmers often operate out of houses and you won't see the terrible kennel conditions the dogs are really kept in. Never arrange to collect the puppy from somewhere such as a service station or other midway point, however plausible the excuse for it might sound. If you have ANY concerns or doubts about the puppy you are buying, walk away! Do not put money into the hands of these unscrupulous breeders, even if you feel sorry for the puppy. The only

Fig. 8.19   Puppy farmers often churn out poorly bred toy breeds, and often at the top of their list are Chihuahuas. Try to research what a show quality Chihuahua should look like, as shown here by Crufts BOB winner 'Ch Coriam Sweet William'.

way to stop puppy farmers is for their market to disappear. Remember, a puppy bought from a puppy farm is highly unlikely to be of show quality and may have serious health problems.

WHY ARE WELL BRED PUPPIES SO EXPENSIVE?

A good breeder will ensure that only the very best dogs are bred from, and, as they are committed to improving the breed, they will only take litters from dogs which have been proven to be good examples of that breed. In order to do this, they invest much time and money in travelling to shows all over the country campaigning their dogs. They will know the pedigrees of their breed-

'Pedigree registration papers'

Be wary of anyone selling puppies with 'pedigree registration papers'. All show dogs have to be Kennel Club registered, so check that the documentation is the official Kennel Club registration. If in any doubt, check with the Kennel Club. It's all too easy nowadays for anyone to produce fake documentation on their computer. Remember, Kennel Club registration is obligatory for show dogs, and only the breeder can register the litter. Refer back to Chapter 1 for information about litter registration.

ing stock intimately, and will choose a stud dog which is the best possible match to their bitch, each complementing the other to produce high quality puppies.

Bitches should have been shown, but it's possible that by the time they breed they may not have earned the high honours that male dogs have achieved. This is partly because bitches have seasons which can affect performance and coat quality, limiting the number of shows that can be attended, and sometimes a bitch needs to have a litter before she can achieve her full show potential. But the stud dog, at least, should have attained his Stud Book number.

Some potentially devastating health problems can now be detected by using DNA testing or x-ray. The Kennel Club website and various breed clubs have details of these health tests, which should be done in each breed before even considering a mating. These health tests are expensive, but good breeders ensure they are done so that identified genetic and known hereditary problems can be eradicated from the breed.

Ensuring that their dogs conform to the breed standard, and that they produce the healthiest puppies possible, costs money. When you pay the going price for a puppy from a good breeder, you can be confident that in return your puppy will have had the very best start in life and have begun the socialization process,

Fig. 8.20 A good breeder will begin standing the puppies as soon as possible. A Sharnphilly Weimaraner puppy at five and a half weeks old.

and perhaps shows promise for a successful career in the show ring, depending on the breeder's assessment as to his suitability.

The final reason why puppies are expensive is the actual cost of breeding. Obvious things include stud fees, progesterone testing (to find out when a bitch is ready to mate), whelping kit, vet care, micro-chipping, food and worming, for example, but there are also costs that may run into several thousands of pounds should the bitch need a Caesarean section or other emergency treatment. Add on to this the fact that the breeder will need to devote nine weeks of their time to caring for the bitch when she's in whelp, and for the first eight weeks of the puppies' lives (twelve weeks in some breeds). A good breeder will stay with the puppies all the time for the first few weeks, and thus be unable to work and bring in a wage.

HOW DO YOU FIND A GOOD BREEDER?

Kennel Club Assured Breeders Scheme

In order to try to help the public to be able to find reputable breeders, the Kennel Club started the Assured Breeders Scheme to promote good breeding practices. In essence, assured breeders commit to performing all relevant health tests for the breed as identified by the Kennel Club, provide written documentation on aspects of puppy care, such as socialization, feeding and worming, and provide a written contract of sale. Whelping facilities should comply with best practice, and scheme members are inspected to confirm that this is so. The scheme is accredited by UKAS (the United Kingdom Accreditation Service) and breeders passing the inspection will be entitled to use that logo. From January 2014 inspections started to be carried out prior to a first litter, and every three years thereafter. The scheme has been in place since 2003, and the UKAS accreditation is a response to some of the criticisms that the Kennel Club did not inspect all accredited breeders.

Although no scheme is perfect, Assured Breeders are more likely to be reputable breeders. But due to the cost of joining the scheme, and some of its limitations (for example, some breeders perform many more health tests than are required by the Kennel Club), a great number of reputable breeders are not members of the scheme. If a breeder is not a member, it should not necessarily be viewed as a black mark against them. In this case, however, a puppy buyer should use their own judgement as to whether the breeder satisfies all the criteria they are looking for.

Fig. 8.21   *Norfolk Terrier bitch puppy. (Photo: Graham Peers)*

The Assured Breeders Scheme, or equivalent, is obviously the way forward to help puppy buyers make the correct choices, but there is still a long way to go before the 'badge' can be relied on. But it needs to attract all reputable breeders to be members, and to be able to weed out the few rotten apples who have managed to attain accreditation.

Initial contact with the breeder

When you have found a breeder, contact them by phone initially. You can expect to be given the third degree as they question you endlessly about your experience of dogs in general, and specifically in the breed you're enquiring about (or similar breeds), your lifestyle, whether you work, have children and/or other pets, and many other questions. This may seem intrusive, but in fact they are simply trying to find out if you will be able to give the right home to a puppy they have bred, or intend to breed. They are trying to ensure that, barring any unfortunate and serious events, the puppy will be going to a new home for life. It is not in the breeder's interest to sell a puppy to a new owner only to have it returned when it reaches the teenage months and starts to destroy the house! Your first conversation with your breeder should start a relationship that extends at least during your puppy's lifetime, and possibly even longer than that. The right breeder can be your mentor for showing, support you at shows, possibly even handle your puppy for you until you gain confidence, and give you advice on health and training. I still exchange Christmas cards and news with the breeder of my first dog, which I purchased in 1985!

When making initial contact with a breeder, you should let them know that you want to show your puppy. They will be experienced in the show world, and should be best able to assess the pups to determine which might be the most likely candidate as a show prospect. When you go along to view the litter, be prepared. Make sure you have read and understood the breed standard, especially if the breed you are looking at is in Category 2 or 3 on the Breed Watch list. When you meet the breeder, talk through any issues to be aware of in the breed, and ensure that they are breeding with the breed standard in mind; you

---

Where to look for a puppy

Do NOT look in the free ads for good breeders! If a puppy seems cheap, then he may not be as advertised. You might be buying a Labrador cross rather than a purebred Labrador. Show dogs are not normally purchased from free ad sites, nor from internet sites offering a number of breeds for sale at the same time. Good breeders with puppies available can be found via the Kennel Club list of Assured Breeders, the Champdogs website or the various breed clubs. If you have visited shows and perhaps admired a particularly stunning dog, you can research his kennel and contact them to see if they know of any related puppies available. Online breed forums are another great source of information.

Fig. 8.22   Griffon Bruxellois puppy. (Photo: Graham Peers)

should also discuss any health problems which have been identified. You should familiarize yourself with the health tests which should have been carried out on both sire and dam. The details of these can be found on the Kennel Club website, along with specific health issues for Category 2 and 3 breeds.

While the breeder is best placed to choose a puppy for you from their litter, they can offer absolutely no guarantees and you have to accept that your puppy may end up without a show career. This applies to whatever level of breeder you go to, from a top breeding kennel to an occasional breeder. Obviously more established show kennels have greater experience, and can point to the successes their dogs have enjoyed. But all too often siblings can appear at the same shows, with one winning first prize and the other being unplaced.

Breeders do not normally allow people to visit their puppies until they are at least four weeks old, and typically not until they are five weeks old due to the risk of infection being brought into the house. So don't insist on an early viewing. Most breeders will be happy to email pictures of the litter. When you do visit, make sure you see the puppies with their mother and check that they all look healthy, with bright eyes and clean bottoms. Puppies sleep a lot, so don't be worried if they're all asleep when you first go in, and be prepared to wait until they are active to make your choice. The breeder should be able to advise you on the best time to go so you can see them romping around.

Make sure you like the look and character of the mother, and ask to see the sire if he is available. Ask to see all the paperwork showing the health test results of both sire and dam. If you know their full kennel names you can check this online on the Kennel Club website before you visit. If the health test results are not recorded online, then check the paperwork – results can take up to three months to be officially recorded. Do not take the word of the breeder unless you can substantiate it in some way.

When you visit, observe the puppies closely. They should be interested in you as a visitor, and not fearful. People often talk about a puppy choosing them, but if you're choosing a puppy to show, do listen to the advice of the breeder. They will already know the temperaments of the puppies, and can advise on the best one for you, taking into account your desire to show and your lifestyle. If you don't have the 'pick of the litter' and most of the puppies are already spoken for, remember you don't have to buy the puppy just because you have visited. On the other hand, some breeders will keep back a very promising puppy specifically because they want it to go to a show home, and they are waiting for the right owner to come along. So if there is only one puppy available, it could be the second best in the litter (the best is probably being kept by the breeder!). But this is a decision that will affect you for possibly fifteen years, so if anything doesn't feel right, walk away.

This is especially important if you want a particular sex. Although in the pet world a large number of dogs are neutered, show dogs, for the most part, are kept entire. If you've set your heart on a bitch, don't take a dog puppy just because it's the only one left, unless you are 100 per cent certain that's what you want.

Good breeders will not sell you two puppies from the same litter except in exceptional circumstances when

Fig. 8.23   A well bred puppy will look healthy, happy and alert. (Photo: Tarimoor)

they can be sure that you really know what you are taking on. It is probably three times more difficult raising two puppies of the same age than raising one.

Contract of sale/puppy contract

A reputable breeder will normally have a contract of sale for the puppy. This may include information about the puppy and his parents, and how the puppy has been brought up to date, with a section on health and welfare. It will give advice on caring for the puppy in his new home. There is normally a clause stating that the puppy should be returned to the breeder in the event that the new owner is no longer able to care for him.

The contract may have endorsements on it. The two endorsements that can be placed are a restriction on registration of any future progeny, or to prevent the issue of an export pedigree. Only breeders can lift endorsements – a common reason for a breeding endorsement is so that the breeder can satisfy themselves that all health testing has been done prior to breeding. This

is particularly important if the dog has been identified as a carrier of a genetic disease, and should only be mated to a dog which has tested clear.

The breeder should go through the contract with you, ensuring that you fully understand it and explaining any endorsement and the circumstances, if any, when they would lift that endorsement. On completion of sale, both you and the breeder should sign a copy of the contract and keep it safe.

BITCH OR DOG?

When deciding to share your life with a dog, gender is an important part of the choice, especially with show dogs. Obviously you can make the decision based purely on personal preference or experience with a particular dog or bitch which makes you lean towards that sex. We've already spoken about showing neutered dogs in Chapter 1, and addressed some of the pros and cons. The majority of show dogs are kept entire, so here we'll look at what it's like to live with and show an entire dog or bitch. Showing your dog will only be a

Fig. 8.24 Quick checklist for buying a puppy.

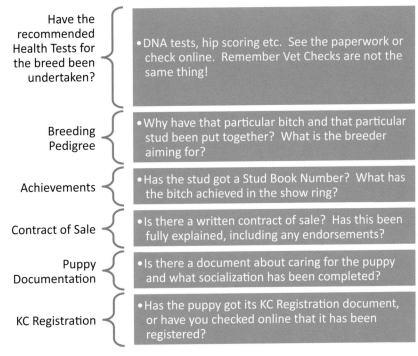

Have the recommended Health Tests for the breed been undertaken?	• DNA tests, hip scoring etc. See the paperwork or check online. Remember Vet Checks are not the same thing!
Breeding Pedigree	• Why have that particular bitch and that particular stud been put together? What is the breeder aiming for?
Achievements	• Has the stud got a Stud Book Number? What has the bitch achieved in the show ring?
Contract of Sale	• Is there a written contract of sale? Has this been fully explained, including any endorsements?
Puppy Documentation	• Is there a document about caring for the puppy and what socialization has been completed?
KC Registration	• Has the puppy got its KC Registration document, or have you checked online that it has been registered?

minor part of your life with him, so when considering whether to get a dog or a bitch you need to be sure that you will be happy with the different behaviours offered by either sex.

Living with an entire dog

Firstly, let's consider some of the pros and cons of keeping an entire male dog.

You will be able to show your dog 365 days of the year if you so wish. In many breeds the male has the more impressive coat and heavier bone structure. While in championship shows (and some open or breed shows) there will be separate classes for dogs and bitches, at the majority of open shows both sexes are judged together. If there is a noticeable difference between the sexes in your breed, then a dog might have the advantage in a mixed class. In any event, to become Best of Breed the winning dog and bitch will have to compete against each other, although in some shows there is also an award for Best Opposite Sex.

The majority of male dogs urinate by cocking their legs. (A minority don't, but this is nothing to be worried

Fig. 8.25 Dogs tend to be bigger and stronger than bitches, and sometimes overshadow them in a mixed class. Dogue de Bordeaux 'Furzeydrong Thundercloud at Emerez'.

about.) This often makes it easier to get your dog to perform when you need him to (just take him to the nearest tree), but some dogs have the tendency to mark anything they take a fancy to, so you will need to be vigilant to make sure this is not someone's picnic hamper or leg!

Some male dogs can be very upset by the smell of bitches in season. If a neighbour has an intact bitch, your male may try constantly to get to her by leaping over fences in your garden, or he will whine and bark constantly. This kind of behaviour is very difficult, if not impossible, to correct; he's not being naughty, it's just his hormones making him act this way. Such dogs may also not perform well at shows if a bitch in season is in the vicinity. And some know when a bitch is about to come into season.

You may have the calmest, most loving dog in the world, but if you use him as a stud dog you may find his character changes. Once the forbidden fruit is tasted, he may well show signs of being a frustrated male, even if he didn't beforehand. Not every dog changes, but it is something you need to consider before allowing him to become a sire.

Living with an intact bitch

The biggest disadvantage of keeping an intact bitch is

that she will have regular seasons. Smaller dogs tend to have seasons more often, but any dog can have seasons at intervals of between four months to a year or more. A lot of people worry about the mess of an in-season bitch, but usually they keep themselves clean, and your furniture can be protected with covers.

During a season any entire dogs coming close to the bitch may be affected by the odours she is producing. This is perfectly natural and a sign she is ready to be mated. You will need to think carefully about whether you can exercise her at this time as dogs can get quite upset if they walk in the same places where a bitch has been. If you do need to walk, you need to find places to go where others are unlikely to exercise their dogs. Even if you aren't put off by causing problems for others, if you walk a bitch in season from your house you may well find yourself besieged by dogs from the neighbourhood who've leapt fences to follow her scent and have set up camp, howling and barking, outside your door! It is not unknown for an entire dog to catch a bitch in season and end up tied on a footpath or the middle of a park.

Apart from the 'mess', when your dog is in season you should think carefully before taking her to a show. Bitches in heat are not allowed to compete in agility, flyball, obedience, heelwork to music events or field trials, but there is nothing in the regulations to prevent bitches in season from attending any conformation show. But this does not mean they should be taken. Dogs, and even some bitches, are very badly affected when an in-season bitch is in the vicinity, and may not show to their best. This is particularly the case at open shows and some championship show classes where both bitches and dogs are in the ring at the same time. It is very uncommon to take a bitch in season to an open show. Bitches in season are often a little under par, so will not show to their best in any event,

Fig. 8.26   This lovely Afghan Hound bitch 'Ch Ratheeli Zazzah' is in full coat, but bitches can drop their coats after a season, taking them out of the show ring for a while. (Photo: David Paton)

Benefits to owning a bitch

There are benefits to having a bitch. If you end up with one of good quality, you may want to breed from her. Bringing up a litter of puppies is very hard work, but as the owner of the dam (mother) you will be able to have the say in who you sell the puppies to, and what you write in the contract of sale. You can put restrictions in the contract, for example, saying the puppies cannot be bred from unless certain criteria have been met (these normally relate to the relevant health tests). If you are breeding from your show bitch, it will normally be with a view to keeping a puppy back to bring on for the show ring, and as the owner of the dam you will be best placed to know which puppy will suit your family best, and hopefully which is the best prospect for exhibiting.

and having a swollen vulva can mean they are more susceptible to picking up an infection.

How long a season lasts can vary from dog to dog, but in most cases you should aim to keep her away from male dogs for around twenty-eight days, or at least until her vulva has returned to its normal size and any discharge has ceased.

As you can see from this, a bitch has a much more limited showing window than her male counterpart, and another complication is that you can never be 100 per cent certain when the next season will be. Some bitches are regular, but others can vary. So you might hold off booking a show thinking you wouldn't be able to attend, but then find she comes in earlier or later than you thought, and you could have gone. You could book shows way ahead, and sacrifice your entry fee if the season starts. Unfortunately no refunds are made if you cannot attend for this reason.

After a season bitches will go through a phantom pregnancy. With many, there are no signs whatsoever, but with some the phantom pregnancy has visible symptoms to a greater or lesser degree and in some circumstances they cause such distress to the bitch that she will need treatment by a vet. One common symptom is enlargement of the mammary glands and nipples. While in long-haired breeds this enlargement can be hidden, and a bitch can happily be shown as normal, in short-haired breeds she might not be looking her best with a saggy undercarriage.

About twelve weeks after a season a bitch can go through a major moult; again, the extent to which this will affect her will often depend on the breed, as well as the individual dog. But bitches are often withheld from shows as they are 'out of coat'. While it could be argued that judges in the bitch classes should take this point into account, a judge is not to know whether the dog naturally has a poor coat, or has just left most of it on the living room floor at home!

Showing a pregnant bitch

The advice of the Kennel Club and British Veterinary Association is that bitches should not travel in the last two weeks of pregnancy. Although pregnancy cannot be confirmed until the twenty-fifth to twenty-eighth day after mating, a responsible breeder will want the best for their bitch, and therefore would refrain from showing for the whole of the pregnancy. Travelling and showing can cause stress, or an infection might be picked up. Either of these could cause reabsorption or adversely affect the growing foetuses.

Summary of the pros and cons of the different sexes

- A dog can be shown at any show chosen by his owner.
- A bitch in season can attend shows, but to retain friends in the showing world you should refrain from doing so until her season has finished.
- Dogs are often the more handsome (in terms of coat and build) than bitches, and may therefore gain the higher places in mixed classes.

So, which sex is recommended?

Owning a bitch or a dog is really a matter of personal preference. Dogs are individuals, so it's hard to say whether one sex is more biddable or trainable than the other, and what people have to say about them often depends on the experiences they have had. If you are still researching different breeds it would be useful to visit a show to get opinions on the differences for showing. Or, if you have chosen your breed, the breeder may well be able to advise you which would be better for your circumstances.

- Bitches can suffer phantom pregnancies and hormonal losses of coat that will affect their chances in the show ring.
- If you own a suitable proven bitch, then you can consider breeding from her. Unlike dogs, bitches are not at such risk of their characters changing simply because they have been mated. If anything, they will become calmer.

KENNEL NAMES AND AFFIXES

Any owner of a Kennel Club registered dog can apply to have their own kennel name. You can re-register your first show dog with your own affix (kennel name) attached at the end, with a linking word such as 'over', 'by', 'for', etc. If you have a bitch who then has puppies, those puppies will be registered with your kennel name at the front. If you have success in the showing world with puppies you have bred, your show name may become well known in the breed (or breeds – it can apply to more than one breed). If you have dogs only, then you will only use your kennel name as an extension to his (or their) existing kennel name(s).

Normally it is only possible to change a dog's name once. The change cannot be made if more than thirty days have elapsed since the dog gained his Stud Book number. Kennel names can be removed if the dog is transferred back into the ownership of the original breeder.

DOGS OWNED IN PARTNERSHIP AND BREEDING CONTRACTS

Buying a pedigree puppy with show potential is not cheap, and you may be offered a puppy to own 'in partnership'. Normally this is with the breeder of your puppy, and means the dog will be registered in joint names. The puppy will live with you, but may be shown either by yourself or by the breeder. The benefit is that the price you pay for your puppy will be a lot less than the full price.

When you own a dog in partnership it is customary to have a breeding contract attached to the arrangement. In the case of a bitch, this may be that you agree, subject possibly to how she turns out in the show ring, to produce a litter of puppies from her, and come to an arrangement about sharing that litter with the breeder in some way. Occasionally the bitch will be returned to the breeder for a period of time so that she can whelp and raise the puppies there. In the case of a dog, you may agree for him to be used at stud, again normally related to his showing performance, either just once or a number of times on bitches that the breeder owns or wishes him to be used on.

You will need to consider a breeding contract very carefully, and make sure you understand everything you are committing to. How will the costs be shared of matters such as insurance and vet bills? Who keeps the stud fees? Who pays for health testing? How long is the arrangement for? A partnership with a good, experienced breeder can be positive, and you can learn a lot from it, with a mentor always on hand for support. But if your relationship with the breeder turns sour, you may find you do not wish to honour the terms you are contractually bound to.

A proper contract needs to be drawn up and signed, and a copy kept, by both parties. All aspects should be covered so that there are no grey areas, even if the arrangement is between friends. Solicitors may need to be involved otherwise a contract may not hold up in a court of law.

Breeding contracts should only be entered into with someone you trust, and whose views you share on dog ownership, showing and breeding. If you are offered a puppy on co-ownership terms be absolutely

Fig. 8.27   Example of a kennel name certificate.

certain you understand exactly what you are committing to.

IMPORTING A DOG

As a novice exhibiter, you will probably find your first show dog within the UK. But some people looking for a particular dog from a specific bloodline may look abroad for a puppy, and then import it to the UK. Breeds native to countries abroad will be more common in their country of origin than in the UK, and in this case your options may be limited unless you look further afield.

Be aware of illegally imported dogs. If you are looking for a breed that is common in the UK, then it's best to buy your puppy here until you have gained experience. You will be able to see the parents, or at least the mother, check the health certificates and research the reputation of the breeder. While it is not illegal to import puppies into this country, they need to be vaccinated against rabies and be microchipped prior to entry. The rules changed in December 2014 so that puppies cannot be vaccinated before they are twelve weeks of age, and they cannot be exported for a further twenty-eight days. This is an attempt to stop the practice of removing puppies from their mothers too

Fig. 8.28   If the Pyrenean Mastiff takes your fancy, you may well need to look abroad for your puppy. (Photo: Pyrenean Mastiffs de Monte Sano)

soon, and vaccinating them too early. (Until a puppy is ten to twelve weeks of age he still has immunity from his mother, and this immunity can interfere with the effectiveness of any vaccination.)

It is, however, not uncommon for the dates of birth on puppies' certificates to be falsified. This creates a real risk of introducing rabies into the country, and of you ending up with a very unhealthy puppy. Under the new regulations a puppy should be at least four months old before he enters the UK, which brings with it another risk – that the puppy may not be socialized properly. If you are importing a puppy, be sure to check what socialization the breeder intends to do in this critical development period.

Although you may need to buy your dog from abroad if the breed you have chosen is not a native British one, try to enter into the same sort of relationship with the breeder as you would if you bought in the UK. If possible, visit the puppy before committing to the purchase. Some very ethical-sounding breeding establishments prove to be anything but when you visit in person. Research any breeder thoroughly.

Registration of dogs imported from abroad

If you import a dog to the UK from another country you will need to register him with the Kennel Club in order to enter shows in this country. Only breeds recognized by the Kennel Club can be registered. Normally you will need to supply a photocopy of a certified export pedigree or a three generation pedigree if the country of origin does not supply the former. You can enter your dog at shows before receiving your Kennel Club registration as long as it has been applied for but you will need to put NAF (name applied for) after his name.

You can only register a dog if you are shown as the owner; in the case of a partnership, all registered owners must apply. Dogs registered with the Irish, Jersey or Guernsey Kennel Clubs need to be registered in the same way as any other imported dog.

IMPORT REGISTER

There are many hundreds of breeds of dogs throughout the world, and of these 210 breeds are currently recognized by the UK Kennel Club. The fact that they are 'recognized' does not mean they can necessarily be shown in conformation shows, however, as they may not be on the Breed Register. This is normally due to there currently being insufficient numbers being shown and bred within the UK and no agreed breed standard. If you have a breed which is on the Import Register you will not find specific breed classes that you can enter at any Kennel Club licensed breed show, although you will be able to compete in working trials, obedience, flyball and agility.

The first stage in obtaining full registration is to have an interim standard approved by the Kennel Club. Once

Fig. 8.30   *The Bavarian Mountain Hound can also show in import classes. Once numbers increase, it may move to the Breed Register proper and have separate breed classes. 'Deertrackers Ula'. (Photo: Suzanne Hall)*

Fig. 8.31   *The Tornjak is a very new breed to the UK. Breeders/owners are keen to increase the numbers so they can get the breed recognized by the Kennel Club.*

Fig. 8.29   *The Cirneco dell'Etna is on the Import Register with an agreed breed standard, which means it can be shown in import classes. (Photo: Graham Peers)*

this has been done for the breed as a whole (normally by the breed club), you can then enter your dog in Imported Breed Register classes at championship and open shows, matches and companion dog shows. If you win you will not be able to go forward to the group or take part in the competition for Best in Show, but you will be allowed a lap of honour around the Best in Show ring.

Getting an imported breed onto the breed register is not a quick process. An application has to be made to have that breed recognized, which requires a lot of information and statistics to be provided. The Kennel Club likes to allow time for a breed to develop in numbers and popularity and become an established breed in this country before moving it from the Import Register to the Breed Register. Factors taken into account include the number of dogs of the breed shown in Import Register classes, the breeding lines in the UK and the size of the gene pool.

Dogs on the Import Register without an interim breed standard

Some dogs are recognized in other countries, and you could enter breed classes there. There are a few breeds recognized abroad that, for a number of reasons, do not want to apply for registration in the UK. So while you have a pedigree dog, you would not be able to show it at a Kennel Club licensed breed show until the breed club, or breed owners, decide to apply for recognition and registration.

Likewise, a couple of breeds recognized by the UK Kennel Club are not recognized abroad. These are the Lancashire Heeler and the Turkish Kangal Dog.

The Import Register is regularly updated. Once an interim breed standard is agreed, that breed will be able to be shown in import classes. The current status of each breed can be checked on the Kennel Club website. If the breed is recognized in the UK there will be a breed standard page. This page may simply carry the statement that the breed does not yet have a Kennel Club breed standard. If it has a breed standard, it will be able to be shown in import classes. The breed will continue to have (IMP) after its name until such time as it is moved to the Breed Register proper.

Breeds on the Import Register
Information correct as at December 2014 – Imported Breeds

Imported Breeds Register without breed standard. (Cannot be shown in KC licensed breed shows)	Imported Breeds Register where interim standard agreed. (Can be shown in import classes at any show where these are on offer)
Azawakh	Basset Bleu de Gascogne
Hungarian Pumi	Basset Fauve de Bretagne
Picardy Sheepdog	Bavarian Mountain Hound
Pyrenean Mastiff	Bergamasco
Small Munsterlander	Cirneco dell'Etna
Spaniel (American Water)	Entlebucher Mountain Dog
	Grand Bleu de Gascogne
	Greater Swiss Mountain Dog
	Griffon Fauve de Bretagne
	Korean Jindo
	Korthals Griffon
	Lagotto Romagnolo
	Mexican Hairless
	Portuguese Podengo
	Segugio Italiano
	Slovakian Rough Haired Pointer
	Swedish Lapphund

CHAPTER 9

GROOMING FOR THE SHOW RING

Your dog will be judged on his conformation and movement, but both you and your dog should be clean, tidy and presentable at any show you go to. It's not fair on judges if they have to run their hands over a dirty, smelly coat. In long-coated breeds any tangles in the fur may cause the feathers not to hang properly, or even hinder the dog moving freely. You've paid good money to enter the show, so make the most of every chance you have to give the judge a good impression of your dog when you take him into the ring.

How much grooming your dog needs will depend on his breed, colour, length of hair, and whether he is single- or double-coated. Dark coloured, short-haired breeds, unless very dirty, often just require a quick wipe over before going into the ring, whereas long-haired dogs need a lot more preparation, such as trimming, and possibly bathing, before being exhibited.

START GROOMING EARLY

Whichever breed you choose, try to get your puppy used to being groomed from the first day. Some

Fig. 9.1 The film star good looks of the Afghan take time and dedication to maintain. 'Wongahurra Manhatten Magic'. (Photo: David Paton)

Grooming pet dogs versus show dogs

While a pet dog needs only to be kept clean and trimmed to ensure he is comfortable, a show dog needs to be prepared in such a way as to make the most of his features, and to present him, as far as possible, as an ideal image of the breed standard. If you don't like spending time brushing and grooming your dog each day, then do not choose a breed that will take a lot of effort to maintain. So in your research about breeds, don't forget to ask about grooming requirements when visiting shows or talking to people about their dogs. Internet searches, YouTube videos and breed clubs may be able to help you find out what a show trim for your breed looks like. When you've chosen your breed, take advice from the breeder where possible about how the breed should be prepared for the show ring.

Fig. 9.2   'Grizzler' is an Old English Sheepdog kept as a pet. As he is not shown, his coat is clipped to keep him cool and for easy maintenance. (Photo: James Grey)

puppies automatically like being brushed, others seem to think that brushes and combs are instruments of torture. Grooming on a table will make it easier for you, and may help stop your pup trying to wriggle away. It doesn't need to be a specific grooming table at the start. Be gentle, make it fun and reward with treats. A potential show puppy needs to get accustomed to being groomed, as well as being handled.

TEETH

As part of your grooming regime, start to get him used to someone looking at his teeth. Saying 'Teeth!' or a similar word while gently lifting his lip each time you groom should help him become used to having his teeth examined and will pay dividends when you eventually take him into the show ring.

You can buy a special toothbrush and toothpaste for your dog, and the sooner you get him used to having his teeth cleaned the better. Do NOT use human toothpaste. The amount of cleaning your dog's teeth will require will depend to some extent on his diet.

Fig. 9.3   The coat of the Old English Sheepdog takes far more maintenance for the show ring. 'Meadowbears True Blue ShCM' winning the Dog CC at the Welsh Kennel Club. (Photo: Graham Peers)

Grooming effort required for different coat types

Coat type	Maintenance

Wire coats (e.g. Border Terrier)

Hand stripping is used on many wire-haired or rough-coated breeds and is the process of pulling out the dead outer coat by hand, leaving the new coat behind. You can either pluck the hair with your fingers and thumbs, or use a serrated-edged blunt knife to help grip the hair, but make sure you do not cut the hair. As the hair is dead it is not painful for your dog, but you may need to get him used to it. Hand stripping will keep a wiry coat the way it should be, whereas clipping or cutting will ruin the texture. Once a coat has been hand stripped, it will take eight to ten weeks to grow back. An alternative is the continuous process of rolling a coat. Rolling a coat means taking only some of the coat out and leaving the rest. After two or three weeks the process is repeated. Eventually this process will trigger new coat growth all the time. Not all groomers hand strip as it is a time-consuming process, so you may have to hunt around to find one who does if you do not want to do it yourself. Never be tempted to clip a wire-haired show dog as the roots of the dead hair will affect the new hair growth, and the new coat will be soft and not right for the breed.

Fig. 9.4   *Sealyham Terriers are hand stripped. 'Tevant Elderflower for Tyniaden'.*

Long flowing or feathered coats (e.g. Afghan Hound, Setters)

Dogs with long flowing coats will need bathing more regularly to keep their coats clean. Daily brushing is required to prevent knots. Most dogs in this category will need regular trimming, particularly on the feet to keep them neat and to trim back the hair growing between the toes. Each breed will need preparation before a show. Feathering will need lots of conditioning to keep the hair soft and silky, and to prevent it drying out.

Fig. 9.5   *Yorkshire Terrier 'Ch Keriwell Dreamweaver'. (Photo: Keith Burgoyne Photography)*

Smooth-coated dogs (e.g. Doberman)

These have the easiest coats to care for. Dark-coloured dogs will need only occasional bathing when they are particularly dirty (or have rolled in something undesirable). Dogs with lighter coats should be presented clean, and may need bathing more often as obviously the dirt shows more. These breeds do moult, and dead hair can make the coat dull. Regular brushing with a rubber grooming brush (or rubber curry comb) or stripping comb will help remove dead hair.

Fig. 9.6   *A short-haired dog such as the Bullmastiff just needs to be neat and clean for the show ring. 'Ch Optimus Holly'. (Photo: Cath Lewis)*

Double-coated dogs (e.g. Malamute, Border Collie)

Double-coated breeds have a combination of long, medium and short hairs with a tough outer coat and a soft, thick undercoat. Although there is some continuous moulting, these breeds have a major shed twice a year. Regular brushing is needed to remove dead hair otherwise mats can form. A slicker brush or undercoat rake can be effective, brushing outwards from the skin to remove the loose hairs in the thick undercoat. Bathing more regularly when shedding will help speed up the process. Using a Blaster to dry the coat can blow away dead hair.

Fig. 9.7 The Samoyed has a double coat. 'Ch Fairvilla Emerald'.

Curly coats (e.g. Poodle, Bichon Frise)

A poodle's coat is a single layer made up of soft and wiry fur which grows continually so needs trimming. Poodles do shed a little, but the hair stays in the coat, twisting round the curls and causing mats if not regularly brushed out. Daily brushing is necessary to remove knots. Other curly-coated dogs include the Portuguese Water Dog and the Curly Coated Retriever. Curly coats are high maintenance. A wire brush and comb used daily will keep mats at bay. Curly-coated dogs will need trimming to prepare them for the show ring. If you are completely new to the breed, then you will probably find it useful in the first instance to watch a professional groomer trimming the coat in the proper way at first.

Fig. 9.9 Adult Standard Poodle 'Tafari Flash Harry'.

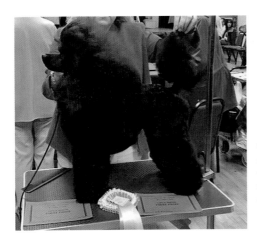

Fig. 9.8 Eleven-month-old Miniature Poodle 'Minarets Here Comes Alice At Silvora' winning Puppy Bitch, Junior Bitch and Best Puppy in Breed at the North Western Poodle Club Show.

Corded coats (e.g. Puli)

Cords form naturally, but to get them presentable for the show ring takes time. The cords begin to form at the adolescent stage. An hour will need to be spent a few days per week to care for the coat and to split the cords (making sure each one is separate and doesn't form mats close to the skin). The coat must be kept free of any debris (leaves, etc.). A corded dog will need to be bathed about three days before the show to allow the coat to dry fully. Shampoo is squeezed through the cords and needs to be washed out thoroughly. Cords may need to be trimmed.

Fig. 9.10   The development of a corded coat: a young Puli puppy. (Photo: Trebettyn Photography)

Fig. 9.11   Puli puppy at six months old with the cords brushed out. (Photo: Trebettyn Photography)

Fig. 9.13 The Bergamasco has flocks (dreadlocks) rather than cords. It takes three years for proper flocks to develop. 'Chique Adulation', 'Chique Christmas Glory' and 'Chique Farfalle'.

Fig. 9.12   Cords now developing. (Photo: Trebettyn Photography)

Hairless dogs (e.g. Chinese Crested)

Hairless dogs are fairly easy to care for. The hair on the feet, head and tail may need light trimming, and some people find moisturizer helps on the skin. In hot sun care needs to be taken that the skin doesn't burn, and it may be necessary to apply sunscreen.

Fig. 9.14   The Chinese Crested is a hairless dog. 'Annamac Perseus at Aucristae'.

Fig. 9.15   The 'just got out of bed' look of the Irish Wolfhound needs regular brushing, and a general tidy-up for the show ring.

GROOMING YOUR DOG YOURSELF

Although it's easier to take your dog to a groomer, it is an enjoyable part of showing if you can prepare and groom him yourself. If you do win a first prize, there's more pleasure in knowing that all the preparation, as well as the handling, was your own work.

You will find it useful to have a grooming table so that you can groom him at the correct height (unless he is a giant breed) and keep him still and secure. Depending on the breed, you will need a range of grooming equipment, including straight scissors, trimming scissors, brushes, combs and clippers. It is a false economy to buy cheap equipment from a local pet shop. Spend as much as you can to get the best-looking trims, which don't look like you've used the garden shears!

Use thinning scissors as much as possible to avoid unsightly straight edges where you have trimmed. Trim a little at a time; you can always take more off, but you can't glue it back on! Straight scissors can be used between the pads of the feet and around the toes and the edges of the ears. If your breed needs clipping, and you will be doing this yourself, invest in a good clipper and blade set, and keep the blades clean and well oiled. Be aware that clipping can sometimes ruin a coat and, for showing purposes, cannot be used in place of the more tedious method of hand stripping or using thinning scissors.

All dogs need a good brush, and which you choose will be partly down to your breed and partly down to personal preference. You might find a grooming mitt useful for a short-coated dog, and will definitely need a comb for long hair.

There is usually a variety of trade stands at shows selling all manner of potions, lotions, shampoos and grooming products, together with a bewildering array of brushes, combs, scissors and every conceivable piece of grooming paraphernalia. It can be a good place to stock up on products you might find useful, and someone is normally on hand to give you advice and help you spend your money!

Finding a groomer

If you have a puppy which needs to be trimmed properly for showing, you may wish to go to a professional groomer in the first instance. Do not simply go to the nearest local groomer as you may well be in for a shock when you collect him. Groomers do not necessarily know the correct way to prepare each individual breed for a show. If you want your dog to have an expert trim, try to find one who has specific knowledge about your breed – you may be able to find one from personal recommendations. Go armed with pictures or descriptions, and make sure they understand what they are doing. Clipping, rather than hand stripping, for example, can adversely alter the texture of a dog's coat.

First impressions always last, so when you walk into the ring you need to have a dog that looks fit and healthy, and a gleaming coat will impress far more than a dull one. Regular grooming and using the right products for your breed will pay dividends. Don't cut corners when buying shampoos and conditioners, and ensure they are formulated for a dog's coat. The pH balance of dog hair is different from human hair and using your shampoo (or even baby shampoo) can strip the natural oils from a dog's coat.

Do not underestimate the effect that a good diet can have on a coat: whatever type of food you feed your dog, make sure it is the best quality you can afford. A poor diet will result in a poor coat. Fish oil, coconut oil or Evening Primrose oil can be given as a feed supplement and will facilitate a gleaming coat as well as keeping the skin healthy.

KENNEL CLUB RULES ON PREPARING YOUR DOG FOR THE SHOW RING

The Kennel Club rules say that 'no substance which alters the natural colour, texture, or body of the coat may be present in the dog's coat for any purpose at any time during the show'. This also applies to anything that alters the colour. In addition, 'any other substance (other than water) which may be used in the preparation of a dog for exhibition must not be allowed to remain in the coat or on any other part of the dog at the time of exhibition'.

The strict interpretation is that any conditioning product you use to prepare your show dog must be thoroughly washed out of the coat before the show day.

There is no doubt that some people use chalk, some people use hairspray. But be warned: if you do use these substances, you could be disqualified and even referred to the Kennel Club for discipline. A person owning or handling a dog in the same breed or class could make a complaint against you, and a sample of your dog's hair could be taken away for examination. Although it rarely happens, it is possible, and you need to be aware of the rules. It is likely that a few people within the breed will be doing the same things themselves, but for your first few shows, and until you

know the ropes, my advice is to follow the regulations to the letter.

The regulations allow for the general committee of the show to order the examination of a particular dog, or dogs.

WET SHOW DAYS

It's going to happen sometime, isn't it? You've groomed your dog to kingdom come and back, he's never looked so good – and show day dawns with persistent heavy rain. Your show might be in an indoor venue, but there'll be mud underfoot in the car park, as well as having to contend with the heavens opening above you!

To be prepared for a wet show day, you should invest in a raincoat for your dog. If you have a dog with feathering or a long coat, then you can purchase an 'all in one' waterproof coat that covers the legs as well. Unfortunately, heads, tails and feet are still exposed, so make sure you arrive at the show early enough to allow sufficient time for him to dry. Take a towel with you to wipe muddy paws.

It may be impossible to keep him dry, especially if you need to take him outside to toilet. You can only go so far to keep your dog tidy on a rainy day, but everyone is in the same boat, and the judge will take it into account.

TRIMMING NAILS

Show dogs should have short nails. Nails that curve and touch the ground affect the natural movement of the dog, and can make the feet appear overlong. Aim to keep your dog's nails trimmed regularly.

Some dogs are nervous of having their feet and nails handled, so start acclimatizing your puppy to having his paws handled from day one, even though you may not need to trim his nails for a while. Nail clippers are the quickest way to trim a dog's nails, but you can also use a dremel (nail grinder), either as an alternative, or to smooth the nails after clipping. There are two types of nail clippers, guillotine or pliers type, and which you use is down to personal preference.

If your puppy, or older dog, doesn't like having his nails clipped there are two methods you can use to get

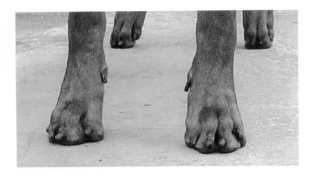

Fig. 9.16 A show dog's nails should be kept trimmed short.

him used to it. The first is by using positive reinforcement. This involves slowly getting the dog used to the nail clippers by rewarding his interactions with them. Reward him for sniffing them, for touching them with his nose, and then letting you put them next to, and then on, his paw. Gradually you should be able to work up to him letting you clip one nail. You should be able to slowly progress to clipping all nails with lots of praise and treats.

The second method is flooding. This means putting the dog into a position whereby he cannot escape from the clippers, either on a grooming table, held firmly between your knees, or being held by another person. Eventually the dog should realize he is going to have his nails clipped, and will allow it to happen. Although it might sound cruel to force your dog to submit to something he doesn't like, he does need to have his nails kept trimmed, even if you are not intending to show him. Dew claws, in particular, need to be kept short, otherwise they will catch and tear, maybe even ripping off the whole claw. Nails that curl under the feet may cause injuries to the legs as he will be forced to walk in an unnatural way.

How to trim nails

Hold the paw securely and apply gentle pressure until the nail is fully extended. Wait for your dog to relax. If your dog has light-coloured nails, you should be able to see the 'quick' (the vein running through the nail). Ensure you cut below the quick. Once you have decided where to make the cut, do it quickly and without hesitation. Being too slow can squeeze the quick and make it painful for your dog. If you haven't trimmed the nails in a while, you might see a distinct hook at the end of the nail. Clip this off so it runs flat with the bottom of the nail.

If your dog has dark-coloured nails you may not be able to see the quick. Take off as little as possible (about 2mm) to avoid cutting into the quick, otherwise it will hurt the dog and the nail will bleed copiously. Keep making tiny cuts on the nail until you see the outside 'shell' of the nail appear, and the texture inside changes to look more meaty. When you see the bottom of the nail change to a darker colour, and/or a white circle appears in the nail, you need to stop. This is the quick, and going further will make your dog bleed.

If you do cut the quick following this method it shouldn't bleed too much, as you are only taking a tiny bit off at a time. You can stem the bleeding by putting the nail into a piece of soap or a bowl of flour, or you can buy a preparation especially for this purpose. If you've cut the quick, then be careful about walking him on hard, rough surfaces for a day or two, otherwise it can open up and start bleeding again.

If your dog has very long nails, then you will need to shorten them in stages. As you cut the nail, the quick will recede a little. To get the nails to the correct length, you should trim a little off them every couple of days. Once the nails are the correct length, then you can keep them short by trimming weekly, or at the interval required for your dog.

Fig. 9.17 When cutting nails, hold the paw firmly.

CHAPTER 10

CRUFTS

A HISTORY OF CRUFTS

Crufts, the biggest dog show in the UK and probably the most famous show in the world, was started by Charles Cruft in 1891. Having cut his teeth on running terrier shows for some years, Cruft decided to hold a show that would be open for all breeds; not a modest man, he named his show after himself. The first Cruft's Dog Show ran over three days and attracted 2,437 entries from thirty-five breeds. Even Queen Victoria's dogs were among the exhibits – a fact which Cruft exploited by offering the public the opportunity to see the royal dogs. There were even classes for stuffed dogs!

Although it was not strictly true, Cruft made good use of some newspaper comments for publicity and in 1892 included the statement 'It is certainly the larg-

est show ever held in this country'. For this second show Cruft even made arrangements with the railway companies to enable dogs to travel from as far away as Scotland to take part.

Crufts has been held annually (with the exception of the war years) ever since, and is internationally recognized as the greatest dog show in the world.

Crufts then and now

In 1891 Cruft's was held on 11–13 February at the Royal Agricultural Hall in London, which was to be its home for many years. The entry fee was 10 shillings per dog, but if two or more dogs were to be entered into the same class, the fee was reduced to 5 shillings per dog. It was a big show with 2,437 entries; there were 473 classes and judging took place in twelve rings.

Fig. 10.1 Crufts! The world's most famous dog show. (Photo: Heidi Hudson © Kennel Club Picture Library)

Price comparison between 1891 and today

Price in 1891	Conversion to Decimal	Rough estimate of value today
6d (6 pence)	2.5p	£1.80
2s (2 shillings)	10p	£7.20
2/6 (2 shillings and 6 pence)	12.5p	£10.37
5s (5 shillings)	25p	£18.00
10s (10 shillings)	50p	£36
£1	£1	£72.00

Having the show running over three (and in subsequent years over four) days allowed Cruft to make money on the entry fees. The show was open between 10am and 10pm, and the entrance fee for non-exhibitors varied between 6 pence and 2 shillings depending on what time they arrived. To attract the public Cruft wanted to ensure all breeds of dog could be seen on their benches on every day of the show.

Dogs had to arrive early on the first day and then had to stay on their benches at the show until 10pm on the final day. In the meantime they were cared for (for free) by the show's own attendants, who exercised them either before 9am or after 5.30pm. If the owner wanted to look after his dogs himself, he had to pay a fee of 2 shillings and 6 pence to obtain a 'Keepers Pass'. Exhibitors could take their dogs home each night, but they had to pay £1 for the privilege, and had to return the dogs by 10am the following morning. On the last day exhibitors could leave early (at 4pm) if they paid 5 shillings, or at 7pm for 2 shillings and 6 pence. As the dogs had to be present on all days, some people simply sent their dogs to the show for the duration of the competition.

It is doubtful whether many of today's exhibitors would approve of the arrangements at the Victorian shows, although the closing date for entries (only fifteen days before the show), and the refund of 75 per cent of the entry fee if entries were cancelled no fewer than eight days before is something we would probably welcome today!

While Cruft was successful in getting the public through the doors (his unsubstantiated claim was that he had 40,000 visitors per day), the quality of the dogs being exhibited was considered poor as there was no Champion class. Although success at Crufts would contribute to the four wins then required for a dog to qualify for a Champion class at other shows, there was no reason for dogs already made up to Champions to attend. The early Crufts attracted a quantity of dogs, but not the quality.

It wasn't until 1928 that the famous Best in Show award was introduced. In its first year this was held without fanfare and was a bit confused. A Greyhound bitch named Primley Sceptre won the honour, but she hadn't won the Hound class the day before! For many years the show wasn't run on the group system, and in 1939 the Best in Show was judged from 180 Challenge Certificate winners.

Cruft died in 1938, and the next year's show was successfully run by his widow. The war years then intervened. In 1942 the Kennel Club bought the rights to hold the now internationally famous and respected Crufts for an alleged £4,000. The first two-day show to be held by the Kennel Club took place in 1948.

Changes were made. Dogs that had been exhibited on the first day of the show did not have to return on the second day unless they were competing for Best in Show. Dogs could enter at 6am and leave at 8pm. This meant that not all breeds were available for the public to see if they visited on just one day, but they still managed to attract 50,000 visitors a day to the show. There were eighty-four different breeds attending – almost double the number of that initial show in the nineteenth century. A total of 4,257 dogs were entered, making 9,412 entries in all.

By 1962 the show had become so popular with

exhibitors that the Kennel Club had to introduce some way to restrict the number of entries, and so puppies under eight months old were banned from entering. This ban lasted until 2014, when Crufts came back in line with other championship shows and lowered the minimum age back to six months.

But the change to the puppy qualifying age did not have a significant impact on the number of entries, and more needed to be done. In 1966 the requirement to qualify was introduced. Now dogs wanting to exhibit at Crufts had to win a prize at a championship show the year before. This caused some controversy, as it was actually contrary to the Kennel Club's own regulations, which state that championship shows must have classes open to all. The Kennel Club got round this by saying it was open to all – as long as they had qualified! In 1972 the qualification was further refined to those winning a first prize, meaning a further rise in the quality of exhibits.

In 1974 Cruft's became simply Crufts, and, due to ever-increasing numbers, five years later the show moved to Earls Court, the extra space facilitating a far greater number of trade stands than before. The reputa-

Fig. 10.3   *Since the 1960s dogs have needed to qualify for Crufts, which means only top-quality dogs can be exhibited. Sloughi 'Dazir Chams d'Al Mahdi'. (Photo: Nick Carter)*

tion for Crufts as being the place to shop for your canine friend commenced and nowadays many people go as much for the shopping as to see the dogs.

In 1990 Crufts was held for the final time in London before moving to the National Exhibition Centre (NEC) near Birmingham. So London lost its last big dog show, and nearly 100,000 visitors attended to mark the event.

Today the whole 25 acres at the NEC are taken over by the show, and various activities such as Discover Dogs, rescue dogs, Police dog team displays, heelwork to music, agility and flyball all take place, alongside the huge numbers exhibiting in the conformation shows.

QUALIFYING FOR CRUFTS

Crufts qualifications can vary slightly from year to year so do make sure you check the current year's criteria on the Crufts website (www.crufts.org.uk). The information below is for 2015. The dates between which you need to qualify also vary slightly from year to year. There is a cut-off date for postal entries, after which there is a period of time where you can still enter online. Manchester is usually the last general championship show which enables people to qualify for Crufts for

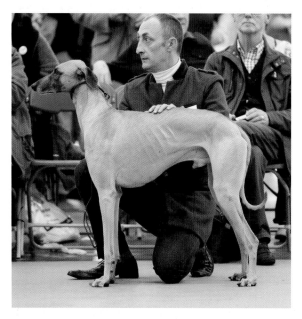

Fig. 10.2   *It's the ultimate aim of all exhibitors to show at Crufts. Sloughi 'Dazir Chams d'Al Mahdi'. (Photo: Nick Carter)*

Fig. 10.4 Nowadays Crufts is vast, with numerous trade stands and canine activities, along with the 22,000 plus pedigree dogs exhibited in the conformation shows. (Photo: Heidi Hudson © Kennel Club Picture Library)

that year before the online entry deadline. As such it is normally a busy show, as people take the last opportunity to qualify.

Qualifying to enter a breed class at Crufts is the first major goal that many newcomers aim for. Qualification is automatic if a dog has won any breed class at Crufts in the preceding year, has gained a Stud Book number, a Junior Warrant, or is a Champion or Show Champion. Otherwise it is only possible to qualify by winning certain prizes in particular classes at shows where Challenge Certificates are on offer for your breed – which places qualify depends upon your breed. There are nearly forty general and group championship shows held throughout the year where Challenge Certificates can be won, together with a number of premier open shows at which some CCs will be available for the more numerous breeds.

If Challenge Certificates are not on offer for your breed at that show, then you cannot qualify, whatever place you achieve, unless your breed is a Bracco Italiano, Havanese or Tibetan Mastiff (2015 qualifications), or a breed that never has Challenge Certificates on offer.

Fig. 10.5   Crufts attracts thousands of visitors each year, all united by the love of dogs. (Photo: Heidi Hudson © Kennel Club Picture Library)

Qualifying for Crufts

This table shows where you can gain qualification for Crufts 2015, and which wins will count.

Crufts Class	Class or Show	Place/Qualification
For Crufts classes with CCs on offer	Championship shows where CCs are on offer for the breed	First, second or third in a breed class for: Minor Puppy; Puppy; Junior; Yearling; Post graduate; Limit; Open; Veteran
	Crufts	First prize in any breed class at Crufts the preceding year
	Hound show (held under the Rules and Regulations of the Masters of Harriers and Beagles Association)	Beagles only – first prize
	Premier open show	Best of Breed
	General or group open show	Best in Show; Reserve Best in Show; Best Puppy in Show
	General and group championship shows where CCs are not on offer, but where CCs are normally allocated for that breed	Best of Breed; Best Puppy in Breed (provided there were more than three breed classes, or more than five for breeds in Stud Book Band E)
	Bracco Italiano, Havanese and Tibetan Mastiff, where Challenge Certificates are not offered.	First, second or third place in breed or Any Variety classes at a championship show for: Minor Puppy; Puppy; Junior; Post Graduate; Limit; Open; Veteran; First prize in any breed class at Crufts the preceding year; Best of Breed at a premier open show (provided there were more than three breed classes, or more than five for breeds in Stud Book Band E); Best in Show, Reserve Best in Show and Best Puppy in Show at a general or group open show
AV Import Classes	General or group championship show – Imported Register classes	Best of Sex and Reserve Best of Sex. Or first, second or third places for: Puppy; Junior; Post Graduate; Open
Overseas Qualifications	Various titles and wins which vary as to country.	

Notes: A breed class means a class for just one breed of dog.
Wins from a class called 'Special', and limited by age, colour, weight, height or type of coat or to members of a society or breeders, are not counted except for Special Puppy and Special Junior classes at Crufts.

Entering Crufts

When you are completing your entry form you will need to supply details of the place and date that you qualified. The class you will be entering will be the one appropriate for the age and qualifications of your dog when Crufts takes place. You may have qualified from a Puppy class, but will need to enter the Junior class as your dog will be that much older. Read the class definitions very carefully, as the classes for puppies and juniors (called 'Special') can have slightly different age ranges than at other shows.

There are other qualifying criteria for dogs entering field trials, special working gundog classes, obedience or agility championships.

WHAT'S IT LIKE TO SHOW AT CRUFTS?

So you've qualified for Crufts! So, what can you expect? For most first-time exhibitors at the biggest show in the UK (and purportedly the biggest in the world) the first thing to expect is excitement and nerves! Try to treat it just like any other show. Yes, it will be bigger, with larger classes, and more people watching the judging, but that's all the difference.

Here are a few key points. 'Not for Competition' dogs are not allowed in the show, so any other dogs you have will need to stay at home. Exhibitors will be given admission passes, and if the dog is co-owned there will be one extra free 'helper' pass (however many owners there are). Any other spectators will need to purchase admission tickets, and you can save money by purchasing these online, rather than on the door on the day. The breed classes take place over four days, with one or more groups on each day. The groups rotate so your breed will not always be on the same day. The group winners compete for the prestigious Best in Show award on the final night. If you want to watch this competition you will need to buy specific tickets, even if you are showing on the final day.

Crufts may well mean a long journey for many exhibitors, and you may wish to stay overnight either before or after your big day. Make sure you book accommoda-

Fig. 10.6   Dogs lined up in the ring at Crufts. (Photo: Heidi Hudson © Kennel Club Picture Library)

Fig. 10.7   Judging proceeds in exactly the same way as for any other show. (Photo: Andy Biggar © Kennel Club Picture Library)

tion early, as hotels fill up a long time in advance. In addition to your entry fee, you will need to pay for the car park (currently £10). The NEC is a very large venue, with a number of car parks. When you receive your

Fig. 10.8   It's a great feeling to take your turn on the 'green carpet'. (Photo: Heidi Hudson © Kennel Club Picture Library)

entry passes you will get an information pack which will tell you which hall you are in; try to head for the closest car park. Shuttle buses run between the car parks and the halls.

The show opens at 7am, and just getting into the car park will take time as you'll be trying to find a space along with thousands of other people. Particularly if you are on your own, it is a good idea to have a trolley to transport your show paraphernalia, as the car parks are a long way from the halls. You can store your trolley under your bench. There are disabled parking facilities

closer to the halls. If your breed is showing later in the day, your information pack will tell you the latest time you can arrive.

Crufts is a benched show. As at any other show where benches are provided, your ring number will be on your bench. The size of the benching varies by breed of dog, but the distance between the benches tends to be more spacious than at other championship shows. If you want to take a soft crate, it must be secured properly to the bench and there is no room for crates to be used as an alternative to benching. Unlike other shows, you are not permitted to remove your dog until 4pm, except in an emergency. Expect a mass exodus at that time, though, and if you want to avoid queuing to exit the car park, you may want to delay your exit.

Your ring will be close to your benching area. Because there are many more people milling around, make sure

Fig. 10.9   Any place at Crufts feels good. Best Saluki bitch 'Glenoak Jazmyn JW'.

Fig. 10.10   Winning Best of Breed at Crufts is a major achievement. This lovely Field Spaniel bitch, 'Sh CH Elgert Aloysisa ShCM', was Best of Breed in 2012 and won the Bitch CC in 2013.

you leave enough time between leaving your bench and the start of your class. All rings are carpeted with that famous 'green carpet'.

A day at Crufts is very long, both for you and your dog. Unless you win your class and go on to other classes, your time actually showing will be quite short. You will be able to visit all the trade stands, watch displays and find something to eat, but much of your time will probably be spent hanging around the benches with your dog. Do take the opportunity to meet up with friends, or make new ones! There will be many experienced hands for whom this is old hat, and there may be people bringing Champions from abroad. But just remember that every dog has his day, and you are always in with a chance!

If you do win your class, you will be able to challenge for the ticket, and to become Best of Breed. Winning this will take you forward to the group judging, which will take place at the end of the day. If you win the group, you will either have to stay for the Best in Show competition (if you are showing on the last day), or arrange to return on the Sunday to take part and possibly achieve the dream of everyone in the dog showing world: to win the esteemed title of Crufts Best in Show!

Fig. 10.11   Group judging in the famous Best in Show ring: the aim for every exhibitor.

CHAPTER 11

AN INTRODUCTION TO SHOWING YOUR DOG ABROAD

In January 2012 the UK Pet Travel Scheme (PETS) was brought into line with those of other countries in the European Union (EU) and meant dogs going to, or returning from, abroad no longer had to go into quarantine. The changes brought in relaxed the pet travel rules and the effect on the dog show world means it became easier to go to shows abroad. Once you've got experience with showing in the UK, you may wish to combine a trip abroad with a show or shows, or even look towards becoming a national or international champion.

If you are considered broadening your show horizons, there are two things you need to consider: first, the legal requirements concerning taking your dog abroad, and secondly, the different awards and titles that you could be aiming for and how they equate to those in the UK.

MICROCHIPPING

Your dog cannot receive a rabies vaccination until he has been microchipped, and it is common for vets to prefer to wait a week after the microchip is inserted before administering the vaccine. Microchips should conform to the ISO standard so they can be checked by transport companies. If your dog's chip doesn't conform you should take your own microchip reader so that it can still be checked. Petlog and Anibase chips are ISO compliant. In this section we're concentrating on showing in Europe, but it's worth noting that if

Taking your dog abroad

While it's a simple matter for us to pick up our passport and go, a little more preparation is needed before taking your dog out of the UK. With the relaxation of the rules in 2012 it became too easy to import dogs (particularly puppies) illegally to the UK. To crack down on these nefarious practices, changes were introduced in December 2014. Dogs travelling abroad need a pet passport, and the amount of information recorded on that document has been increased and is less able to be tampered with. If you already have a passport issued before December 2014, it will continue to be valid. As well as his passport, your dog will need to be microchipped (if not already), receive a rabies vaccination, and, depending which country you are visiting, treatment for tapeworm on his return. You will need to factor in the time involved for these arrangements and should note that the rules shown below apply to the Republic of Ireland, as well as to any other country, and that dogs can no longer enter Eire without a passport. There are different rules when taking more than five dogs abroad if you are travelling to enter a competition.

you are taking your dog to the USA, you will probably need to get another chip as the standard there is for ten-digit microchips. The European standard is fifteen digits.

Once your dog has his microchip and has been vaccinated against rabies, you must wait a further twenty-one days before you travel. Changes made in 2014 mean puppies cannot have this vaccine until they are at least twelve weeks old. To maintain the protection against rabies the UK requirement is that a booster vaccination is required at three yearly intervals. If you are planning to reside in a European country for more than three months, most countries in the EU require rabies boosters annually.

PET PASSPORTS

Any dog travelling abroad must have a pet passport issued by the Local Veterinary Inspector (a government authorized vet). There should be one at your usual vet practice (if not, they will know where you should go). The passport is normally issued twenty-one days after the rabies vaccine has been given, and must include the microchip number. The vet issuing the passport must record and retain, for a period of three years, certain information about both you and your dog. This includes your name and contact details, plus your dog's name, breed, sex, colour, date of birth and any notable characteristics, plus the location of his microchip (they can move round the body). The vet must also complete a page in the passport with his name and details. Passports issued before 14 December 2014 remain valid even though they do not have all the information recorded.

TAPEWORM

In France, Germany and other parts of continental Europe a tapeworm is found which can cause a serious, sometimes fatal, liver disease in humans. In order to keep the UK clear of this tapeworm, dogs returning from affected countries must be treated to ensure the tapeworm eggs are not shed here.

Unless you are coming back to the UK from Ireland, Finland, Malta or Norway you will need to have your

Fig. 11.1   *Your dog will need a pet passport if you are taking him abroad.*

dog treated for tapeworm by a vet; this is not something you can use over-the-counter treatments for. Unless you are only going abroad for less than five days, this means you will need to find a vet in the country you are visiting. The treatment must be given between 24 and 120 hours (one and five days) before your scheduled arrival in the UK. Details of the treatment must be recorded in the pet passport whenever you want to enter the UK and the information to be recorded includes the name and manufacturer of the product used to treat your dog (which must have praziquantel or equivalent as the active ingredient), the date and time of treatment, and the vet's stamp and signature. You cannot enter the UK until a full 24 hours have passed since the treatment was given, and if you delay for more than 120 hours after treatment, it will have to be done again.

Tapeworm treatment if you're only travelling to a single show

If you are going abroad just for a show, you will probably not be away for more than a day or so. In this case you will need to have the tapeworm treatment in the UK before you go, but the same rules apply in that your return must be within the 24–120 hour window. The Department for Environment, Food and Rural Affairs (DEFRA) has recommended that a further treatment is administered twenty-eight days after return.

TAKING MORE THAN FIVE DOGS ABROAD

Obviously here we are interested in showing abroad, but it is worth noting that if you are taking more than five pets abroad and NOT entering a competition, you need to comply with additional rules including travelling from a registered premises, using an authorized transporter and registering on the TRACES system. People taking more than five dogs to enter a competition are exempt from these extra requirements.

Transporting more than one dog to a show

The legislation on the movement of dogs between countries changed in December 2014 to prevent dogs being imported for sale under the guise of being for non-commercial reasons. At the time of writing, the changes were still being consulted on, so please check for any new requirements on the DEFRA website listed under the Pet Travel Scheme.

As it stands, if you are taking more than five dogs to take part in competitions, exhibitions or sporting events or training, then you will need to have with you written evidence that the dogs are entered into the event. You may also be asked to sign a declaration confirming you are exempt from the additional requirements.

You cannot transport more than five dogs under the age of six months old. There may be spot checks to examine your documentation.

Fitness for Travel health certificate

Unless exempt, you can only transport five or more dogs abroad using certain transport companies and routes. The transport companies (including sea, air and rail) are responsible for checking documentation. Each dog will require a Fitness to Travel health certificate. This certificate has to be applied for at least ten working days before you travel and is issued by the Animal Health and Veterinary Laboratories Agency (AHVLA).

TRAVELLING WITH DOGS

Travelling to France can be fairly easy if you use the Channel Tunnel as both you and your dog can stay in the car. But if you are travelling elsewhere, or decide to take the ferry, you may need to leave your dog alone in the car, in which case having him secured in a crate is probably the safest way. Rather than leaving him for the first time on the ferry crossing, practise leaving him in the crate and building up the time he's left on his own so that by the time you travel he is used to staying in his crate and doesn't feel abandoned. You could use an Adaptil collar on him to help reduce his stress levels. Do tell the ferry operator when you board the boat that you have a dog or dogs in the car so that you can park in the coolest part of the ferry.

On the Stena Line pets can travel in kennels on the car deck on all routes between Britain, Ireland and Holland. Kennels are issued on a first come, first served basis, and are accessible throughout the journey; dogs can be exercised under controlled conditions. The kennel costs an extra £15 at current rates.

If you intend to fly, your dog will need to travel in a suitable container in the cargo hold of the plane. Containers must fasten securely, and must have a water and food container that is accessible from the exterior; your dog must be able to stand and sit up without touching the top of the crate, and he should not be able to get his nose or paws out. Your airline will

Dogs in cars

The rules for carrying dogs in cars can vary from country to country, so make sure you are aware of the requirements before you travel. The UK Highway Code states that dogs must be 'suitably restrained so they cannot distract you while you are driving or injure you if you stop quickly'. This is advisory (and common sense), but not a legal requirement, although if you cause an accident it will probably count towards driving without due care and attention. In some European countries the rules are stricter and the law prohibits dogs travelling loose in vehicles. Make yourself aware of specific requirements before you travel. DEFRA has a useful document 'Protecting the welfare of pet dogs and cats during journeys' which may be helpful.

have information about acceptable types and suitable sizes of container. Some airlines have restrictions on transporting brachycephalic breeds.

SHOWING ABROAD

The Federation Cynologique Internationale (FCI) is a worldwide canine organization which ensures that breed standards and judges are mutually recognized by all of its eighty-nine members. It also partners with other countries which issue their own breed standards and train their own judges. The UK, like other countries that are not members of the FCI, has national breed clubs which are responsible for their own breed standards and these are used in competition in those countries. The standards try to keep conformity with the FCI standard, but may differ where there are concerns about some of the requirements.

With the exception of the United Kingdom, all the countries of the EU, including Eire, are members of the FCI.

FCI groups

The first difference concerns groups. In the UK we have seven breed groups, but under FCI rules there are ten, as shown in the table below. The Breed Showing Information Guide at the back of this book shows to which FCI group the breeds recognized in the UK belong. The FCI also recognizes some breeds that are not recognized by the UK Kennel Club.

Fig. 11.2   Array of rosettes at a European show. (Photo: Laura Kolbach)

FCI Groups

Group	Breeds
Group 1	Sheepdogs and Cattle Dogs (except Swiss Cattle Dogs)
Group 2	Pinscher and Schnauzer – Molosoid Breeds – Swiss Mountain and Cattle Dogs
Group 3	Terriers
Group 4	Dachshunds
Group 5	Spitz and Primitive Types
Group 6	Scenthounds and Related Breeds
Group 7	Pointing Dogs
Group 8	Retrievers – Flushing Dogs – Water Dogs
Group 9	Companion and Toy Dogs
Group 10	Sighthounds

Judging system

There are only six main classes into which you'll be able to enter your dog, although breed club shows sometimes hold a Baby Puppy class for dogs aged between four and six months. One important point is that you can only enter ONE breed class, unlike in the UK where you can enter more than one. It is therefore important that you enter the class that is most appropriate to the age of your dog.

The way dogs are judged and awarded prizes is very different from the UK. The judges will look at all dogs, and then go over them in the same way as you'll be used to. But EVERY dog is then graded by the judge; the grades are:

- Excellent: this grade is awarded where the dog is a close match to the ideal of the breed standard. It is in excellent condition, has good posture and a good temperament. Minor faults are ignored, as no dog is perfect.
- Very Good: again, the dog must be typical of the breed, with well balanced proportions and in correct condition. Dogs must show class.
- Good: a dog awarded this grading will be a good representation of the breed, and his good points should outweigh his faults.

- Sufficient: a dog which may be out of condition, but still corresponds to the breed standard.
- Cannot be judged: this grading is for dogs which don't move properly for the judge, either through jumping up or lameness, or where the judge cannot properly go over him. It is also given where a judge suspects either that the exhibitor is trying to deceive him, or that operations have been performed to alter the dog's features. If this grading is awarded, the judge has to state the reason in his report.
- Disqualified: this grading is given to dogs which show aggression, do not have two descended testicles, or have major faults that mean they do not correspond to the breed standard or have faults that could threaten their future health.

A grade card, marked by the judge, is given to each exhibitor. In most countries the exhibitor is also given a coloured ribbon that can be placed on the lead.

Places are awarded to the four best dogs, provided they have achieved at least a 'very good' rating.

Puppy class gradings

Puppy classes are graded slightly differently, with puppies graded as Very Promising or Promising instead

Fig. 11.3   Dogs graded Excellent can be given a red ribbon to display on their lead. Belgian Shepherd Dog (Groenendael) 'Grondemon Krusader'.

Fig. 11.4   Cairn Terrier Finnish Champion 'No Copyright Catch Me If You Can'.

Awards

The ultimate award that can be gained via FCI shows is the title 'International Beauty Champion'. Similar to our Champion and Show Champion titles, this can be achieved by gaining four CACIBs (Certificat d'Aptitude au Championnat International de Beaute de la FCI) under at least three different judges in three different countries. Two may be under the same judge, or in the same country, making the four in total. There must be a gap of at least a year and a day between the first and last CACIBs being awarded. Some breeds need a working qualification as well, before being able to claim the International Beauty Champion status (INT CH).

of Excellent, Very Good and Good. The other grades (Sufficient, Cannot be Judged and Disqualified) still apply.

Some people think this is a far better system than that used in the UK, as every exhibitor finds out what the judge thought of their dog. However, as in the UK, judging is subjective, and what one judge thinks 'excellent' another may think only 'good'.

CACIB

A CACIB can only be won at an international show. As with Challenge Certificates in the UK, the number of CACIBs that are available per breed per show is governed by the number of entries expected per show. There will be no more than two CACIBs per breed (one of each sex), and sometimes just the one. Judges will award a prize card to the winning exhibitors which states that the dog has been proposed for a CACIB. Final confirmation is needed by the FCI, which will issue a certificate. The certificate will be made available for download on the FCI website, but it might take a few months to appear.

Only dogs which have been awarded 'Excellent' status in the following classes can be awarded a CACIB, although dogs graded excellent do not necessarily get the CACIB award.

- Intermediate class
- Open class
- Working class – can only be entered by dogs which have a WCC (Working Class Certificate)
- Champion class – only dogs holding one of the following titles can enter: International Beauty Champion, International Show Champion, National Beauty or Show Champion of an FCI member country or a National Beauty or Show Champion of a country which has signed a letter of understanding with the FCI. (NB: If you want to enter the Champion class, you must provide proof of your dog's Champion status when you register with the FCI.)

If a Reserve CACIB is on offer, it will be given to the dog which came second to the dog given the CACIB, as long as he is graded excellent. If the dog awarded the CACIB is already a Champion, the Reserve winner can have his award made up to a CACIB. This is done by applying to the FCI using a form on their website.

When judging the CACIB, it is up to the judge which dogs he calls back into the ring. Some judges only call back the dogs placed first in each class, while others ask for all the dogs graded excellent to compete.

CAC

A CAC (Certificat d'Aptitude au Championnat) is a grading given by individual member countries of the FCI. To earn the title of National Champion, a dog must achieve

Fig. 11.5   Breeders team being judged in Sweden. Judges are international – this competition is being judged by two English judges.

at least two CACs won at different shows in the same country. Different countries have different criteria for their titles of National Champion. In most European countries you need four CACs to be a National Champion, and possibly a working title as well (depending on breed), or a lower number of CACs and a working title. Different time limits, age and residency restrictions can also apply. The kennel club of the country in question will be able to tell you the requirements for gaining their national title and it is not unusual for the criteria to include completing a National Aptitude Test. Details of the various kennel clubs can be found on the FCI website.

Recognizing an FCI award in the UK

A CAC is normally considered to be equivalent to a UK Challenge Certificate, and a CACIB to an International Challenge Certificate. For a dog registered in the UK, claims for an international title must be submitted to the Kennel Club, and the dog must already be a British Champion or Show Champion.

Fig. 11.6   A CAC rosette.

Best of Breed and Best Opposite Sex

As well as the CAC and CACIB awards, FCI shows may also offer Best of Breed and Best Opposite Sex awards. The Best Junior, the winner of the CACIB and the best veteran from both sexes (but only if they have been graded 'Excellent') then compete for

Fig. 11.7 Shows abroad have large numbers of cups to be won.

Best of Breed. The judge then awards Best Opposite Sex.

SHOWING SURGICALLY ALTERED DOGS ABROAD

Different countries have different regulations with regard to the showing of docked or neutered dogs, and may have different breed specific legislation. The criteria can be obtained from the relevant kennel club or embassy.

IRISH SHOWS

To explain how national kennel clubs can have their own system for awards under the umbrella of the FCI, it's useful to take a look at overseas shows in more detail; we have chosen the Republic of Ireland because many people from the UK make the crossing of the Irish Sea to exhibit there.

Northern Ireland

Just a reminder that Northern Ireland is part of the UK. There are no special travel requirements and you do not need a pet passport. But there is a difference from the rest of the UK: in Northern Ireland shows can be held under either Kennel Club regulations or those of the Irish Kennel Club (IKC). You should check carefully under which regulations the shows are being held. If it is an IKC show, you will need to register your dog (or dogs) with the Irish Kennel Club. Once you have registered, you can show in any country that is a member of the FCI using your IKC registration.

Showing in the Republic of Ireland

Just as the Kennel Club is the governing body for dog showing in the UK, so the Irish Kennel Club is responsible for the registration of pedigree dogs and licensing shows in the Republic of Ireland. All shows in the Irish Republic are run under FCI rules, and you must register your dog with the IKC in order to be able to exhibit.

The show types (open and championship) are very similar to those in the UK, and can be general for all breeds or restricted to one group or breed, but as they are operating under FCI regulations there are ten groups as shown in the table earlier in this chapter.

The breed classes are the same as for all FCI shows, and entry into only one breed class is allowed per dog. Dogs and puppies are graded as previously described.

Green Stars

Green Stars are awarded to the top dog or bitch in each class, and a Reserve Green Star may be awarded to the exhibit which came second only to the dog that won the Green Star. Green Stars and Reserve Green Stars can only be awarded to dogs which have been graded 'Excellent'. A Green Star is equivalent to the UK Challenge Certificate.

The dogs and bitches which have won Green Stars then compete for Best of Breed. Best of Group and Best in Show judging follows, as under the UK system.

Puppies which have been graded 'Very Promising' and have been placed first in their class then compete for Best Puppy in Breed, and the winner subsequently competes for Best Puppy in Group and Best Puppy in Show. Unlike the UK system, a puppy cannot win Best in Show.

The Best Veteran in Breed also competes for Best of Breed if he is graded Excellent; if he wins this, he goes through to Best in Group and Best in Show. If the Best Veteran in Breed does not win Best of Breed, he competes for Best Veteran in Group, and, if there is such an award on offer, Best Veteran in Show.

Similar to the UK's Junior Warrant system, dogs aged between six and eighteen months can gain a Junior Diploma. A Junior Diploma card is available from the Irish Kennel Club, and the judge confirms each place awarded by signing the card. A total of twelve points are required from both open and championship shows.

A further award of Junior Champion can be earned if the dog achieves first place in five Junior breed classes and is graded 'Excellent' at championship shows.

Annual Champion

The dog or bitch which gains the most Green Stars in its breed (as long as the number is more than five) is given the title Annual Champion. This entitles the owner to put the year in which the dog achieved this title after his name. If there is a tie, then the award takes into account the most Best of Breed wins, and the dog with the highest wins.

Fig. 11.8   Junior Champion Havanese 'Ch Blevwil Cast a Glimpse at Berrywood', Jr Ch CW 2014.

Fig. 11.9   Irish Champion Brittany 'Sh CH IR/Sh CH Eastonite Bracken'.

Fig. 11.10   Irish (and most European) shows are held at outdoor venues so wet weather gear is essential.

Irish Champion

The highest award in Ireland is Irish Champion. To achieve this accolade, the dog must win seven Green Stars from seven different judges at Irish Kennel Club championship shows. One of these stars must be gained after the age of fifteen months.

The Irish Circuit

The Irish Circuit is a series of five championship shows which take place over one week in August. The locations are Navan (near Dublin), Clonmel, Killarney, Limerick and Tralee. The first show at Navan is open only to breeds in FCI Groups 1, 2 and 5. The shows are held on Saturday, Sunday, Tuesday, Thursday and Saturday, and obviously require accommodation to be booked, and travelling arranged between them. All the shows are outdoors, so this will need to be borne in mind if you have a light-coloured or long-coated breed to keep clean!

Travelling to and from the UK and completing the circuit will take up nine or ten days, but will be an experience to remember.

ENTERING SHOWS ABROAD

The Irish Kennel Club has information about shows you can enter, or there are websites such as dogshowentry or Fossedata for shows in Ireland. The FCI has a list of European shows on its website.

Dogs from overseas who wish to compete in UK

Showing abroad

When you arrive at the show, you will need to have with you your pet passport and registration certificate as these will be checked along with your dog's microchip. There will then be a vet inspection. This all takes time, and there are often queues for these checks. Make sure you leave enough time so you do not miss your class. Shows are normally held outside, and no benching is provided. This can prove challenging on hot or wet days, so make sure you are prepared with crates, sunshades or large umbrellas! Whereas in the UK you can choose your position in the line-up in the ring, at shows overseas exhibitors have to line up in numerical order of their ring numbers. Often breeders will have tents that are used as social gathering points for exhibitors of dogs bred by them, so you may be able to meet up with friends.

shows need to obtain an Authority to Compete (ATC) from the Kennel Club and provide this number on their entry form. Likewise, dogs registered with the UK Kennel Club have to register with an FCI kennel club in order to compete in Ireland or Europe. Once you have registered with an FCI kennel club, you can enter shows in other countries using FCI rules on the back of that first registration.

CHAPTER 12

THE FUTURE OF DOG SHOWING IN THE UK

The twenty-first century is an exciting time in the world of dog showing. The Kennel Club is keen to open up the sport to as many pedigree dog owners as possible, and changes now being brought in will give newcomers the chance to find out what showing is about, and encourage new and old exhibitors to continue exhibiting their dogs.

The original rules and regulations of the Kennel Club were drawn up at its inception in the nineteenth century, and have been subjected to amendment since that date, usually with minor changes being introduced on 1 January each year. Major changes are less common. However, during the closing months of 2013 the Kennel Club set up a working party to look into ways of raising both attendance and the popularity of dog showing, in an effort to ensure the dog show scene today fits with the needs of people in the twenty-first century. Following consultation, some changes to the show regulations were brought in from January 2015, and it seems likely that there will be minor tweaks or even major amendments to the rules that govern dog showing in the UK over the next few years.

This book already incorporates the amendments that were brought in early in 2015 (namely the ability to have two sets of Challenge Certificates awarded on the same day at the same venue, and the two-year suspension of the beaten dog rule) but these are summarized below for ease of reference. Further changes are being proposed with reference to the overall allocation of Challenge Certificates, and the detail is likely to become clearer following the publication of Stand! There are also a number of other areas where exhibitors might see a change over the next couple of years. Possible areas for amendment are discussed below.

KEEPING UP WITH THE CHANGES

Although the Kennel Club show regulations provide official guidance for everybody involved in showing, in this interim period proposed changes will be introduced and explained via Frequently Asked Questions on the Kennel Club website, and show schedules will be amended to reflect the alterations. Once the changes have bedded in, the show regulations will be updated.

The Kennel Club will keep exhibitors informed of future initiatives on its website and for up-to-date information the following page should be bookmarked: http://www.thekennelclub.org.uk/activities/dog-showing/already-involved-in-dog-showing/exhibitors. The dog press (*Dog World* and *Our Dogs*) will also keep exhibitors up-to-date with the latest news. Changes can also be found on www.trishhaill.co.uk.

CHANGES BROUGHT IN FROM JANUARY 2015

Two sets of CCs to be awarded on the same day at the same venue

The shows at which Challenge Certificates are awarded can be few and far between for some breeds, and for any breed may be available at some distance from where an exhibitor lives. Although the entry fees are not considered prohibitive, the expense of travel, and possibly overnight accommodation, may be off-putting to some people.

In order to try to reduce the amount of travelling, the rules have been changed to allow breed clubs to team up with societies running championship shows so that they can hold the two shows together, on the same day and at the same venue. This will enable exhibitors to compete in one or both shows for their breed with the chance to win a CC at both. As there will be different judges, a dog beaten in the championship show would not be considered a beaten dog at the second show.

This change was brought in with effect from January 2015. How successful it will be remains to be seen. Clubs and societies will need to work together to make it work, but a venue at the other side of the country will still be remote and perhaps difficult to get to. With the current allocation of CCs breed clubs may feel they could have a better geographical spread of opportunity if they keep their breed shows at a different location. Exhibitors may, of course, agree that it's a better use of their time to be able to enter into two shows at the same time and thus minimize their travel arrangements. This change does give the opportunity for more flexibility, but, like anything new, it may need time to bed in.

Two-year suspension of the beaten dog rule

Prior to the new arrangements, dogs beaten in a stakes or Any Variety class were considered beaten dogs in their breed classes. Although they could continue to become Best of Breed, they were unable to proceed to group judging, and would lose out on the chance of becoming Best in Show.

From January 2015, for a period of two years, the Kennel Club is suspending this rule, together with the requirement for a dog showing in a stakes or Any Variety class to have entered, and exhibited in, a breed class first. This means that the stakes and Any Variety classes are considered as completely separate entities. Not being considered for first place by the different judge in the AV classes will no longer penalize dogs in the breed judging, and people can decide to enter a show purely to exhibit in an Any Variety or stakes class.

While in essence these changes appear quite simple, the original requirements are referenced throughout the regulations. The two-year trial period will enable the regulations to be redrafted to reflect the alterations depending on the success and effect of the trial.

CHANGES UNDER CONSIDERATION

Increasing the number of all-breed championship shows

Only four shows can award CCs in all breeds for which CCs are available. These shows are Crufts, the Birmingham Dog Show, the Scottish Kennel Club and the Welsh Kennel Club. From January 2015 the wording in the regulations describing these shows as 'representative shows' will be changed to 'all-breeds championship shows' to enable other shows, which satisfy certain conditions, to also award CCs in all breeds.

Core breeds to be allocated CCs at all general championship shows

Another proposal being seriously considered is to allocate CCs to all 'core breeds' (that is, those in Stud Book Bands D and E) at all general and possibly group championship shows. Increasing the number of CCs available would potentially lead to some less numerous breeds, whose historical origins mean they have a higher number of breed clubs, ending up with more CCs than a far more numerous breed, which, being newer to the show scene, has possibly only one breed club. The anomalies will need to be worked through. Currently the allocation of CCs can change annually, so changes to how they are distributed (and making available additional CCs) is proposed to be agreed for the 2017 allocation, and, in order for show societies to be better able to plan, will then be set for a period of five years from 2018.

Encouraging people to try showing and keeping existing exhibitors

The main reason why this book came about was that the dog showing world can be complicated. Knowing how to present your dog in the ring is one challenge, but finding out what you're supposed to be doing and why is another. Recognizing this, the Kennel Club is considering 'Have a Go' dog shows, which would include practical advice on handling, and information about the judging process and dog shows in general. In addition to the practical sessions, the Kennel Club will be making more comprehensive information available online.

OTHER POSSIBLE CHANGES

Allowing people to enter open and limited shows on the day of the show (for age-restricted and open classes only)

Many exhibitors would probably like to be able to have the opportunity to enter classes at an open or limited show on the day itself. Even experienced exhibitors miss the closing date for shows at times. A bitch may be expected to come into season so the show was not entered, but she may not have started by the show date! Such a change might even attract newcomers to the show: they may see signs advertising it and decide to give showing a try. People coming in on the off-chance, or encouraged by friends, may not be aware of the strict closing dates that we have at the moment. It would be up to show societies and clubs to decide whether to accept entries on the day, but this could be problematical. Firstly, there may be a financial shortfall if the number of entries falls. Currently people pay their money to enter, whether or not they decide to turn up on the day. For a society running a show in an outdoor venue on a miserable rainy day, they may find the amount of entry money decreases if a number of people leave it to the last minute to decide whether to turn up. Although to start with people can continue to enter in advance, if this becomes common practice it may become the norm, in these classes, to leave entry to the show date.

Also, of course, a full catalogue could not be produced, and exhibitors would not know either the number of dogs in each class, or the names of their competitors.

Rosettes and prize cards

The entry fee for a championship show is around five times more than the entrance for an open show. At the latter, places will be rewarded with a prize card and a rosette. At the former, unless winning the top prizes, you will receive only a card. If you want a rosette to mark your win, you will need to buy one from a trade stand. Being placed at a championship show is an honour that many people feel should be rewarded by a ribbon to mark the occasion. Many exhibitors, especially those new to showing, feel disappointed when they find they are not given a rosette at championship shows.

Introduction of a Champion class

At the moment there is no Champion class in UK shows. Champions go into open classes, which, of course, they are likely to win as they have already proven multiple times that they deserve to be a Champion. Dogs with the potential to become Champions end up getting the Reserve Challenge Certificate (RCC) – this is, of course, an honour in itself, as to award this place the judge must be satisfied that the RCC winner is deserving of the Challenge Certificate should the top placed dog be disqualified for some reason. But it means that potential Champions continue only to get the Reserve place (or even lower), due to the number of Champions entering the only class they can. There are dogs with literally tens of tickets!

A Champion class is proposed which will take those dogs which have won three Challenge Certificates out of the open class, leaving the way clear for other dogs to come through. On the face of it, this seems a good idea, but many exhibitors feel that it would devalue the Challenge Certificate if the winning dog was not actually the best dog on the day!

Benching to be scrapped

Some people love benching as they have somewhere away from the hustle and bustle of the show where their dog can be safe and secure, and relax until his class. Others feel that they want their dog with them at all times, and do not agree with tethering him to a bench or prefer to use their own crate. People with multiple dogs generally find benching easier.

If benching were not provided, then entry fees may well be lower, but there could be some health and safety issues at larger shows. People would, or could, bring their own crates, which may or may not be as secure as benching, and the same size area would have to be provided for people to set them up.

Judges

There is a view that there are too few judges able to award CCs, and that the same faces appear too often on the championship show circuit. It has been suggested that the amount of experience necessary to award CCs is lowered, to enable more people to be able to judge at that level.

It is definitely true that a new judge under whom people have not shown before attracts a larger entry as no one is sure of his interpretation of the breed standard, and all feel they have a chance. Alternatively, a judge who is too well known can cause a lower number of entries as people whose dogs he has not placed in previous shows tend to stay away.

CONCLUSION

I've heard someone say that nothing will change as the 'old hands' will be against it. Well, that's the case in any walk of life. What's familiar is comfortable, and once you've learned one set of rules it is hard to adapt to another, but changes are coming.

Only just over fifty years ago Crufts changed its rules so that people had to qualify their dogs in order to enter. That was quite a drastic change if you think about it –

but imagine how many dogs would be entering today if something hadn't been done to limit the numbers. Everyone wants to show at Crufts, but isn't it just that bit more special when you know you've earned the right to be there, rather than just paying your money and turning up?

Dog showing is a wonderful sport. It isn't elitist – people from any walk of life can join in. The cost of a purebred puppy is sometimes far less than the cost of one of the new 'designer' breeds, and once you've got a dog, the cost of maintenance during his lifetime is the same whether he's a registered pedigree or not (as long as you're comparing dogs of a similar size).

It would be a shame if exhibitor numbers continued to decline, and making shows more accessible, giving new pedigree dog owners the chance to 'have a go', and widening the opportunity for other dogs to win CCs, rather than keep rewarding the same ones, might be ways of attracting people to the sport, and retaining their interest as their dogs grow and mature.

Change is inevitable, but major changes will be slow in coming, which is why the Kennel Club is looking at short-, medium- and long-term options to bring the sport of dog showing into the twenty-first century.

For any newcomer to the world of dog showing, finding your way round the current regulations is hard enough. I've included this chapter as food for thought on what is happening, and what might come to pass. As in any walk of life, there will be things you think are excellent about the sport, and things you would like to see changed. As you gain more experience, you might start to think about doing something about it, perhaps by becoming a member of a breed or show society, or taking a more active part in shows through stewarding or even judging!

BREED SHOWING INFORMATION GUIDE

CURRENTLY RECOGNIZED BREEDS, AND INFORMATION AND TIPS ON SHOWING

When the judge takes his first glance at the dogs presented in the ring, he will expect to see them standing in a way that shows off their conformation. How they are stood depends on their breed, and the work they were originally bred for. Some dogs have the back legs extended and head forwards in an alert position – much like you'd see on a walk when they spot something that attracts their attention. Others stand four square: i.e., all four legs are directly beneath their body.

There are two ways of presenting a dog. One is hand stacking, which is where the handler stands or kneels and places the dog's feet in the correct position, and then continues to hold him in that pose. The other is where the dog is walked into a natural stand. As long as the dog attains the proper stance, in many breeds it doesn't matter whether the exhibitor has taught him to stack or free stand, and even in breeds which are normally stacked a number of judges like to see a free stand after the dog has been moved round the ring. In many cases, how you choose to present your dog will depend on what works best for you and him.

An all-rounder judge may ask you to do something differently from a breed specialist. He may, for example, ask to judge your dog on the floor, rather than on the table, or ask you to free stand your dog rather than stack him. If the judge asks you to do something differently, *do not argue with him*; just try your best to comply with his instructions.

Show leads are another area where it's often down to personal choice as to which to use, but in some breeds there are types of lead that are predominantly used. There are several things to remember when selecting a lead. Firstly, the judge should be looking at your dog, and not at the lead, so use a colour or style that is not distracting and which blends in with the dog. Secondly, all exhibitors need to be able to control their dogs, so those with larger breeds will need stronger collars and leads, and possibly check or semi-check chains. And lastly, there is some tradition which dictates the most common leads used with the different breeds. Most gundogs, for example, will be shown on a leather slip lead.

In the next pages we will look at each of the currently recognized breeds and the most common ways of showing them. The table also shows which UK Kennel Club group the breeds belong to, as well as the FCI group for those interested in showing overseas. This information is a guide only, and more detailed information can be obtained from breed clubs and ringcraft classes. There are two breeds which are not recognized by the FCI, and these are marked NR.

In the table below, IMP denotes that the breed is on the Import Register (*see* Chapter 8). The breeds marked with an asterisk cannot be shown at conformation shows until a breed standard has been agreed with the Kennel Club. The information was up to date as at 1 December 2014.

Breed	Showing Information	UK KC Group	FCI Group Category	Breed Watch Category
Affenpinscher	Shown on a loose lead, and only stacked when on the table. Most exhibitors prefer round leather leads with half-check leather collars with a swivel in the lead section. The chain must be lightweight. Some are shown using an all-in-one nylon half-check collar and lead.	Toy	2	1
Afghan Hound	Stacked side-on to the judge, with one hand gently supporting the lower jaw. Ideally the Afghan is walked into the desired stance and any adjustments made quickly and quietly if needed, including smoothing down any parts of the coat that need attention with a brush or your hand. Front legs should be well under and rear legs back, showing good sweep from hip to hock. Leads used are generally thin, half-checks. Tails in the UK are relaxed and down when stood. The Afghan is moved at a steady pace on a loose lead to show maximum reach and drive. Head and tail should be raised naturally when moving. If it is breezy, face the dog into the wind so that the coat is blown back from the face, and if the ground is uneven or sloping always face uphill! *Figs 8.26, 9.1*	Hound	10	2
Airedale Terrier	Stacked four square on the floor. The lead is usually a half-check in black leather. Should have powerful drive from hind legs.	Terrier	3	1
Akita	Normally shown stacked, four square, and baited from the front. Shown on a double choke or choke chain and should be moved at a moderate speed on a loose lead. *Fig. 5*	Utility	5	1
Alaskan Malamute	Can be either free standing or stacked. The size and strength of the breed and its heavy coat means the lead has to be practical, but the type is up to the exhibitor. Common leads are a slip or choke chain or a martingale.	Working	5	1
Anatolian Shepherd Dog	Generally shown stacked but free stood after moving. When stacked, the Anatolian is not excessively stretched and the tail does not have to be held up in the wheel position. All show lead types are acceptable. At the trot, the gait is powerful yet fluid. When viewed from the front or rear, the legs turn neither in nor out, nor do feet cross or interfere with each other. When viewed from the side, the front legs should reach out smoothly with no obvious pounding. The withers and backline should stay nearly level with little rise or fall. The rear assembly should push out smoothly with hocks doing their share of the work and flexing well. This breed is reserved or aloof around strangers. In manner, they are proud and confident, although reserved and unenthusiastic about show ring exhibition. When alert, the tail is carried high, making a wheel. Both low and wheel carriage are acceptable when gaiting.	Pastoral	2	1

Breed	Showing Information	UK KC Group	FCI Group Category	Breed Watch Category
Australian Cattle Dog	Usually shown free standing, four square, although a few handlers stack. Should move freely. The lead is the exhibitor's choice, but should complement the coat colour and not detract from the appearance of the dog.	Pastoral	1	1
Australian Shepherd	Can be either stacked or free standing, four square. Preferably moved on a loose lead at a steady trot, not too fast. The lead is usually a thin lead and chain or half-check but not a normal collar and lead.	Pastoral	1	1
Australian Silky Terrier	Can be stacked or free stood – whatever works best to get a level topline, alert expression and erect ears. Presented to the judge on the table – sometimes on the table they will not put their ears up fully, but this should not be penalized. They require a lead that can be kept in place directly behind the ears to prevent the hair from becoming untidy.	Toy	3	1
Australian Terrier	Free standing when stood on the floor, but stacked on the table. Recommended lead has a catch which can be moved up or down the neck so that it is comfortable but secure. *Fig. 6.23*	Terrier	3	1
Azawakh* (IMP)	These are difficult dogs to show, and need to be trained from a very young age to accept and tolerate being in crowds of people, meeting strange dogs and being touched. Breed specialist judges do not excessively touch the dog to feel the muscles and condition as the distant and reserved Azawakh does not naturally tolerate physical contact by strangers. Some judges do not even try to look at the dentition, but ask the handler to present the teeth and the bite. The judge should approach from the side, and not from the front. The Azawakh should stand naturally with his hind legs in a rectangle under his pelvis. A common mistake by newcomers in the UK (and the practice in the USA) is to extend the hind legs, which pulls the topline down. The topline should be straight. A thin nylon leash or leather leash with a thin martingale collar can be used.	Hound	10	1
Basenji	Normally stacked on the table and on the floor, but some exhibitors do choose to free stand. They move on a loose lead. The normal lead would be a Double D chain collar on a nylon or leather fine lead.	Hound	5	1
Basset Bleu De Gascogne (IMP)	Can be free standing or stacked. The show lead is preferably a thin chain or leather slip lead that can be opened to the base of the neck to show off the head, neck and shoulder.	Hound	6	1

Breed	Showing Information	UK KC Group	FCI Group Category	Breed Watch Category
Basset Fauve De Bretagne) (IMP)	Stacked in line-up and generally free stood after moving. Four square, aiming for level top line, good hock angulation, not stretched, tail held in sickle shape, gentle curve, not straight up or out behind. Always tabled. Show leads can be slip or half-check but they should be plain, no bling, but not too fine as Fauves pull to sniff the ground. Plain leather generally in tan to match and blend into the coat colour. Should be a happy hound with quick movement but not racing, with tail up and wagging in a sickle shape, but not curved over the back. *Figs 2.8, 2.21, 4.5, 6.10*	Hound	6	1
Basset Griffon Vendeen (Grand)	Stacked and judged on the floor. Show leads can vary although the most popular include a leather slip collar or half-check collar, a thin leather slip lead or a chain.	Hound	6	1
Basset Griffon Vendeen (Petit)	Stacked and should be judged on the table, although some judges will request that the dogs are judged on the floor. Various types of show lead are used including a leather slip collar or half-check collar, a chain or a thin leather slip lead.	Hound	6	1
Basset Hound	Stacked on the ground. When returning to the judge they are also stacked, although some all-rounder judges may ask for a free stand. The exhibitor normally kneels behind the dog supporting the head under the chin. A practice coming from the USA is for the exhibitor to stand and hold the head up with the collar and lead. Ramps, which are used regularly abroad, are starting to be introduced in the UK, and are becoming very popular. The most popular choice of lead is a rolled leather half-check. Leather leads with beads are used occasionally, but the general thought is that a Basset is a solid, practical breed and a fancy lead does not really suit.	Hound	6	3
Bavarian Mountain Hound (IMP)	In the UK the Bavarian Mountain Hound is shown free standing, presented side-on to the judge four square on a loose lead. They can be stacked initially but never held in position. Should move on a loose lead allowing the dog to find its own pace so the natural carriage of the head and tail can be seen with a clear topline. As a guide the hound normally strides out faster than a trot but not galloping. A common show lead is leather, and thin enough to not spoil the line of the neck. *Fig. 8.30*	Hound	6	1
Beagle	Judged on the table. In the ring they can be free standing or stacked. Main show leads used are a fine chain and lead, a fine leather slip lead, a fine nylon/cotton slip lead or a half-check collar and lead in leather or nylon. *Fig. 1.2*	Hound	6	1

Breed	Showing Information	UK KC Group	FCI Group Category	Breed Watch Category
Bearded Collie	Traditionally the Bearded Collie was shown free standing but the current trend is for the majority to be shown stacked; both methods are acceptable. Front legs should be well under the dog and it should never be over-stretched at the rear. Movement is free, supple, smooth and long-reaching. The overall effect is that of a dog covering plenty of ground with the minimum of effort. Choice of show collar/lead is normally a lightweight chain slip collar with an appropriate lead attached, or a three-quarter slip collar, again with lead of choice attached.	Pastoral	1	2
Beauceron	Free standing, and the show lead can be whatever the handler is comfortable with. The main thing to remember is not to 'chop off' the neck line or restrict the movement. Black is best as it complements the colour of the dog.	Working	1	1
Bedlington Terrier	Can be either stacked or free standing. Exhibitors use a very fine lead to match the coat colour. The movement should be light and slightly mincing as explained in the breed standard. They require grooming and trimming.	Terrier	3	2
Belgian Shepherd Dogs (Groenendael) (Laekenois) (Malinois) (Tervueren)	Free standing. Most breed specialist judges and exhibitors prefer to show the dog facing outwards at the end of its lead to show alertness, which is an essential breed characteristic. The handler stands behind the dog allowing him to show a keen watchful trait with ears high up and an alert enquiring look. Some judges, however, prefer dogs shown side-on and baited. The breed is normally shown on rolled leather show sets: a rolled leather lead and rolled leather half-check collar. *Figs 2.16, 11.3*	Pastoral	1	1
Bergamasco (IMP)	Can be stacked or free standing. They are a large breed and handlers sometimes have a problem stacking if they are not able to stretch along the length of the dog. Given the unique coat texture, if using a collar it must be a fine American-style no-tangle chain otherwise it will tangle or tear out the coat. A sturdy, fine leather slip collar with a matching leather lead is the alternative. Bear in mind the need to remain in control of the dog at all times! *Pic 9.13*	Pastoral	1	1
Bernese Mountain Dog	Free standing and should be stood four square giving the best outline and showing off height to length ratio, reach of neck, slope of shoulder and ideally a medium turn of stifle. Exhibitors show on a variety of leads, but a slim leather slip lead or a fine choke chain on a leather lead is ideal. Some exhibitors use a classic wide leather collar and lead.	Working	2	1

Breed	Showing Information	UK KC Group	FCI Group Category	Breed Watch Category
Bichon Frise	A table dog usually shown stacked, the handler using the lead to hold the head up. The tail should be carried over the back of the dog and can be held by the exhibitor if necessary. A kindness collar is preferable for showing, with whatever lead the exhibitor finds most compatible with their dog. Bichons are gay, lively happy dogs and should move energetically, head held high, and moving with reach and drive.	Toy	9	1
Bloodhound	Stacked with the tail held high in a scimitar shape. The lead will be a check chain or a very sturdy slip lead.	Hound	6	3
Bolognese	This is a table dog which can be either stacked or free standing. The show lead should be small and fine. A chain collar is not recommended. Their movement should be very brisk and active. The breed is shown in its natural state and is never trimmed for the show ring.	Toy	9	1
Border Collie	Usually shown in a slip chain and thin leather lead. They must never fly their tail over their back, but move with grace and athleticism. When they set off, they should lower the head and move with very little lift of paw. Both free standing and stacking are acceptable. *Figs 1.24, 2.17, 6.14, 6.15*	Pastoral	1	1
Border Terrier	Shown on the table. This is a smart breed which looks best moving freely on the lead and ideally not strung up. Most exhibitors free stand, but some stack. Mainly shown on a white slip lead, but if the neck is dark they look better on a black lead. Should move freely, gracefully and with style, and all legs moving straight ahead, neither toeing in nor out.	Terrier	3	1
Borzoi	Generally stacked, but the judge may ask for the dog to free stand after moving to determine that the dog can stand four square without aid from the handler. Slip leads in leather or cord, or a fine chain and lead, are most commonly used. The Borzoi should be moved on a loose lead to allow correct head carriage. Movement should be powerful with long and low front extension in front through the shoulder, and drive from behind. Cow hocks, hackney gait, or high-lifting goose-steps should be penalized. Temperament is aloof but this should not be mistaken for shyness. Any nervous or aggressive behaviour towards other dogs or the judge should be heavily penalized. *Fig. 1.3*	Hound	10	2

Breed	Showing Information	UK KC Group	FCI Group Category	Breed Watch Category
Boston Terrier	This is a table dog which should be free standing, but some people do stack. The Boston is a smart breed and looks best moving freely on the lead and not strung up. They are mainly shown on a white slip lead, but not all have the full white collar and if the neck is dark they look better on a black lead. They should move freely, gracefully and with style, all legs moving straight ahead, neither toeing in nor out.	Terrier	3	2
Bouvier des Flandres	Can be shown either stacked or free standing. They are usually shown on a rolled leather slip lead or leather lead with half-check collar.	Working	1	1
Boxer	This breed can be stacked or free standing with the exhibitor keeping the dog's attention with bait. They can be held under the neck by the handler, but stringing up with the lead tight under the neck is more common in the USA. They should have a strong powerful movement with noble bearing, reaching well forward and with driving action of hindquarters. *Figs 2.9, 4.3, 6.4*	Working	2	1
Bracco Italiano	Can be either stacked or free standing, depending on the dog and exhibitor. The lead is predominantly a slip lead, sometimes a half-check.	Gundog	7	1
Briard	Stacked. The majority of exhibitors use a fairly fine check chain with a slim leather or nylon lead. Some people use half-checks. Slip leads are never used with this breed.	Pastoral	1	1
Brittany	Can be either free standing or stacked. In France they tend to be stacked. The lead is usually a thin chain with a thin leather lead, but it is up to the exhibitor's preference. *Figs 1.19, 6.19, 8.13, 11.9*	Gundog	7	1
Bull Terrier	Shown on the floor and should be free standing. The preferred show lead is a white rope slip lead.	Terrier	3	2
Bull Terrier (Miniature)	Judged on the table, and shown free standing in the ring. Generally exhibitors use a white webbing slip lead or thin chain and leather lead. Other colours are sometimes used depending on the colour of the dog. *Fig. 2.29*	Terrier	3	2

Breed	Showing Information	UK KC Group	FCI Group Category	Breed Watch Category
Bulldog	Free standing and always presented front on to the judge, with the back two feet slightly drawn in to the front. This breed is not stood four square – you should always be able to see the back feet through the front legs. The movement is known as a barrel roll and is unique to the bulldog. The lead should be a fine snake chain with a thin lead or thin slip lead to show the arch of the neck. While bulldogs are mostly examined on the ground, it is becoming increasingly common to use ramps. *Figs 2.23, 2.24, 5.32, 7.5, 7.6*	Utility	2	3
Bullmastiff	Can be stacked but should always be presented three-quarters on to the judge. Should stand four square and need little adjustment after moving out. Head can be lifted when standing but on the move should be carried roughly level with the top line. Should be moved on a loose lead; a check chain and leather lead is recommended. Slow and steady pace, not flying around the ring! *Figs 5.3, 9.6*	Working	2	1
Cairn Terrier	In the UK the Cairn is shown free standing on a loose lead, and is never stacked except when on the table being examined by the judge. They should be moved at a trot, but not too fast and preferably on a loose lead. Cairns are normally shown on a light leather lead with a half-chain or light check chain. Some exhibitors use nylon leads. *Figs 1.26, 11.4*	Terrier	3	1
Canaan Dog	Usually stacked square. The handler holds the lead above the head, and holds the tail so it curls over the back. The lead is the exhibitor's choice; a thin chain collar and clip-on lead is good for dogs which are steady and dependable, with a martingale type collar and lead for dogs (especially puppies) which might pull back.	Utility	5	1
Canadian Eskimo Dog	Free standing. It is desirable to use a choke chain or half-choke chain when showing. *Fig. 4.6*	Working	5	1
Catalan Sheepdog	Can be stacked or free standing. Examples of leads include a bracelet check chain and leather lead, or half-check collar; it's important to avoid anything that would snag the coat. Shown in its natural coat with no trimming whatsoever. Should be shown in clean condition, but not subjected to regular bathing as this softens the coat.	Pastoral	1	1
Cavalier King Charles Spaniel	Free standing four square and not stacked. They should be walked freely in the ring, and not held tightly on the lead. A reasonably lightweight lead is preferable. *Figs 5.2, 6.29*	Toy	9	1

Breed	Showing Information	UK KC Group	FCI Group Category	Breed Watch Category
Cesky Terrier	Judged on the table. Usually shown on a check or half-check collar.	Terrier	3	2
Chihuahua (Long Coat) (Smooth Coat)	Shown free standing, and judged on the table. There is no recommended show lead, but should be a light lead. Should move briskly without a high step or hackney action. It is particularly important with this breed to make sure a puppy is show quality. Potential exhibitors should visit shows to see the type being shown. *Fig. 8.19*	Toy	9	1
Chinese Crested	Judged on the table. They can be either free standing or stacked. The recommended show lead is a half-check. *Figs 1.11, 3.3, 6.2, 9.14*	Toy	9	2
Chow Chow	Normally free standing four square. Will often stand for bait. Generally Chows are shown on the floor although the Kennel Club has just granted permission for them to use a table/ramp. Most Chow exhibitors use a rolled leather collar plus a stout leather lead as they are very powerful once they decide not to co-operate. Movement is very specific with its stilted gait from the hindquarters. They should step out at a reasonable pace but should not be raced around the show ring. The best advice for newcomers to the breed is to get their Chow socialized from a very young age so they are used to being approached and handled; also, practise showing the mouth, which must also be opened to check the black tongue and dark pigmentation around the gums, roof of mouth, etc. When approaching Chows, always tickle them under the chin first and never attempt to pat them on the head until you are properly introduced! *Figs 6.26, 7.3*	Utility	5	3
Cirneco Dell'Etna (IMP)	Usually presented free standing, but sometimes stacked. Some judges in the UK ask the breed to be presented on the table, but the table is not used in their country of origin. The most common lead is a fine lightweight show lead matching the coat colour. *Fig. 8.29*	Hound	5	1
Collie (Rough)	Free standing. Recommended leads are a rolled leather half-check, a rolled leather slip lead, or a thin chain with a leather/fabric lead. *Fig. 1.25*	Pastoral	1	2
Collie (Smooth)	Usually shown free standing in the UK. Exhibitors prefer a light choke chain and a narrow leather or nylon show lead. The Smooth Collie is moved at a brisk trot to demonstrate his reach and driving movement.	Pastoral	1	2

Breed	Showing Information	UK KC Group	FCI Group Category	Breed Watch Category
Coton de Tulear	Judged on the table, and free standing. The lead is down to individual preference, but should have an adjustable neck with satin padding under the chin.	Toy	9	1
Dachshund (Long-Haired) (Smooth-Haired) (Wire-Haired)	Judged on the table. Most are stacked with very few free standing. They are usually shown on checks or half-checks with fairly narrow leads.	Hound	4	1
Dachshund (Miniature Long-Haired) (Miniature Smooth-Haired) (Miniature Wire-Haired)	Judged on the table. Most are stacked with very few free standing. They are usually shown on checks or half-checks with fairly narrow leads. Miniature Dachshunds can be weighed by the judge at the discretion of the show society. If they are to be weighed a notice informing exhibitors of this must be included at the beginning of the relevant breed classification in the schedule.	Hound	4	2
Dalmatian	Free standing, ideally on a loose lead. The usual show lead is either a complete slip lead in leather or nylon, or a half-check collar and lead. The colour is usually black for black-spotted Dalmatians, and brown for liver-spotted.	Utility	6	1
Dandie Dinmont Terrier	Judged on the table. When standing in the line-up some dogs are free standing, but the majority of exhibitors kneel beside the dog and present them stacked. Dandies can be shown on a number of leads, from slip leads and half-check collars to conventional collars and leads. *Fig. 4.8*	Terrier	3	1
Deerhound	Free standing in a natural state. It should be clean and brushed, but not heavily stripped. Deerhounds are shown on a loose lead and should not be strung up. *Fig. 3.5*	Hound	10	1
Dobermann	Can be shown stacked or free standing. The type and length of lead are down to personal preference. The dog should run freely. *Figs 5.1, 6.22*	Working	2	1
Dogue de Bordeaux	Stacked facing the judge in the UK, but some overseas judges prefer them to free stand. A slip lead is recommended. *Figs 4.7, 8.17, 8.25*	Working	2	3
English Setter	Shown stacked with handler holding head and tail. Can be shown on a loose lead, but generally they are shown on a tighter lead. The lead is usually a leather slip lead. Should trot round the ring elegantly. *Fig. 1.8*	Gundog	7	1

Breed	Showing Information	UK KC Group	FCI Group Category	Breed Watch Category
English Toy Terrier (Black & Tan)	The breed is initially presented side-on to the judge and free standing to emphasize the dog's head carriage, unique top line and construction. The lead is either held up above the dog's head or loose around the shoulders. The breed is examined by the judge on the table where it is usually stacked to ensure control, and often baited to encourage an alert expression and high-set ears. The breed standard asks for movement 'akin to an extended trot' so exhibitors have to move the dog at a brisk pace to allow the dog to demonstrate this gait. Fine rolled leather leads with silver, brass or black chains are usually used for showing. *Fig. 2.27*	Toy	3	1
Entlebucher Mountain Dog (IMP)	Can be free standing or stacked. By nature they are cautious of strangers, so it is important they are trained for the show ring and judges should not loom over them. A loose lead is necessary to show free easy movement with a good drive from the hindquarters. As a new breed to showing, there is not yet a preferred look, but exhibitors often use a half-check show set, but start puppies on a slip lead. *Fig. 3.4*	Working	2	1
Estrela Mountain Dog	Usually stacked. Some handlers prefer to free stand, but this is unusual. The dog should not be overstretched. Often leather or corded slip leads are used. The dog should never be 'strung up', and should be led around the ring on a loose lead.	Pastoral	2	1
Eurasier	Free standing, and legs should not be placed by the handler. Various show leads can be used, including fixed check rolled leather collars or a metal check which lies flat and doesn't trap hair.	Utility	5	1
Finnish Lapphund	A free standing or stacked breed with very little or no adjustment required. The tail can be either dropped or held over the back when standing, as long as it goes up over the back on the move. Moved at a steady trot or fast walk on a loose lead, but not too fast as they tend to change into a gallop quite easily. They should have an effortless gait, covering the ground well. They are usually shown on a light lead with a half collar or thin check chain.	Pastoral	5	1
Finnish Spitz	Free standing. Usually shown on a half-check show lead.	Hound	5	1
Fox Terrier (Smooth)	Free standing and should not be stacked except on the table for the judge's examination. A leather or nylon lead with half-chain or full chain check is normally used for the show ring. Smooth fox terriers do need trimming around the head, neck and tail, which can be done carefully with clippers or with thinning scissors.	Terrier	3	1

Breed	Showing Information	UK KC Group	FCI Group Category	Breed Watch Category
Fox Terrier (Wire Haired)	Wire Haired Fox Terriers are examined by the judge on the table. The breed is stacked in the ring. A variety of leads are used, with a white slip lead being most common. By tradition professional handlers have been involved in exhibiting the breed. *Fig. 1.18*	Terrier	3	1
Foxhound	Free standing, although young or new handlers can stack. A half-check chain or leather collar looks best, with a strong enough lead to hold this powerful rear-drive breed when moving. Movement should be free with symmetry and balance. Foxhounds are bred to run 80 miles plus daily, so should be full of power and drive. *Fig. 1.1*	Hound	6	1
French Bulldog	Judged on the table. Preferably free standing in the line-up, but some exhibitors kneel and stack as is the norm abroad. This breed should move freely with drive and is usually shown on a half-check. A short tail is required and in some other countries this breed is weighed.	Utility	9	2
German Longhaired Pointer	Always shown free standing. The tail is not held out and is carried horizontally or just below the line of the back. The head may be held to keep the dog still during the judge's examination. A lightweight show lead is preferable. The lead should be held loosely so as not to restrict the natural movement. Should have free, long striding, stylish and graceful movement with good forward reach and powerful drive from the hindquarters. The breed combines power with grace, pace with style, and displays a quiet and equable disposition. *Fig. 8.6*	Gundog	7	1
German Pinscher	Can be either stacked or free standing. Moved on a loose lead at a fairly fast pace. Show lead normally thin leather but the choice is what's most comfortable for the handler.	Working	2	1
German Shepherd Dog	Presented side-on to the judge with the two front legs positioned perpendicular to the ground and parallel to each other. The toes of the rear foot furthest from the judge should be placed so that they are in a vertical line with the front of the pelvis. The rear foot closest to the judge should be positioned so that the metatarsus is in a vertical position, not angled and definitely not overstretched. The neck chain should be positioned low on the neck during the individual presentation, walking and gaiting. As German Shepherd Dogs are trotting dogs, at specialist events the majority of the judging is done during gaiting. Therefore the unique gait of the German Shepherd Dog, displaying great energy and vitality while covering the maximum amount of ground with the least amount of effort through a firm topline, is paramount to its assessment. *Fig. 2.15*	Pastoral	1	3

Breed	Showing Information	UK KC Group	FCI Group Category	Breed Watch Category
German Shorthaired Pointer	This breed is always stacked, with the handler holding the head, which should be forward to show the neck, not upright. Tail is held straight out, which is easier with docked dogs. With undocked dogs handlers either let the tail hang naturally or hold it out. Dogs are moved at a trot, preferably on a loose lead. *Fig. 3.17*	Gundog	7	1
German Spitz (Klein)	Table dog. Free standing on the ground.	Utility	5	1
German Spitz (Mittel)	Table dog. Free standing on the ground. *Fig. 3.16*	Utility	5	1
German Wirehaired Pointer	Can be stacked or free standing. The choice of lead is the exhibitor's preference.	Gundog	7	1
Giant Schnauzer	Stacked or free standing, and both options should be trained. Judges may have a preference for how the dog should be shown, and handlers should observe previous classes if possible to see which the judge prefers. The type and length of the lead are the choice of the handler.	Working	2	1
Glen of Imaal Terrier	Judged on the table. Must be shown on a lead that can control the dog; a slip chain is preferred by many exhibitors. This breed looks best free stood, but stacking is often resorted to.	Terrier	3	1
Gordon Setter	Usually stacked, and handler may stand or kneel. Must stand with a level topline. Handler will place one hand under the jaw, and hold and extend the tail with the other. Hind legs will be slightly extended to show good bend of stifle but must not be exaggerated or cause the topline to slope. The head and neck should not be pulled upright using the lead. Should be moved on a loose lead at a steady gait, but not too fast, to show drive from behind. *Fig. 4.9*	Gundog	7	2
Grand Bleu de Gascogne (IMP)	Can be either free standing or stacked. The show lead is preferably a thin chain or leather slip lead that can be opened to the base of the neck to show off the head, neck and shoulder.	Hound	6	1
Great Dane	Shown free standing on a fine leather loose slip lead. The action when moving should be lithe, springy and free, covering the ground with drive. *Fig. 8.1*	Working	2	2
Greater Swiss Mountain Dog (IMP)	Shown free standing in the UK, but may be stacked on the continent. The show lead is up to the handler. *Fig. 1.7*	Working	2	1

Breed	Showing Information	UK KC Group	FCI Group Category	Breed Watch Category
Greenland Dog	Preferably shown free standing. A good strong leather lead is the best choice. Other materials can be used, but strength is the number one consideration as these dogs are extremely powerful.	Working	5	1
Greyhound	Shown stacked on a thin leather lead. The movement should be a long and low stride which covers plenty of ground. *Figs 5.33, 6.31*	Hound	10	1
Griffon Bruxellois	Judged on the table. Should be shown free standing – stacking is frowned upon. The usual type of lead used is a fine martingale. *Fig. 8.22*	Toy	9	1
Griffon Fauve de Bretagne (IMP)	This breed is shown stacked on the floor. It can be presented free standing and will normally be shown on a slip lead or half-check lead. The coat is tidied in order to give a clean outline but should not be over-groomed or sculpted. The dog should ideally be moved on a loose lead but this is a personal preference.	Hound	6	1
Hamiltonstovare	Free standing. The usual lead is thin leather with a chain collar. They should move on a loose lead.	Hound	6	1
Havanese	Shown stacked, either by the handler or self-stacked, with the tail curved over the back (it may be held in that position by the handler). The Havanese should be gaited on a loose lead, at a moderate pace, so the typical springy gait can be demonstrated. The tail should be held in an arch over the back during movement. Any appropriate show lead can be used. *Figs 5.12, 8.4, 11.8*	Toy	9	1
Hovawart	Free standing and moved on a loose lead. Many exhibitors choose a complete leather slip lead or a three-ring slip, but the lead is mainly down to individual choice.	Working	2	1
Hungarian Kuvasz	Information not available as the breed is not currently shown in the UK	Pastoral	1	1
Hungarian Puli	Judged on the table. Can be either free standing or stacked on the floor, and shown on a half-check leather collar. *Figs 9.10, 9.11, 9.12*	Pastoral	1	1

Breed	Showing Information	UK KC Group	FCI Group Category	Breed Watch Category
Hungarian Pumi* (IMP)	Usually judged on the table in FCI countries, but some judges don't use the table. The Pumi is an aloof breed and does not like strangers hovering over it while on the ground. Can be either stacked or free standing. When stacked, the natural structure should be shown without exaggerated pulling of the hind legs rearwards. Exhibitors can use whichever lead their dog is most comfortable with: FCI exhibitors prefer a half-chain, rolled leather or a very thin American collar. Bling leads are not used as this is a herding dog. Movement should be sprightly, alert and ready to spring into action.	Pastoral	1	1
Hungarian Vizsla	Stacked and usually shown on a leather slip lead. They should move with a graceful, elegant movement at a lively trot. *Fig. 0.1*	Gundog	7	1
Hungarian Wire Haired Vizsla	Normally stacked holding the head under the chin and the tail in the required position. Some people will bring the lead under the jaw to hold the head up, but that doesn't look so natural. It is perfectly acceptable to free stand, but it is not the norm. Show leads are personal preference and range from fine leather slip leads to ones with a fine chain or a slim rope.	Gundog	7	1
Ibizan Hound	Can either be stacked or free standing; when free standing, the exhibitor stands in front of the dog holding his attention. Most exhibitors use a narrow slip lead. Best moved on a loose lead brought from under the chin to keep the head up. Should not be moved at a fast pace. The movement should be a long far-reaching stride at the extended trot, with a slight hover before putting the foot to the ground. The breed tends to be reserved with strangers, and is dignified, intelligent and independent.	Hound	5	1
Irish Red & White Setter	Stacked in the ring with the handler's right hand gently holding the head up a little, and the left hand holding the tail straight out. A soft narrow slip lead is preferred. This breed moves positively with drive and a smooth action. *Fig. 4.11*	Gundog	7	1
Irish Setter	Stacked in the ring with hind legs extended, the handler kneeling or standing behind them holding the head and the tail. The judge often expects a free stand after moving. A dark brown leather slip lead is the most common lead used. Should have a driving, balanced movement with perfect co-ordination. *Figs 1.20, 2.12, 5.29, 6.1*	Gundog	7	1

Breed	Showing Information	UK KC Group	FCI Group Category	Breed Watch Category
Irish Terrier	Free standing, and look their best when naturally interested in the other exhibits or activities going on around them which encourages good use of ears and stretching of the body to give the correct racy outline. The American style of handling using bait to attract their attention is creeping in, but strictly this is not the way an Irish Terrier should be presented. The breed can be presented to the judge on the table or the floor depending on judge and handler preference. It is useful to train for both options. An ideal show lead is a double slip chain collar or part chain with the neck piece in leather. The lead would be fine leather. *Fig. 8.12*	Terrier	3	2
Irish Wolfhound	Stacked. The object of showing a giant breed is to display your ability to control such a large beast, therefore a slim leather lead is recommended. Shown on the move with a loose lead; 'stringing-up' is not desired. When stacked, the front legs should be in line with the shoulder, and the rear legs not too stretched, showing muscle tone and tuck-up to the best advantage. Movement in the ring varies; as it is a galloping breed, some judges want it shown at speed, others can assess its qualities with a more relaxed gentle jog! *Fig. 9.15*	Hound	10	2
Italian Greyhound	Judged on the table. Generally stacked, and handlers can stand or kneel. Can be shown on a loose lead, but most are shown with the lead held above their head. They should move at a brisk walking pace. Show leads are fine leather half-checks or slip leads. *Fig. 3.15*	Toy	10	1
Italian Spinone	Stacked to show off their square outline. Normally shown on either a rope/fabric or leather slip lead. The lead is then placed back on the shoulders when stood. Docked Spinone are stood with their tail held out level with their top line; undocked dogs are stood with the tail left down. The movement should be a free relaxed gait, so unlike many other gundogs they are not shown moving at a high speed. They are moved on a loose lead and not strung up.	Gundog	7	1

Breed	Showing Information	UK KC Group	FCI Group Category	Breed Watch Category
Japanese Akita Inu	This breed is presented in the traditional Japanese way 'head on' to the judge at a 45 degree angle to allow all of the key features such as body depth and proportion, strength of back, tail set and carriage to be seen, and allowing the dog to demonstrate his confidence and aloofness to the judge: essential character traits. The lead is a specially designed leather collar, a small link, close-fitting check chain and traditional Japanese tassel lead usually made from either silk or cotton thread. It is very long and has a rope-like appearance with a large tassel on the end of the handle. It is a replica of the leads used by the Samurai and adds to the overall appearance because the handler can stand well away from the dog. The 'Japanese' collar places the ring for the lead on top of the neck instead of underneath. Properly fitted, it will enhance the features of the head by framing the face with neck hair, so adding to the rounded appearance of the skull: a highly desirable feature as described in the breed standard. The check chain should fit onto the neck leaving only a small amount of chain spare so that it holds its position in front of the collar when the dog is presented in a static position. The correct pace for the dog is a rhythmic trot which allows the judge to see a resilient action when viewing the dog from the side. When moving away from the judge it is expected that the dog can hold a straight line and show convergence of the limbs towards a centre line, thus creating a single track of footprints. *Fig. 2.11*	Utility	5	1
Japanese Chin	Free standing. The recommended lead is a thin half-check or slip lead.	Toy	9	1
Japanese Shiba Inu	Judged on the table, most commonly stacked but can be free standing. The American half-choke is probably the most common lead, but some people prefer 'bling'-type leads. In the UK and Japan white Shibas can be shown, whereas in the US and FCI countries they are not recognized. Movement should be a lively, athletic gait with head and ears held erect and tail set on their back. A Shiba should push from the front, not the rear end.	Utility	5	1
Japanese Spitz	Judged on the table, free standing. Most exhibitors use a half-check. *Fig. 4.2*	Utility	5	1
Keeshond	Free standing, but often require bait of some sort to keep their attention. It is usual to use a rolled leather show lead combined with a rolled leather collar or half-choke. *Figs 5.9, 6.18*	Utility	5	2

Breed	Showing Information	UK KC Group	FCI Group Category	Breed Watch Category
Kerry Blue Terrier	Free standing, but the handler will hold the dog's head up with the lead. A rolled leather collar and lead is often used. *Fig. 5.7*	Terrier	3	1
King Charles Spaniel	Should be shown free standing. Show leads are the exhibitor's choice. These are very friendly dogs, although on some occasions they can be a bit possessive of their owners. Their coats do not have to be clipped. Their movement should be sound. They should have a domed head, a good reach of neck, and their nose, ears and eyes should be in a straight line, well cushioned under the eyes; other attributes include a level top-line, short in back, good spring of rib and good bone.	Toy	9	1
Komondor	Usually shown free standing on a loose lead, whichever type suits the dog and handler.	Pastoral	1	1
Kooikerhondje	Shown free standing on the floor in their country of origin and the UK, but sometimes the judge will go over nervy puppies on the table. They are most commonly shown with a half-check collar and appropriate thin lead, often white or tan depending on the colour of the dog. Can be aloof with strangers so plenty of early socializing is essential, both with people and dogs, to prepare them for the ring.	Utility	8	1
Korean Jindo (IMP)	Shown on a loose lead and can be either stacked or free standing side-on to the judge. A slip lead or half-check collar is used, with length of lead to suit the handler. The dog should be allowed to move freely.	Utility	5	1
Korthals Griffon (IMP)	Judged on the table, but presented to the judge in a free stand. Generally a long slip lead of the woven type is preferred, but often a general walking slip lead is used. Both would be made from man-made materials in green, brown or black.	Gundog	7	1
Lagotto Romagnolo (IMP)	Can be free standing or stacked, but always presented side-on to the judge. Should move on a loose lead and at a good pace. An all-in-one slip lead is recommended, either leather or fabric. Breed experts and Italian judges know the importance of ear carriage, so even if stacked in the ring, it is recommended to free stand and bait at the end of the movement in the hope that the dog will prick his ears up when the judge takes his final look.	Gundog	8	1
Lakeland Terrier	Judged on the table. Stacked. Recommended collars and leads are cloth or fine rolled leather as chain can damage the hair. Lakelands should move freely, straight and true, neither toeing in nor wide. Should drive with the hind legs with a stride capable of covering ground. Should have a perfect scissor bite.	Terrier	3	1

Breed	Showing Information	UK KC Group	FCI Group Category	Breed Watch Category
Lancashire Heeler	Free standing with the handler standing to the front or slightly to the side of the dog and moved on a loose lead, normally using a half-check collar in nylon or leather. Judged on the table, with the handler lightly holding the lead near the neck to steady the dog. Mostly shown using titbits or a toy, and judges often use something to attract them to check their ear carriage, which can be erect or tipped with a slight lift. The tail is not held up, and can be up or down, but usually comes up on the move. This breed does not need to be over-handled on the table, particularly around the head, as their smooth coat means the judge can see what he needs to see with just a quick going-over of the body to check the flatness of skull, fore chest, level topline, front and rear angulation and musculature. The front feet can turn out slightly, which would enable the dog to turn quickly while doing the job he was bred for: that is, getting in low to nip the heels of cattle and quickly turning and ducking out of the way of flying hooves. The back should not be too long in the loin, with the dog being just slightly longer than his height at the withers; the hind legs should be parallel both standing and moving, and the gait should be brisk and easy on the move. *Figs 3.2, 8.2*	Pastoral	NR	1
Large Munsterlander	Can be stacked or free standing, and shown on a slip lead or half-check. Not trimmed except to tidy the feet. *Figs 6.12, 8.11*	Gundog	7	1
Leonberger	The judge can request the dog be stacked or free standing. Some judges will expect the dogs to be stacked when they are first seen, and then free standing on return to the judge. The most common lead is a link chain collar and a strong but fine lead.	Working	2	1
Lhasa Apso	Stacked. The coat should be trimmed to touch the ground with no excess. The hair on the head must be left natural: no bands, bow or clips are allowed in the ring. The lead is completely down to the exhibitor's preference. Most use a push-down show lead or martingale lead, although some prefer half-check chains.	Utility	9	1
Lowchen (Little Lion Dog)	Judged on the table. Can be stacked or free stood in the ring. They should be shown on a half-check or whichever lead the dog is used to. They should not be strung up, and should be moved at a steady pace.	Toy	9	1
Maltese	Judged on the table, and can be stacked or free standing. Most exhibitors use a Kindness lead. When moving, the breed should have a proud head carriage, with a driving movement, but appear to glide across the ground.	Toy	9	1

Breed	Showing Information	UK KC Group	FCI Group Category	Breed Watch Category
Manchester Terrier	Judged on the table. Some people free stand their dogs, and others place the feet into position. At the end of moving round the ring, the dog is usually presented to the judge free standing. Most exhibitors use a black or dark brown leather show lead with an integral half-check collar. *Fig. 6.25*	Terrier	3	1
Maremma Sheepdog	Free standing. A variety of leads can be used depending on dog and handler preference, but a check chain and leather lead or a thin rope lead are the most common. Their movement should be free flowing with head and tail carried low so as to form a straight line from head to tail.	Pastoral	1	1
Mastiff	Stacked. There is no standard show lead. Leads have to be extremely robust. Some use a soft leather show collar and matching lead, but others use a chain. It can be a problem to find large enough collars! *Fig. 7.4*	Working	2	3
Mexican Hairless (Xoloitzcuintle): (Intermediate) (IMP) (Miniature) (IMP) (Standard) (IMP)	Standard Xolos are examined on the ground, while intermediate and miniature Xolos are presented on the table. All varieties are presented side-on to the judge, with the back feet slightly drawn out from the rear. This breed is not stood four square – you should always be able to see the front feet through the rear legs, with a slight slant to the back starting just behind the shoulders. Free standing and stacking are permitted. All three sizes (hairless and coated) are exhibited together. The dog should move freely with a long, elegant, springy step; the trot is quick and flowing with head and tail carried high. Hindquarters have free and strong movement. The lead should be a fine one – either snake chain or a leather slip lead to show the arch of the neck.	Utility	5	1
Miniature Pinscher	Shown free standing, and should never be stacked. Examined by the judge on the table. The breed standard calls for complete self-possession. The most commonly used lead is a soft leather half-check. The 'Min Pin' is characterized by its precise hackney action and fearless animation, and is known as the 'King of the Toys'. *Fig. 2.13*	Toy	2	1
Miniature Schnauzer	Judged on the table. Can be stacked or free stood, but some judges do not allow stacking. Show leads are usually thin and adjustable, and the usual colour is black.	Utility	2	1
Neapolitan Mastiff	Can be stacked or free standing. The show lead is down to personal preference. This breed often paces, with a bear-like movement in walk and a feline movement in trot. Pacing is not considered a fault under experienced judges.	Working	2	3

Breed	Showing Information	UK KC Group	FCI Group Category	Breed Watch Category
Newfoundland	Can be stacked or free standing. In the UK the breed is mainly stacked, but in the US many are free standing. Front feet should be in a vertical line below the withers, with the hind paws placed about an inch behind the vertical line from the hip joint. Should run on a fairly loose lead at a pace which suits the dog. The hind feet should step into the track left by the front feet. Show leads tend to be a very fine, thin check chain with a fine, thin leather lead. Dark brown or black is used for black dogs, but some use coloured leads on white/black dogs. Should be bathed before a show and properly trimmed. *Figs 6.11, 8.3*	Terrier	3	1
Norfolk Terrier	Judged on the table and stacked. Should move on a loose lead. This is a very busy breed and should not be expected to stand still for long periods. *Fig. 8.21*	Terrier	3	1
Norwegian Buhund	Should be shown free standing in profile to the judge, with the handler standing at the dog's head in front of the dog. The dog is encouraged to hold his tail high, look alert and stand square. The most common lead is a check or snake chain or half-check. They should be moved on a loose lead with a nice, light and free movement.	Pastoral	5	1
Norwegian Elkhound	Free standing. Exhibitors normally use a rolled leather half-check collar and a fine leather lead.	Hound	5	1
Norwich Terrier	Judged on the table. Shown on a loose lead on the floor. Stacking or touching the dog while on the floor is very much frowned upon, as it is considered they should show themselves. Experienced judges do not expect the breed to stand still while on the floor – the dogs are allowed to move around. The choice of lead is down to dog or handler preference, but they are not usually shown on leather slip leads.	Terrier	3	2
Old English Sheepdog	Free standing. They are usually shown on a light chain collar with a material lead. *Figs 9.2, 9.3*	Pastoral	1	2
Otterhound	Free standing. The lead should be whatever best suits the hound, enabling sufficient control for it to stand freely and to move out with typical stride and show freely. Otterhounds have a low boredom threshold and the puppies remain very tired after the stress of a day's showing. They should not be over-shown and their owners must keep it fun for them.	Hound	6	1

Breed	Showing Information	UK KC Group	FCI Group Category	Breed Watch Category
Papillon	Judged on the table, stacked, but free standing when shown in the ring. Most dogs are shown on fine rolled leather show leads, although some exhibitors use nylon leads. *Figs 1.9, 1.29, 1.30, 5.31*	Terrier	9	1
Parson Russell Terrier	In the UK Parsons are shown either free standing or stacked. They should be moved at a brisk walk, preferably not over-strung as they should have a ground-covering gait. Parsons are normally shown on a light leather lead with a half-chain or with a light check chain or nylon show lead. *Figs 1.21, 1.22*	Terrier	3	1
Pekingese	Shown stacked on the ground and on the table, facing forward as they are a head breed. After individual examination, they are lined up along a succession of tables still facing forward for the judge's final look and placement. Breed specialists often move them before assessing them on the table as they are notoriously aloof and stubborn. Most people show them on a loose leash around their shoulders so as to keep their mane full and intact. Handlers can take brushes into the ring with them to keep brushing the full leonine bloom into their manes and to fan their tails over their back. Judge should also pick the exhibits up on the table to ascertain that they are 'surprisingly heavy for their size'. The breed is characterized by a slow, dignified, rolling gait which must never be hurried or rushed around the ring. *Fig. 5.10*	Toy	9	3
Pharaoh Hound	Free standing. Leads are a matter of personal choice, but most people use lightweight slip leads or a smart half-check. Some exhibitors like to 'string up' their dog round the throat to stretch the neck, but a slack lead/collar looks more natural. Some judges prefer the dog to be run on a loose lead, but some continental judges like to see a taut lead when on the move.	Hound	5	1
Picardy Sheepdog (IMP)*	This is a very new breed to the UK and numbers are currently low. The breed can be stacked or free stood to stand four square for the judge. It is a wary breed and needs to be approached slowly. They dislike being handled by a stranger, so going over the dog needs patience and time. They should not be shown on a tight choke chain.	Pastoral	1	1
Pointer	Pointers are stacked, and normally a leather lead is used. When stacked, the lead is placed over the shoulders to enhance the shoulder placement. They should be moved on a loose lead so they can move freely and at a pace to cover the ground, with head up and tail lashing from side to side. *Figs 2.7, 2.25, 6.5, 6.13, 6.16*	Gundog	7	1

Breed	Showing Information	UK KC Group	FCI Group Category	Breed Watch Category
Polish Lowland Sheepdog	Free standing. The most common show lead is a check chain and lead.	Pastoral	1	1
Pomeranian	Free standing with feet four square. The head should lie right back into his shoulders, looking up at his handler, and his tail plume should lie over his back, carried flat and meeting his ears, giving the desired round shape. Examined on the table. Movement should be free, brisk and buoyant; some move on a tight lead, some on a loose lead. Lead type is personal preference but generally a light, delicate lead is best. Pomeranians should be extrovert, lively and show great intelligence.	Toy	5	2
Poodle (Miniature)	Usually a stacked breed, but some do free stand. Shown on a rolled leather collar or a light chain, holding the head up and with the other hand holding up the tip of the tail. Most people do free stand when coming back to the judge after moving. Movement should be a gentle trot, not too fast, light and free, with head held high and tail up showing a level top line. Measured with a fixed bridge measure appropriate for the size of the dog. *Fig. 9.8*	Utility	9	1
Poodle (Standard)	Can be stacked or free standing, with both methods acceptable. Leads and collars are a matter of personal choice, but a high proportion are shown on fine chain collars, with a fine lead of either leather or fabric. They should be shown on a loose lead, never strung up, and at a speed which shows the dog's extension when seen in profile. The movement is free and light-footed, never heavy, and the handler must not run at a speed too fast for the dog. Standard Poodles are extrovert, love attention and love being shown. If they don't enjoy it, it will show in their demeanour. *Fig. 9.9*	Utility	9	1
Poodle (Toy)	Table dog. Can be stacked or free standing four square. Measured with a fixed bridge measure appropriate for the size. All traditional trims are acceptable as long as there is sufficient length of coat to demonstrate colour and quality. Shown on a lead and collar or chain appropriate for the size of the dog.	Utility	9	1
Portuguese Podengo	Judged on the table, either stacked or free standing. When stacked, the tail is held so that it is sabre-shaped.	Hound	5	1

Breed	Showing Information	UK KC Group	FCI Group Category	Breed Watch Category
Portuguese Pointer (IMP)	Usually stacked. As it is a small breed, handlers often kneel. The tail should be held level with the topline, or very slightly above. It is a rustic breed and not fancy or elegant. Bitches are generally less 'showy' than dogs, which tend to be more exuberant and thus have better ring presence. In Portugal leather slip leads tend to be used, while other exhibitors prefer a fine check collar and lead.	Gundog	7	1
Portuguese Water Dog	Usually presented as a stacked breed, four square, with head and tail held high. Tail should be held over the back in a ring. The Portuguese is a swimming breed, so the chest is deep and wide; this shows in the front as the legs are set quite apart. The gait is a light and lively trot with good reach and drive. The tail should always be carried over the back on the move. In the UK and all of Europe the dog has to be presented in the 'lion trim', which was the traditional clip used by the fishermen on the boats of the Algarve; in the USA they are also shown in a 'Working Retriever' clip.	Working	8	1
Pug	Judged on the table, free standing. Normally shown on traditional show leads with a loose chain collar, not a check collar! *Fig. 7.1*	Toy	9	3
Pyrenean Mastiff *(IMP)	Stacked square with the choke chain held up towards the occipital for examination by the judge. Can be shown using a heavier form of show check chain such as a serpentine chain if trained to lead calmly from an early age. Movement is at a moderate trot on a loose lead. *Fig. 8.28*	Working	2	1
Pyrenean Mountain Dog	Normally stacked, but can be presented free standing. The judge will often want to see a free stand after moving. This breed should be confident and well balanced, moving with elegance and appearing to float around the ring. While there is no particular recommended show lead, these dogs are strong, and a half-check with leather lead is normally used. The collar should be rounded so as not to pull the hair. Some people prefer white leather to blend in with the dog. *Figs 4.4, 5.16*	Pastoral	2	2
Pyrenean Sheepdog (Long Haired)	Free standing. They should not be presented to the judge on the table, although sometimes the judge requests this. They are shown on a half-check show lead.	Pastoral	1	1

Breed	Showing Information	UK KC Group	FCI Group Category	Breed Watch Category
Retriever (Chesapeake Bay)	Most exhibitors free stand, but some prefer to stack. Either is acceptable. No specific lead is recommended, although some prefer half-check slip leads in leather or nylon webbing, or plain slip leads. The breed should reach out in movement and has a tendency to single track at the correct speed. Generally happy dogs, though aloof, but generally well behaved in company. It is predominantly a working dog and generally not recommended as a novice owner's dog.	Gundog	7	1
Retriever (Curly Coated)	Either stacked or free standing in the ring, standing square with a level topline. They are strong, upstanding dogs with a degree of elegance. The neck is strong and slightly arched, of medium length, free from throatiness and flowing freely into well laid back shoulders. Feet should be in line with the withers, with the hocks extending out from the root of the tail. Movement should appear as an effortless, powerful gait with good extension and drive. At speed, the legs tend to converge. The tail should be carried level with the back and not 'flagged' or 'gay', and the dog should move freely. Generally shown on a thin lead and collar. The curly coat is of paramount importance and the body should be covered with a mass of tight small curls.	Gundog	8	1
Retriever (Flat Coated)	Free standing; should never be stacked. Bait can be used with discretion. Exhibitors use black thin leather or nylon show leads, mostly in black. *Fig. 8.18*	Gundog	8	1
Retriever (Golden)	Can be free standing or stacked. Recommended that the dog is shown on a loose lead, often a slip ring type in various materials, and of a colour that blends in well with the dog. The dog should not have a collar on when showing, just the lead. For a stronger dog a slightly thicker circumference is better for the handler to grip. *Figs 8.7, 8.8*	Gundog	8	2
Retriever (Labrador)	Free standing, four square. Most exhibitors use a thin rope slip lead, but some use leather, particularly on stronger dogs. The breed should be powerful in the rear, driving from the back; they should have a good correct reach of movement and hold their topline on the move. Tails should be turned over the back. *Figs 2.1, 2.19, 8.14, 8.23*	Gundog	8	2

Breed	Showing Information	UK KC Group	FCI Group Category	Breed Watch Category
Retriever (Nova Scotia Duck Tolling)	Free standing in ring, and should be animated. A rolled leather half-check or chain is often used, but some use slip leads. The breed should be jaunty and single track at speed. Moved on a loose lead with the head almost level with the back. The tail should be carried above the level of the back. A Toller tail is a feature of the breed and can be carried over the back in an arc. Tollers do not need to have white markings and shouldn't be over-groomed.	Gundog	8	1
Rhodesian Ridgeback	Stacked on a loose lead, or with the lead up under the chin. The colour of the lead usually matches the dog, and can be a brown/black slip lead or check collar. It is moved at a steady pace, showing extension. As an athletic/endurance hound, they should appear fit and muscular. *Fig. 2.41*	Hound	6	1
Rottweiler	Most exhibitors use a slip lead or American collar in cloth or leather. The breed should free stand, but initially some stacking may be needed to get the correct profile. Front legs should be straight down, the rear legs should not be over-extended. Bait can be used to bring the dog's head forward, smoothing and elongating the neck. After moving, the judge will expect a free stand on a loose lead. *Figs 1.14, 5.30*	Working	2	1
Russian Black Terrier	Can be free standing or stacked. Free standing is better as it shows the dog is balanced. No particular type of show lead is recommended.	Working	2	1
Saluki	Stacked, usually on a taut lead with the tail left to fall naturally. Run on a loose lead. There is no recommended type of lead, but it should be light and must not interfere with the dog's ear feathering. *Figs 5.19, 6.27, 10.9*	Hound	10	1
Samoyed	Free standing four square, with ears up and tail over the back. Presented to the judge side-on. Feet and legs should never need to be placed or stacked. The handler normally stands in front, facing the head. Shown on a loose lead at trotting pace, or at a brisk walk for the handler. They should not race around the ring. Normally they are shown on a round rolled leather-stitched collar and lead, or an all-in-one round nylon half-slip. *Figs 4.13, 9.7*	Pastoral	5	1

Breed	Showing Information	UK KC Group	FCI Group Category	Breed Watch Category
Schipperke	Free standing both on the table and on the floor. Usually shown on a slender check chain or half-check collar. This breed is easily distracted and very alert, so be sure not to 'train' their personality out of them early on, otherwise your puppy will be bored and ultimately will not show well as he matures. They usually bait very well for any treat you may want to use. This breed comes in solid colours: black is predominant, but gold and cream are often found. Prior to 2007 the breed was docked; now their tails are left on and they have a spitz-type tail. *Fig. 5.6*	Utility	1	1
Schnauzer	Can be stacked or free standing, but some judges have a preference so it is useful to train both. The lead is down to personal preference. Some run their dogs on a long lead and some short; it all depends on what the handler feels comfortable with.	Utility	2	1
Scottish Terrier	More commonly stacked nowadays in the UK, but can be free standing. The lead needs to hold the head up so a slip lead is most commonly used. This breed should be alert, using its pricked ears, and should carry the tail up. They should move freely, striding out well. The handler needs to walk briskly but not run.	Terrier	3	1
Sealyham Terrier	Usually stacked but some do free stand. Presented to the judge on the table. The usual type of lead is a slip lead. The breed should move at a brisk and vigorous pace with plenty of drive.	Terrier	3	1
Segugio Italiano (IMP)	This breed is uncommon in the UK, and is mainly a working dog. Can be either stacked or free standing. They should move at a loose but active trot.	Hound	6	1
Shar Pei	Can be free standing or stacked. While the dog is being examined, exhibitors sometimes ask the judge if they may show the bite, and open the mouth to show the black tongue that is a feature of the breed. Shar Peis should be moved at a good speed to show drive from the rear quarters.	Utility	2	3
Shetland Sheepdog	Shown free standing on a loose lead and should stand four square in profile to the judge. They are handled on the table. On the ground the dog should stand alert and attentive to the handler, and never be strung up. A fine leather or nylon half-check lead is usually used. The dog should be moved at a steady pace on a loose lead, and should single track. *Figs 2.20, 2.42, 6.28*	Pastoral	1	2

Breed	Showing Information	UK KC Group	FCI Group Category	Breed Watch Category
Shih Tzu	Stacked and examined on the table to begin with, and then moved at a reasonable pace, not too fast, preferably on a loose show slip lead made of nylon. Exhibitors never use a collar and lead. The movement should be free, with front legs stretched well forward; the hind legs should reach well under the body and be driven out with a strong thrusting action and a slight kick, showing the whole pad.	Utility	9	1
Siberian Husky	This breed should not be stacked and should be brought into a free, natural stand. Tails should never be held over the back. Some exhibitors may use bait to attract the dog to show off the alert expression. Trimming of any part of the coat is not permissible. They can be shown on a full check chain, or half-check. Some exhibitors choose a slip or clip lead. The lead should not be pulled up high round the neck, nor be used to help hold the dog's head up when standing. Leads should be loose on the free stand. They should be smooth and seemingly effortless on the move, and so should be gaited on a loose lead at a moderately fast trot. Topline should remain firm during gaiting. The neck should not be carried high, but should stretch out in front as the dog moves on. *Figs 2.14, 5.17, 6.3*	Working	5	2
Skye Terrier	The handler usually kneels on the ground behind the dog, and the dog is shown in a natural stance with the head up and ears alert; the front legs should be straight, and the topline (back) should be level; the hind leg facing the judge is slightly back, and the tail is left down. This is the stance the Skye would automatically adopt when watching something. When walking, he should be on a loose lead but should keep his head up, his topline should remain level and his movement should be free and effortless; the judge should be able to see the pads of the dog's hind feet as he moves away. The tail should be carried as a continuous line from the back or slightly higher, but should never be curled over the back.	Terrier	3	1
Sloughi	Generally stacked, although some will walk into a stand. Four square, with hocks perpendicular to the ground, and a straight line down from the withers to the back of the front leg/paw. Most exhibitors use a standard slip lead, leather or chain. Sloughis are notoriously wary of people they don't know, so can be difficult to show. Judges shouldn't approach them head on, but slightly from the side and confidently. Movement is not 'flashy' but economical, free, smooth and effortless. The front paw should not extend beyond the nose. *Figs 10.2, 10.3*	Hound	10	2

Breed	Showing Information	UK KC Group	FCI Group Category	Breed Watch Category
Slovakian Rough Haired Pointer (IMP)	Can be stacked or free standing. Leads vary, but as they are strong dogs most show people use leather slip leads.	Gundog	7	1
Small Munsterlander* (IMP)	This is predominantly a working breed and not yet shown in the UK. Abroad the breed is free standing.			
Soft-Coated Wheaten Terrier	Can be stacked or free standing. When moving around the ring they are sometimes strung, but most exhibitors prefer a loose lead. A common lead is leather with a slip chain around the neck. Wheaten Terriers are not table dogs.	Terrier	3	1
Spaniel (American Cocker)	Judged on the table. Stacked on the table and on the floor. There is no recommended lead. *Fig. 3.19*	Gundog	8	2
Spaniel (American Water)* (IMP)	Information not available as the breed has not yet become established in the UK.	Gundog	8	1
Spaniel (Clumber)	Normally presented stacked, although occasionally free standing. Needs to be shown clean and trimmed, but trimming should be minimal (tidying the feet, ears and tail). Usually shown on a white slip lead so that it does not detract from the dog. *Fig. 7.8*	Gundog	8	2
Spaniel (Cocker)	Judged on the table and usually presented stacked, although some exhibitors like to free stand their dogs. There is no recommended show lead but a thin leather or nylon slip lead with a slider is the most popular. *Fig. 8.15*	Gundog	8	1
Spaniel (English Springer)	Stacked. There is no commonly agreed type of lead, although most exhibitors use a slender slip-type lead in either soft leather or fabric. *Figs 8.9, 8.10*	Gundog	8	1
Spaniel (Field)	Can be stacked or free standing. Should have a level topline, not sloping, and should not be overstretched at the rear, with rear pasterns perpendicular to the ground. Frequently shown on a leather slip lead or martingale, which should be held loose around the ring. Should be moved steadily round the ring, allowing the slow unhurried drive to be seen. *Fig. 10.10*	Gundog	8	1

Breed	Showing Information	UK KC Group	FCI Group Category	Breed Watch Category
Spaniel (Irish Water)	Most exhibitors prefer to walk the dog into the stand, and then present either free standing or with the lead held at the top of the neck behind the skull. They are never stacked. Show leads differ, but most use either a fine leather slip lead, or a half-check martingale.	Gundog	8	1
Spaniel (Sussex)	In the UK Sussex Spaniels are presented stacked. Many exhibitors use a lightweight slip lead.	Gundog	8	1
Spaniel (Welsh Springer)	The Welsh Springer is normally shown stacked. Many exhibitors use a white leather slip lead. *Fig. 4.12*	Gundog	8	1
Spanish Water Dog	Ideally free standing, but can be stacked. Acceptable to hold out the tail level, or slightly higher, than the topline. A loose lead is preferred on the move, but a taut lead is accepted, particularly with younger/stronger dogs. The coat should be presented rustically, with absolutely no aesthetic trimming, combing or brushing. Cords should have wispy ends and should be shaved off once or twice a year to an even length all over. The movement is brisk and powerful with good ground coverage. A short stepping movement with a lack of drive and reach is undesirable. *Fig. 2.28*	Gundog	8	1
St Bernard	Some exhibitors stack but a good dog will look his best when he is free standing. The lead used is either a check chain with a longish lead or a narrow leather check and lead combined. The breed's temperament should be good and never aggressive. The breed standard requests an unhurried gait.	Working	2	3
Staffordshire Bull Terrier	Always judged on the floor, and can be stacked or free stood. Traditionally they are stood head on to the judge facing into the centre of the ring, and are moved at a walking pace. Various show leads are used, ranging from leather collars and leads decorated with traditional SBT brasses, to leather slip leads, half-check collars and leads, and often some quite sparkly leather collar and lead sets.	Terrier	3	2
Swedish Lapphund (IMP)	Can be either stacked or free standing. The lead is a matter of personal choice, but a half-choke and leather lead is most often used.	Pastoral	5	1
Swedish Vallhund	Can be stacked or free standing, and presented on the table for the judge. Movement is free and active, with the elbows fitting closely to the sides, and the forelegs moving well forward without too much lift, in unison with powerful thrusting hind action. Shown on a light lead and half-check or check chain.	Pastoral	5	1

Breed	Showing Information	UK KC Group	FCI Group Category	Breed Watch Category
Tibetan Mastiff	Normally stacked four square with the hindquarters slightly extended. Only a few exhibitors free stand their dogs as the breed is not particularly food motivated. The most popular lead is a rolled leather half-check collar with a matching lead.	Working	2	1
Tibetan Spaniel	In Ireland, the UK and parts of Europe these dogs are free stood but in Scandinavian countries they tend to stack and hold the dog's tail – this is rarely seen in the UK except with a dog that is lazy with his tail. A good tail set is therefore important. Tibetan Spaniels are put on the table for the judge to go over. Slip leads are commonly used, and they should move on a loose lead. Tibetan Spaniels are a head breed and should have a beautiful soft expression, no coarseness and no wrinkles, a beautiful coat, fringes and tail plunges.	Utility	9	1
Tibetan Terrier	A table dog, either free standing or stacked when in show stance on the ground. Can be shown on various show leads suitable for the breed's size, mostly with the lead coming from above rather than on a loose dropped lead (but some exhibitors do show like this too). Movement should be free-flowing with good reach and drive. Any colour can be shown apart from liver or chocolate, as these colours will not have the required black pigment on nose and eye rims. The coat should be double in adults, presented clean/well groomed and is never cut for the show ring. *Fig. 2.10*	Utility	9	1
Turkish Kangal Dog	Free standing with the lightest lead possible for that particular dog. This is dependent on each dog's size and weight, and so is often a normal lead.	Pastoral	NR	1
Weimaraner	Stacked but often free standing when returning to the judge. This breed is shown on a loose lead to show off the free effortless movement. Leather, webbing or chain slip leads are most popular. The dog must be shown in fit, hard condition to show his good muscle tone. *Figs 1.27, 1.28, 6.8, 8.20*	Gundog	7	1
Welsh Corgi (Pembroke and Cardigan)	The Corgi is shown either free standing or stacked while being judged on the floor. They are then stacked on the table for the judge to go over. They should have a free and active movement. They tend to be shown on either a thin check or slip check with a fine lead. The Corgi should be outgoing and friendly, never nervous or aggressive.	Pastoral	1	1

Breed	Showing Information	UK KC Group	FCI Group Category	Breed Watch Category
Welsh Terrier	Judged on the table. Usually shown on a check or half-check collar.	Terrier	3	1
West Highland White Terrier	This breed is stacked on the table when presented to the judge. On the ground some are free standing and some are stacked. The colour of the lead is always white.	Terrier	3	2
Whippet	Stacked on the ground and the table with front legs under the body. The hind legs should be placed so that the stifles are sufficiently bent with the hocks perpendicular and parallel. Most exhibitors use half-check collar and lead sets. *Figs 1.4, 4.10, 8.16*	Hound	10	1
Yorkshire Terrier	In the UK they are shown free standing on the exhibitor's own box (often wooden and/or a travelling crate) with a red cover – normally velvet. They are shown with a red bow in their topknot, and with a red lead which is made of very small, thin, silky material that slips over the head and is pulled up to make the dog secure. The judge will go over them on the table. Exhibitors should move at a walking pace round the ring. *Figs 2.22, 9.5*	Toy	3	1

GLOSSARY OF COMMON TERMS

Bait   Bite-sized dog treat

Bite   The manner in which the upper and lower jaws meet

Bobtail   Stump-like or very short tail

Breeder   The name of the owner of the dam of a puppy at the time of his birth

Brisket   Chest

Castration   The operation on a dog (male) to remove his reproductive organs

Challenge   When the unbeaten dogs at a show compete for Best of Breed

Close behind   With the hocks close together when moving

Conformation   Each breed has a detailed breed standard which refers to the structure and appearance of the ideal match to the breed standard. Good conformation is where a dog matches well to the standard; poor conformation is where the dog deviates too far from the standard

Crabbing   Moving sideways

Dam   Female dog (mother)

Dewlaps   Lips of the dog (also known as flews)

Docked   Tail size reduced to prevent injury in working gundogs. Can only be done with permission

Drive   A strong forceful action from the hindquarters

Dual Champion   A Show Champion and a Field Trial Champion (or a combination of Champion status in other disciplines)

Elbow Scores   The results of x-rays of the elbows; it is advised that breeding stock should have scores of 0

Entire   A dog which has not had his reproductive organs removed

Fault   A fault is where the dog deviates from the breed standard

Feathers   The longer coat found hanging on the underline, the back of the legs and the ears

Flank   The side of a dog

Flews   See Dewlaps

Gait   The description of how a dog moves

Hackney action   The front legs have a high-stepping movement

Hawe   Showing the second eyelid

High in rear   When the rear quarters are higher than the front quarters

Hip scores   The results of x-rays of the hips

Hock   The joint on the hind limb between the pastern and the lower thigh, known as the rear pastern

Intact   A bitch which has not had her reproductive organs removed

Lay back   The angle at which the shoulders are set in relation to the body

Leathers   The skin on the ears

Level bite   The upper and lower incisors meet

Loin   The area between the croup and the ribcage

Loose movement   Clumsy movement often caused by poor muscle development

Lower thigh   Also called the second thigh, this is the area from the stifle to the hock

Lumbering   Ungainly movement

Mean hip score   All the hip scores of the dogs in the breed divided by the number of dogs scored to produce a mean average for the breed. All breeders should use this as a guide to keep the hip scores of puppies low

Muzzle The area of the dog forward of the eyes

Neutering   The term used for the operation to remove the sex organs of a dog or bitch

Occiput   The highest point at the back of the skull, which is often quite prominent

Overbite   The gap left between the teeth when the upper incisors overlap the lower incisors

Pacing   Both legs on the same side move together

Pads   Area under the feet

Pastern   The region of leg (metatarsus) extending from the hock to the foot on the hind leg, and the metacarpal area of the foreleg

Pigment   The natural colour of each dog

Pounding   Front legs hit the ground hard

Rear angulation   The angles between the pelvis, thigh bone and lower thigh

Ringcraft   Training for show dogs and handlers

Roach back   A topline which is arched and convex

Sabre tail   A tail carried low and slightly curved

Scissor bite   Where the upper incisors overlap the lower incisors, and the rear of the top teeth should touch the front of the bottom teeth

Second thigh   *See* Lower thigh

Shoulder angulation   The angle between the scapula and the humerus

Single tracking   The dog moves as if running along a line: the legs converge on the centre line of balance

Sire   Male dog (father)

Sound   The movement is good viewed from front, rear and side

Spay   The operation on a bitch to remove her reproductive organs

Stifle   The knee joint

Stop   Area from the back of the skull to the muzzle

Stud   The dog who mates the bitch. If successful, he will be the sire of her puppies

Sway back   A topline which is sunken or concave

Topline   The line from the withers over the back loin to the croup

Trot   Diagonal legs move in unison

Tuck up   Area beneath the loin showing the waist

Undershot bite   Lower incisors extend beyond the upper incisors

Undocked   Full tail

Withers   The place at the shoulders where the neck and back meet

COMMON ABBREVIATIONS

AKC	American Kennel Club	FT	Field Trial
ATC	Authority to Compete	FTCh	Field Trial Champion
AV	Any Variety	G	Graduate
AVNSC	Any Variety Not Separately Classified	G1	Group 1 – first place in Group
		G2	Group 2 – second place in Group
BB	Best Bitch		
BD	Best Dog	G3	Group 3 – third place in Group
BIG	Best in Group	G4	Group 4 – fourth place in Group
BIS	Best in Show		
BOB	Best of Breed	GB	Graduate Bitch
BOS	Best Opposite Sex	GD	Graduate Dog
BP	Best Puppy	GWT	Gundog Working Test
BPIS	Best Puppy in Show	HC	Highly Commended
C	Commended	HD	Hip Dysplasia
CAC	Certificat d'Aptitude au Championnat – equivalent to a Challenge Certificate	IMP	Import
		IR	Import Register
		J	Junior
CACIB	Certificat d'Aptitude au Championnat International de Beaute de la FCI – International Beauty Champion	JB	Junior Bitch
		JD	Junior Dog
		JH	Junior Handler
		JW	Junior Warrant
CC	Challenge Certificate – also referred to as a ticket	KC	Kennel Club
		KC Reg	Kennel Club Registered
CH	Champion	L	Limit
Ch & FTCh	Champion and Field Trial Champion – also known as a Dual Champion	LB	Limit Bitch
		LD	Limit Dog
		M	Maiden
Dual Champion	A Show Champion and a Field Trial Champion (or a combination of Champion status in other disciplines)	MB	Maiden Bitch
		MD	Maiden Dog
		ML	Mid Limit
		MLB	Mid Limit Bitch
ED	Elbow Dysplasia	MLD	Mid Limit Dog
FCI	Federation Cynologique Internationale – Worldwide Canine Association	MP	Minor Puppy
		MPB	Minor Puppy Bitch
		MPD	Minor Puppy Dog

NAF	Name applied for	Sh CH	Show Champion
Neut	Neutered	ShCM	Show Certificate of Merit
NFC	Not for Competition	SY	Special Yearling
O	Open	SYB	Special Yearling Bitch
OB	Open Bitch	SYD	Special Yearling Dog
OD	Open Dog	UG	Undergraduate
P	Puppy	UGB	Undergraduate Bitch
PB	Puppy Bitch	UGD	Undergraduate Dog
PD	Puppy Dog	V	Veteran
PG	Post Graduate	VB	Veteran Bitch
PGB	Post Graduate Bitch	VD	Veteran Dog
PGD	Post Graduate Dog	VHC	Very Highly Commended
RBIS	Reserve Best in Show	WT	Working Trial
RBOB	Reserve Best of Breed	Y	Yearling
RBPIS	Reserve Best Puppy in Show	YB	Yearling Bitch
RCC	Reserve Challenge Certificate	YD	Yearling Dog

REFERENCES

Kennel Club Show Regulations 2013

Kennel Club Code of Best Practice for Judges (2012 Edition) (including Guide for Judges and Ring Stewards)

Kennel Club FAQs:

- Awards
- Dog Show Awards
- Breed Watch
- Judging
- Category Three Breeds
- Two CCs on the Same Day at the Same Venue
- Unbeaten Dog Rule

Multilateral Consultation of Parties to the European Convention for the Protection of Pet Animals (ETS 125),10.3.1995

Bateson, P. (2010). *Independent Inquiry into Dog Breeding*. London: Dogs Trust

Taking your pet abroad – https://www.gov.uk/take-pet-abroad-pet-passport

Regulations for FCI Dog Shows and Complementary Rules for World and Section Shows, FEDERATION CYNOLOGIQUE INTERNATIONALE (FCI) (AISBL), *Place Albert 1er, 13, B–6530 Thuin (Belgique), tel: +32.71.59.12.38; fax: +32.71.59.22.29; internet: http://www.fci.be*

Pet Travel Scheme Changes from December 2014: https://www.gov.uk/government/publications/pet-travel-guidance-on-changes-to-the-eu-scheme-from-29-december-2014

USEFUL ADDRESSES

Kennel Club
1–5 Clarges Street, Piccadilly, London W1J 8AB .
Telephone: 01296 318540   Website: thekennelclub.org.uk/

FCI
FCI Office, Place Albert 1er, 13, B-6530 THUIN, BELGIQUE
Telephone: +32 71 59 12 38   Website: www.fci.be/en/

Pet Travel Scheme Helpline
East & West Block, Whitehall Place,   London SW1A 2HH
Telephone: 0370 2411710   Website: gov.uk/take-pet-abroad/overview

Our Dogs
Our Dogs Publishing, Northwood House, Greenwood Business Centre, Regent Road, Salford, M5 4QH
Telephone: 0844 504 9001   Website: ourdogs.co.uk

Dog World
The Dog World Ltd, Williamson House, Wotton Road, Ashford, Kent, TN23 6LW
Telephone: 01233 621877   Website: dogworld.co.uk

Dog Show Central (for details of many available shows and links to schedules)
Website: Dogshowcentral.co.uk

Fosse Data (schedules and online entry)
Tripontium Business Centre, Newton Lane, Newton, Rugby, Warks, CV23 0TB
Telephone: 01788 860960   Website: Fossedata.co.uk

Higham Press (schedules and results)
Higham Press Ltd, New Street, Higham, Alfreton, Derbyshire DE55 6BP
Website: Highampress.co.uk

Dog.biz (online show entry)
Website: www.dog.biz/

Southern Canine Imaging
Old Stables, Beckford Lane, Southwick, Portsmouth, UK
Telephone: 01329 230052

The Show Dog Company
www.theshowdogcompany.co.uk/

Hide and Collars
Telephone: 01430 879072   Website: www.hideandcollars.co.uk/

Junior Handling Association
Mrs L. Cartledge, Ryslip Kennels, Binfield, Bracknell, Berkshire RG42 5NL
Telephone: 01344 424144 (daytime only)   Website: www.jha-dog.co.uk

USEFUL WEBSITES

Top 10 Dog Poisons
http://pets.webmd.com/dogs/guide/top-10-dog-poisons

2011 AAHA Revised Vaccination Protocol
http://healthypets.mercola.com/sites/healthypets/archive/2011/10/27/new-canine-vaccination-guidelines.aspx

Dog Walking in England – Paws Outdoors (England)
www.forestry.gov.uk/dogs

I Judge Dogs
www.ijudgedogs.co.uk

Dog Crates, Cages and Puppy Pens
www.croftonline.co.uk

UK Agility
www.ukagility.com

Obedience UK
www.obedienceuk.net

INDEX